No One Else

Advance Praise for *No One Else*

'This searing memoir of a gay man from a country that criminalizes homosexuality is intertwined with a first-hand account of the struggle for basic human rights by gays as well as by women sex workers, two groups similarly outlawed in India. Dube unsparingly exposes a complex web of hypocrisy, corruption and brutality in this work of grave, vital importance.' – Kiran Desai

'An extraordinary book that triumphs on many levels, personal and social ... Above all, it is a sensual and passionate story about the search for love, the "endless flowing river in the cave of man", that animates all our lives.' – Sudhir Kakar

Praise for *In the Land of Poverty: Memoirs of an Indian Family, 1947–1997*

'A deeply illuminating study of poverty in India, seen in concrete detail [and] made vividly real by remarkable descriptive skill.' – Amartya Sen

'Devastatingly effective.' – Pankaj Mishra, *Times Literary Supplement*

'An extraordinary study of the human dimensions of poverty and development. Destined to become a classic.' – Shashi Tharoor

'Siddharth Dube's argument is relentless, like the poverty he describes.' – Arundhati Roy

'A sensitive, ideology-free analysis of the poor and their history [that] stands out for its boldness and narrative accuracy.' – *Outlook*

'A fine biography [that will] leave an indelible mark on a reader's conscience.' – *India Today*

'Sharp, convincing and absolutely to the point [...] deserves the widest possible commendation.' – Susan Ram, *Frontline*

Praise for *Sex, Lies and AIDS*

'Lucid, compelling and indefatigably researched.' – *The Telegraph*

'Impassioned and lucid analysis.' – *Far Eastern Economic Review*

'Riveting.' – Suneetha Kadiyala and Tony Barnett, *Economic and Political Weekly*

'A deeply disturbing book [written] with language and passion that leave you wrung out.' – Dilip D'Souza, *Frontline*

No One Else

A Personal History of Outlawed Love and Sex

Siddharth Dube

HarperCollins *Publishers* India

First published in India in 2015 by
HarperCollins *Publishers* India Limited

Building 10, Tower A, 4th Floor, DLF Cyber City, Phase II,
Gurugram Haryana – 122002, India
www.harpercollins.co.in

P-ISBN: 978-93-5029-713-1
E-ISBN: 978-93-5029-714-8

2 4 6 8 10 9 7 5 3 1

Typeset in Adobe Jenson Pro 11/14.6
by Jojy Philip, New Delhi

Printed and bound at
MicroPrints India, New Delhi

For Basant Kumar Dube,
my marvellous father and friend,
who insisted, foremost, that we always tell the truth.

Loneliness I gave myself,
loneliness they gave me,
the small tithe I paid the lightning
of my God, sweet and tremendous.

My play of give and take
with clouds and with the winds
and what I knew trembling,
of secret springs.

– *Final Tree* by Gabriela Mistral

1

Shame

In retrospect, it's clear that these most enduring themes of my life were present so many years back in that single night, which is why I recollect it all with such clarity even decades later. But I could only see it with a child's eyes then, simply, directly, without interpretation, without thought of what it might mean for the future.

The year was 1971 or 1972, and I was about ten years old. I was at the Grand, Calcutta's most sumptuous colonial-era hotel. The orchestra had burst into a rousing flourish, and everyone moved to the sides of the ballroom as a light-skinned woman, petite but full-bodied, wearing just a shimmering two-piece bikini and a veil, emerged magically from somewhere.

The woman began to dance her way slowly down the length of the vast room, her movements languorous yet purposeful, as she removed the veil and used it as a fluttering prop for caressing and seducing. She was flaunting her near-nakedness, the expanse of smooth skin and soft curves magnified by the glitter of her bikini. I was entranced.

It struck me that, unlike the other striptease dancers I had seen (my parents often brought me along with them so I wouldn't have to be left with my ayah), this one never pressed herself against the men in the audience. Instead, she consciously held the gaze of man after man for a measured moment, but then moved on almost dismissively.

She is like a snake charmer, I thought to myself in wonder. And indeed, all the men, including my father, standing across from my mother and me, seemed hypnotized by the dancer in a peculiar, unsettled way, almost as if they were struggling to keep themselves from grabbing her.

The dancer approached me, and I immediately pressed against my mother, finding comfort in her familiar scent and the soft folds of her sari. In the past, to my burning embarrassment and the amusement of the adults, some Park Street nightclub dancers had done a watered-down version of their bump-and-grind routine against me, no doubt singling me out because I was the only child present.

But this one just passed us by, shimmied to the end of the room, and then—to a loud, collective gasp from the partygoers—threw off her bikini top to reveal peculiarly small breasts. In another flash, to an even louder gasp from the adults, she pulled off her bikini bottom—and, as she twirled naughtily out of the room, I spied what seemed to be a penis!

There was silence for a long minute—and then an explosion of clapping and laughter from the adults. But I was in turmoil. Had I made a mistake? Had I imagined the penis? A woman with a penis! It couldn't be!

When things eventually quietened, I tugged at my mother's arm and asked, 'Mama, Mama, was that a woman or a man?'

My mother stroked my hair lovingly, and said in a voice bright with amusement, 'Yes, it was a man!'

Though I recounted the incident to my wonderstruck, envious brothers when they returned from boarding school for the holidays, back then I never thought of it any more frequently than I thought of the other stripteases I had witnessed, or regarded it any differently from the others. Being a child, I didn't know that it had marked my first precocious introduction to some of my life's preoccupations—the beguiling possibilities of gender beyond the conventional bipolarity of male and female, and the mysterious, limitless permutations of sexual desire. It was only as an adolescent, years later, that memories of it came rushing back with disquieting clarity, and I realized that I had seen something of myself in that unusual dancer, in her androgyny and in her power to enthrall men.

Just a year or two before that striptease at the Grand, I had become aware that I was a girly-boy, a sissy, different from other boys, and despised and ostracized by them.

At the age of eight, I joined La Martinière, one of Calcutta's most revered secondary schools. Within a few days, I began to grasp that this school bore no resemblance to Miss Higgins's, the tony elementary school where I had studied up to that point. While the homely bungalow that housed the elementary school had made me feel secure and carefree, the main buildings at La Martinière were forbidding, cathedral-like edifices, over a century old. High walls and impassable gates enclosed the grounds. The massive buildings housing the assembly hall and senior classrooms had towering pillars that only served to underscore my puniness. Even the steps that led up to the assembly hall were intimidating, each one so tall and deep that I couldn't climb from one to the other in a single stride. It all seemed to be designed expressly to humble us children.

And there were no girls here like there were at Miss Higgins's. Not one. They were all at a sister school across the street. I had known that I was joining 'La Martinière for Boys', but in my state of anticipation those words had not registered.

I felt the absence of girls as a difference in atmosphere, which seemed more boisterous and yet darker than at Miss Higgins's. When school ended, I would watch them spilling out of the gates on the far side of the street, always looking so much happier than we boys did. I often longed to join them.

Soon, I became aware that I was not popular with my new classmates. Whenever I sat down next to someone in class or tried to strike up a friendship, I sensed I was being rebuffed. At first, I wondered whether this was because my new environment was so regimented. We wore identical uniforms of white shirts and shorts, black lace ups with knee-high socks, and a school tie of gold stripes on black, held in place with our house pin. (Mine was a bright yellow, for Macaulay House, named after Lord Thomas Babington Macaulay, the 19th century imperial politician and lawmaker, whose legacy of criminalizing homosexuality later proved to be the cause of my most abiding adult fears.)

At the morning assembly, we stood in neat rows and sang Christian hymns after we had recited '*The Lord's prayer*'. In our classrooms, we sat at identical wooden desks and chairs, springing up anxiously when the teacher entered to sing 'Good morning, Sir!' or 'Good morning, Ma'am!' in unison, and then quickly sitting down in silence. There was little time for fun before or after school hours. So I thought my friendliness might have seemed inappropriate, given the circumstances.

However, I soon realized that the class was essentially divided into two groups: a number of studious or quiet boys like me at the front, and a larger group of the more 'boyish' kind in the rows behind. The ones at the back looked tougher and bolder than us. While the boys around me were cautiously friendly, this larger group in the back disliked me with a vengeance. In fact, I was the main target of their antagonism. Whenever I stood up to answer a question, they sniggered. When I turned around, I caught belligerent looks. On the few occasions I ventured into their rows, I was shoved away by whomever I approached while the rest laughed at my humiliation. Eventually, I stopped making overtures to them.

Things continued like this for a few months. And then one day, as I stood up in class to answer a question, I heard a threatening chorus of hate-filled whispers from behind: 'Sissy! Sissy! Sissy!'

A wave of shame swept over me. They were right to call me that. I recalled how silent my parents fell when I had recently paraded into our living room adorned with my mother's jewellery. Not only did I have earrings, necklaces and bracelets on, I had also secured a pendant in my hair like a Hindu bride. I pranced around like a filmi siren, shaking my hips, stamping my bare feet in Kathak-like movements, my hands twisting and turning seductively. I even gyrated sinuously on the floor in an imitation of Helen, that gorgeous vamp.

I remembered the numerous times my mother had found me feeding and cradling my cowboy-Indian action figures as if they were dolls. Or playing nurse with our long-suffering dogs, swaddling them in improvised bandages. With sharp shame, I also remembered how I had preened whenever my parents' friends remarked what a beautiful girl I'd have made, how I looked just like my luminously beautiful mother with my long-lashed eyes and fine skin.

At that exact moment, standing there at my classroom desk and hearing the other boys calling me 'sissy', I began to see myself as a freak. I was overcome with self-loathing as I realized the many occasions on which, unthinkingly, I had shown my parents what a girly-boy I was. Now, much worse, I realized that the larger world saw me as only that.

Things only worsened over the next few years. Of all the boys in my class who got picked on, I became the prime target of ill will. Among the others bullied were two fat ones, several tiny ones, and one other somewhat girly-boy. They were called 'fatso' or 'sissy', had pieces of chalk flung at them, or were shoved around when the teacher wasn't there. But this happened infrequently. I was the only one who was unfailingly the focus of hostility.

Making matters worse, I became known as a girly-boy in other classes as well. It seemed to me as if everyone in school had been told to despise me. Older boys shouted 'sissy' as I walked past, or stopped mid-conversation to stare at me with distaste. A few times, when I inadvertently caught someone's eye, things got uglier. The taunts got louder and louder: 'Sissy', 'Sissy! Sissy!', 'Girly girly girly!', 'Go to the girls' school!' These groups would move threateningly towards me even as I tried to beat a retreat. Though these incidents were relatively few over the course of my years there, and never escalated into physical violence, they were enough to make me feel constantly apprehensive.

My mother soon noticed from my increasingly subdued behaviour that I wasn't enjoying La Martinière. She didn't question me about it, no doubt because she assumed that I was merely facing the routine challenges of school life. Moreover, given that she was facing struggles of her own, she probably no longer had the emotional strength to be as attentive as she was earlier.

Her marriage to my father, once a powerful romance between strong-willed equals, had begun to unravel. My father relished Calcutta's cosmopolitan life and rose meteorically in the prosperous tea industry. But my mother, ascetic and serious-minded, was a misfit in this brown sahib world of elite British mores and corporate wealth, with its constant round of parties, golf and polo matches. Her fear that she was losing him to one or another flirtatious memsahib tipped over into constant, feverish suspicion.

I had become my mother's staunchest ally in their conflict, viewing her as the wronged victim and my father as the offender. Every day, I would mirror my mother's attitude towards my father. When she bristled at him, I was rude too, turning away if he spoke to me. If they fought and she wept, I shrank from him too, looking at him as if he were evil incarnate. This unaccustomed hostility towards my father, coming after years of loving him, left me unhappy and off balance.

And yet, despite my closeness to my mother, I couldn't discuss with her the daily humiliations I faced at school. Given my now antagonistic relationship with my father, there was no likelihood of discussing my problems with him. More than anything else, I wanted to avoid drawing their attention back to my shameful problem. I felt it was I who was despicable and needed to change, not the boys who hated me.

Hence, I found my own ways of coping as best as I could. I would arrive at school only when the classes were about to begin. I kept to myself and avoided getting in the way of the boys who taunted me. I didn't react to their stares, their comments, or the chalk they flung at me. Though I would be shaking with apprehension, I'd try to appear calm and walk away unhurriedly, as if I were doing so out of choice and not fear. That act of defiance helped me salvage some sense of dignity, despite being near tears and achingly aware that I was an outcast.

It was a difficult transition because, despite the eroding of my parents' relationship, my childhood had been happy and almost carefree until I joined La Martinière. I had not given a thought to whether I was boyish or not in my mannerisms and looks in the cheery mix of boys and girls at Miss Higgins's, where I found myself quite naturally at the centre of most things. Moreover, at home, I had felt no different from my brothers, Pratap and Bharat, and despite being the youngest I had confidently established my boundaries.

While I was usually happy to follow my brothers' lead, I would get notoriously feisty whenever I felt that they were treating me unfairly. My jaw would jut out, I would glare, and I'd talk right back to them. My brothers still take pleasure in reminding me that my standard comeback was, 'Ya, so?!'—in other words—'What are you going to do about it?' Consequently, my brothers christened me 'Yaso', and while it no doubt honoured my fighting spirit, it also made me sound unfairly truculent. Tellingly, my other moniker—given to me by my parents' friends—was 'pondpaka chele', a vivid Bengali expression that translates into 'ripe-ass kid' or 'precocious brat'. This should testify to just how mischievous I was in those early years.

But on joining La Martinière my once-headlong approach to life turned into an unrelenting battle with self-consciousness. To protect myself from further ridicule and shame, I began to ferociously weed out every girly trait that I could see in myself. I desperately wanted to be a regular boy, left with no damning evidence of who I actually was.

I noticed the way other boys handled objects—firmly, roughly, or casually—rather than in the gentle way that came naturally to me, and I tried to do the same. I suppressed my longing to play the doctor, nurse or mother during play-dates with friends, or even when I was alone at home.

While passing by a mirror, I would suppress any stray thought that reminded me that I looked so like my mother. I would announce to my parents' friends that I attended 'La Martinière for Boys', placing heavy emphasis on the last word. Decades later, I realize how hilarious this assertion must have sounded to them.

In trying to purge these central aspects of my personality, I developed a lasting sense of shame and self-loathing. So focused was I on adopting what I imagined was appropriately boyish behaviour that it wasn't until decades later that I began valuing the aspects of my personality that I thought effeminate—my loving nature; the fierce protectiveness that I felt towards my eldest brother Pratap, who had been left badly handicapped by polio; and my love for animals, which made me refuse to eat meat.

The psychological conflicts set in motion at this juncture of my life might have been impossible for me to cope with if, like some gender-atypical children, I had desperately longed to change my sex. But, looking back at those childhood years, at least as far as I can tell through the complexities of my own mind, I've never strongly felt 'that I had been born into the wrong body, and should really be a girl', as the great British writer Jan Morris—who was James Morris before a sex-change operation—wrote. Nor do I recall experiencing any of the other feelings that strongly gender-atypical children experience: disgust at their own genitals, the conviction they will grow up to be the opposite sex, and a strong desire to be so.

In contrast, as best as I can understand it, I would have opted for an amorphous, undefined gender, something that fluidly combined the best qualities attributed to boys and girls, and later, adult men and women. In a setting free of gender-prescriptive prejudice and fears, like the one I was in before joining the boys-only La Martinière environment, I would have simply continued to be this combined self: a carefree boy with some 'girlish' traits.

Quite a few of these traits seem to have emerged from a specific genetic predisposition, rather than from any volition on my part. Indeed, they are still an innate part of my being as an adult: my somewhat pretty looks, my gentle nature, and my strong nurturing instinct.

Other stereotypically 'feminine' behaviours that I was drawn to as a young child—wearing women's clothing, dancing seductively, or beautifying myself with make-up and jewellery—seem to spring partly out of instinctive aesthetic appreciation and partly because I modelled aspects of myself on beautiful, intelligent women, such as my mother and Sophia Loren. I did relish these interests of mine, but I never felt the urge to pursue them all the time. Not only was I passionate about many stereotypically 'boyish' things, such as playing with model racing cars and fighter planes, for instance, but my keenest desire as a child was to go swimming or to play with our dogs, not to cross-dress.

So, while I genuinely doubt that I ever wanted to change my gender and sex and become a girl, I am equally sure that I would have blossomed in a childhood environment where these differences didn't matter—where I could be the way I was without having to feel ashamed and worried that some of my actions were 'girlish'.

And yet, even while living through these difficult years of my life, I didn't actually think of myself as being unhappy or unfairly victimized. I coped with the persecution I faced at La Martinière as well as the bitter battles between my parents by daydreaming about a peaceful enchanted place, populated only by noble wild animals (especially tigers and elephants) that lovingly protected my mother and me. A lot of my waking time was spent in this world, sometimes to the point where it felt more real to me than the one that was now rife with anxiety and threats.

My mother was a great source of calm. After school hours, she and I spent much of our time together. With my brothers away at boarding school and things worsening between my father and her, we became even closer. Because of the problems at home, my father would absent himself for increasingly long periods of time, touring the tea plantations in Assam and north Bengal. I savoured being with her and was never bored, even when we spent day after day by ourselves.

It seemed to me that she had a magical way with animals. Our dogs would willingly do everything she asked of them, their eyes fixed intently on hers to see if they had succeeded in pleasing her. In the garden outside our Lord Sinha Road flat, dragonflies seemed to choose to settle on her outstretched hands. She would tie a fine thread to their tails, so that I could hold them for a while—pet fairies flying on a string—before she released them unhurt. At the kids' section at the nearby Calcutta Club, the chital stag—who had been brought

Provided by author

My mother, Savitri

there when he was still a fawn—would unfailingly come to nuzzle her, though he would ignore me. Our shared love of nature kept us ceaselessly happy together, poring over wildlife books and outdoing each other in identifying the koel's call, even through the din of traffic in crowded Chowringhee.

I also spent a lot of time immersed in my books. My mother was a voracious reader, and so I became one too. Every few days, we'd replenish our stock from the libraries at Calcutta Club and the British Council. I loved books about animals: Tarka, the otter in the English countryside; Flicka, the American mustang; and White Fang, the heroic wolf-dog. My two favourites were set in the wilds of India—Kipling's *Jungle Book* and an illustrated book about Chendru, a Bastar adivasi boy, and his pet tiger cub.

But I found nearly any book engrossing, and read everything I could lay my hands on—works that were appropriate for my age and, because my mother didn't censor my reading, the ones meant for adults too. I didn't understand a great deal of the adult books, but this didn't keep me from loving them. So, at the age of ten, I was reading Enid Blyton's Famous Five series and Frank Richards' Billy Bunter series as well as westerns by Louis L'Amour and potboilers by Harold Robbins. Jacqueline Susann became an enduring favourite, first for her tribute to her poodle, *Every Night, Josephine!*, and then for the steamy *Valley of the Dolls*.

Publicly, I read historical and literary romances by Daphne du Maurier and Georgette Heyer, thinking that my mother would assume that I liked them for their literary qualities. But in my bathroom, with the door locked, I read her Barbara Cartland and Mills & Boon novels. I loved the unceasing romance. I loved the handsome, complicated heroes they featured. I read them in secret because I now knew, from my experiences at La Martinière, that only girls were supposed to like them. I began to spend so much time in the bathroom that my mother wrote on the door, in indelible red paint, 'This is not a library!'

This isolation was punctuated during twice a year, when life reverted to a close approximation of the glorious earlier years of my childhood: before my brothers went off to boarding school, before my parents' relationship began to fall apart, before I joined La Martinière and learnt that I was a girly-boy, before I became ashamed of who I was. These were the holiday months, every summer and winter, when my brothers returned from school.

All the noise around the house would help revive my mother's spirits. My father would be around most of the time. My parents would fight rarely, and sometimes not at all, for those months, and I was spared the anguish of having to take sides against my father. Instead, there was once again a sense of love at home. What we children wished for desperately seemed to come true, however implausible it may have seemed for the rest of the year: our parents loved each other, they loved us, and we loved them and each other.

The company of my brothers made me feel normal once again. We would spill out everywhere together, playing 'cowboys and Indians' and 'cops and robbers'. We dragged our much-loved dogs into our games. Sally, our spotlessly white German Shepherd, was particularly stage-worthy, born for playing the role of our indomitable protector against all the threats of this world.

In the living room, our imaginations were set afire by the enormous tiger skins (from our father's hunting expeditions) spread across the floor. When we stood astride them, or sat on their stuffed heads—stretched in a fierce permanent snarl, complete with daunting incisors and raspy tongues—we became Mowgli, Tarzan or the Phantom. The high point of our afternoons was going swimming at the Calcutta Club. Once in the cool embrace of water, we three consummate swimmers were like a pod of dolphins, flashing past the other kids, confident and joyous, always together.

Driving home as a family from the club, my father—after gruelling sets of tennis, followed by drinks with my mother and friends—would flirt with her. The attraction between them in those moments was evident even to us kids. He made mischievous sexual allusions while my mother pretended to be offended. We, for our part, acted as if we could understand everything clearly. My parents' favourite music played once again at home: Connie Francis, Eartha Kitt, Frankie Lane, Begum Akhtar, and the soulful soundtrack of *Mumtaz Mahal*.

Come bedtime, we kids would settle heavily into our single beds, with the dogs at someone's feet or on the floor, the air-conditioner humming loudly, and the door to my parents' bedroom left reassuringly ajar. Then Papa would settle down on a low chair, at the level of our eyes, to tell us riveting bedtime stories about our zamindar ancestors in the Uttar Pradesh badlands.

In one of them, set in medieval times, a magical giant cobra lifted one of our ancestors onto its hood, thereby preventing our clan from being wiped out in a murderous late-night assault by rival zamindars. In another story, my widowed grandmother and teenaged father, armed with shotguns, rode off on horseback at dawn to a relative's haveli to wrest back jewellery that the latter had wrongly laid claim to.

A particularly dark story that our father rarely told us, but of which we remembered every detail, was about how his own father—newly married and barely into his twenties—had been murdered by cousins trying to usurp his inheritance. But even here, good eventually won—our treacherous relatives had not known that our grandmother was pregnant with our father, her first and only child.

Despite the grim tenor of most of these stories, I felt safe and secure. Even at that young age, I understood that the moral of Papa's stories, which he wished us to absorb, was that it was our family dharma to endure even the most terrible suffering without complaint. This was the core message of my father's favourite texts, the Bhagavad Gita and Kipling's 'If', copies of which he kept not only at home but also in his office. However shattering the blows faced in life, we boys—like our grandmother and father—were to remain superhumanly brave, and to never resort to lying or dishonesty. On the contrary, we were supposed to do good for others without giving any thought to self-interest.

In these moments, my father seemed to embody the kind of firm goodness his stories spoke of, revealed in the steadiness of his gaze even when his eyes were soft with affection. Despite the palpable awkwardness between him and me, persisting from the months of strain that had preceded the holidays, I knew for a fact that he loved me too. I knew that I was safe with him, and that he would give his life to protect everyone in his family. So even when I faced hardships in school and later in life, my father's protectiveness and our family history of suffering and fortitude gave me the strength to endure them.

Looking back, I realize that neither of my parents ever admonished me for my feminine traits. I don't recall them commenting on even the most obvious of these incidents, such as my vampish dance

Provided by author

My father, Basant

performance, let alone rebuking or urging me to change myself. Even in these moments, there was nothing more than silence and a blank look on their faces. I didn't sense any anger or hostility.

The absence of censure from my parents was of enormous positive importance. As an adult, when comparing my childhood experiences with others who also had gender-atypical traits as children, I realized how lucky I was. The majority of the people I spoke to, in India and abroad, told me that their parents persecuted and shamed them. One of my Delhi friends used to be beaten mercilessly, abusively called a hijra—the common term for India's traditional male-to-female transgenders—and locked up in isolation for hours by his parents, all because he insisted on shaving his legs and wearing dresses.

It made me wonder why my parents handled this matter more kindly than others from their era. I know that my mother always half-wished that I was a girl so that I could remain at home with her and be the loving confidante that she desperately sought. This longing probably contributed to her setting aside any discomfort she felt about my behaviour. In my father's case, despite his being a manly man in the Victorian colonial mode, it's possible that not having a father himself led him to follow his natural instincts as a parent, making him less bound by convention.

And though they looked like quintessential products of their class, my parents were more unconventional than many of their friends. They broke social rules, big and small. In an age of arranged marriages, theirs had been a love marriage. My mother spurned jewellery and make-up, and was drawn to teaching yoga rather than to parties. My parents thought nothing of taking us children to striptease performances, flirting with each other in our presence, letting us read adult novels with explicit sexual content or, in my father's case, teaching us bawdy British songs like 'Roll me over in the clover'. Perhaps this freethinking streak made them more capable of withstanding the fears that other parents felt about their children's gender-atypical behaviour.

Their response was close to the best that could be expected, given the times. Even if they had been actively supportive, and sought to give positive direction to me as a gender-atypical child, child psychology services barely existed in India in that era. Indeed, the times were such that very few parents of their generation in the USA, western Europe, or elsewhere in the industrialized world would have been any better placed to face up to this challenge. Gender-atypical children were viewed by most psychological and medical professionals as deviant characters most likely to grow up to be homosexual. Given the oppressive stigma attached to homosexuality and the laws criminalizing it, their approach was to 'cure' children through aversion therapy and electric-shock treatment. These so-called 'treatments' were brutal and ineffective.

However, while my brothers and I remained very close, they eventually began to see me as a girly-boy, like the students at my school. One day, when some of my parents' friends were visiting, Bharat—to whom I was particularly attached as we were just fourteen months apart in age—blurted out: 'Siddharth reads Barbara Cartland and Mills and Boons! And he plucks his eyebrows. Look at them!'

Everyone turned to look at me. I sat there in shock, and then said in a trembling voice, 'I don't.' (I was referring to plucking my eyebrows; they are naturally arched and tidy by some twist of androgyny.)

'Yes, he does!' insisted Bharat in his most convincing voice. I was close to tears. Somehow the conversation moved on, perhaps through my parents' conscious efforts.

Forever after, through my childhood and teen years, Bharat would repeat these announcements to adult audiences at unexpected moments. I would sit speechless, at the most mumbling in protest. While I knew that this was just Bharat's bull-in-a-china-shop way momentarily getting the better of him, my sense of shame was so intense that I could never speak about it to him. I thought bringing it up would only confirm that I really was a girly-boy. So we never discussed this matter, and consequently I was subjected to such embarrassment every once in a while. Each incident, however infrequent and trivial, made me feel different from my brothers and somehow markedly inferior, despite our strong bonds of affection.

By the age of nine or ten, I began to be attracted to boys and men. The first person I recall being attracted to was one of our drivers. It was a vague kind of desire, not the powerful sexual pull that I began to experience a few years later. I'm not even sure why I found him attractive. He wasn't handsome, and his skin exuded the sour odour of cheap alcohol. (His drinking led to him getting dismissed in a few weeks.) My desire had something to do with his dissolute style as well as a somewhat transparent, creamish nylon shirt that he often wore, displaying smooth, hairless flesh.

I'm not sure what I felt first, romantic desire or sexual desire. I know I first experienced romantic desire through the pulp novels I was reading. I longed for the heroes to love me obsessively, to sweep me away—preferably on a magnificent Arab stallion—to the land of happily-ever-after. It was an inexplicable yearning, an ache of some strange kind. I didn't know where it came from, but there it was one day, a painful longing that made me feel as if I had been separated from an unknown someone that I now continually pined for.

Even though the books only depicted romance between men and women, I didn't really wonder if this implied that I had to transform myself into a woman. I only concluded that I had to be alluringly feminine, because it was feminine charm that drew the heroes to the heroines instead of the other women.

Similarly, I first felt sexual desire through reading. There was a constant undercurrent of sex in the Barbara Cartland novels, hinted at in hot-house language but never explicitly described. It was stronger still in *Valley of the Dolls* and the Sidney Sheldons, but it was only in the Harold Robbins books that I found regular snatches of explicit sex. I fixated on the description of the men's bodies, their cocks, what they did, the pleasure they felt. I came across a thrilling section where a man recalled having sex with a handsome black man. I was beside myself with excitement.

Sexual desire became another yearning within me, and this one was a force located in my groin—single-minded, insistent and attention seeking. It led me to discover the joys of masturbation, an inexhaustible source of pleasure. And though I was furtive about this practice, locking myself up in the bathroom, the fact that my parents treated sexual matters openly and casually spared me the common trauma of thinking that the act itself was sinful or dirty.

At that early point, and for many years later, I did not wonder whether other boys—my brothers, for instance—fantasized about men or women, or whether the nature of my new-found desires had any link to my feminine behaviour. Such was the blissful ignorance of childhood, not knowing that my desires too, like my femininity, made me disgracefully and dangerously different from most other boys.

2

A Boy's World

Ironically enough, my first great experiences of desire and romance occurred in an atmosphere marked by brutal physical and sexual abuse. It was when I left home at the age of eleven, in 1973, to go to the Doon School. This famed bastion of boys-only education, India's Eton, was where all the men in my family had gone since its founding in the last decades of the British Raj. I soon came to realize that I had left behind a world in which I was victimized for my femininity only to enter one where it made me an object of both desire and condemnation.

I had joined Doon desperately hoping that I could start over again as a regular boy in this new setting. So, from my very first day there, in trying to create the impression that I was just like everyone else, I boasted, shoved and strutted, mimicking the tough boys who had dominated La Martinière.

My aggressive behaviour made an immediate impression, though not the kind I had been aiming for. Within the very first days, I ended up in fist fights with classmates as well as school seniors. Bharat, who was then in his middle years at Doon, sought me out to warn me that several boys—including his peers—had complained to him that I was obnoxious. I must behave better, he said, clearly wondering why his gentle brother had suddenly turned rogue. I usually heeded Bharat's advice, but because there was no other way to hide the fact that I was a girly-boy, I decided to persist.

As it happened, my disguise didn't take long to fall apart. It was too alien to me to be kept up for long. And, more practically, I was quite simply not the strongest even among my peers. A month into my stay at Doon, I was defeated in a fist fight. I'm not sure what sparked the confrontation, but I still remember its course as if it had ended just minutes ago.

It was with a boy of my age, but taller and better built. We fought in our changing room, a small chamber adjacent to the bedroom that we shared with three other newbies. Every inch of wall space had uniforms and pajamas hanging from wall hooks, rows of shoes were lined up below, and a long towel rack occupied the window area. There was just enough space left for two brawling boys of our size. We boxed each other on the face and stomach. We hit hard. We tore at each other's hair. He knocked me to the ground. We wrestled. I fought as hard as I could—because I had everything to lose.

But I was outclassed. The fight ended with all my strength exhausted, and him sitting astride me, scornfully remarking that I wasn't half as tough as I acted. I didn't cry, but lying on the floor there, I felt that sinking dread from my La Martinière days coming over me again. Now that I had lost a fight, they were going to figure out that I was 'girly' and start despising me.

Doon was a place out of time, a place out of place. An elite British school had been transposed to the Himalayan foothills to groom us, sons of privilege, into the vanguard of 'Macaulay's Children'—'a class of persons, Indian in blood and colour, but English in taste, in opinions, in morals and in intellect', as Lord Macaulay had so precisely described the goal of his imperial education policy, begun in 1830s British India.

A peculiar mood of constant apprehension and fear blanketed the school. It stemmed from the relationship between the school's senior-most class and the rest of its cohorts. Outside of our hours in the classroom, these seniors governed our lives as prefects in a system that dated back unchanged to the very founding of the school in 1935, when India was still a colony, replicating the prefectorial systems of Eton and Harrow, where Doon's first headmaster and his deputy had taught before moving here.

Our residential dorms, where we lived and slept, had been made the prefects' fiefdom, places they ran with only minimal interference by the housemasters. The prefects supervised us through our tightly regimented days, virtually every waking hour of which was carved out by the clamour of large brass bells unceasingly ordering us from one activity to another. We sprinted from our dorms to the academic buildings, the playing fields, and the arts and crafts workshops, speedily getting in and out of unending sets of uniforms.

We obeyed the prefects unquestioningly because they enjoyed practically unrestricted powers when it came to administering punishments. These were levied if we were late in answering any bell through the day, if we did not execute every uniform to perfection—whether it concerned the knot of our ties, the sheen of our shoes, or the precise height of our knee-high socks—or even if they arbitrarily disliked something about us.

The physical punishments included long sessions of extra PT, jackknives and star-jumps, crawling on all fours on gravel paths, and remaining in the convoluted murga position for an unbearably long time. The corporal punishments that they were allowed to administer included brutal practices such as 'putting'—where they whacked our backsides with hockey sticks or cricket bats, often using the stick's edge to inflict even more pain. All these punishments were carried out in the absence of teachers, allowing the prefects to be as brutal as they wished.

Their power and our oppression were multiplied by the tradition of 'fagging', a practice that was also adopted from elite British schools.

Under this system, boys in the junior grades worked as house slaves for the seniors by unquestioningly attending to every task put before them—from making their beds, shining their shoes, lugging pails of hot water for their baths, even massaging them if required. The more powerful a senior in the prefectorial hierarchy, the larger would be the number of 'fags' attending to him. Fagging gave seniors additional licence to humiliate and abuse juniors at every turn. So, from our perspective as juniors, the school administration seemed to have given the prefects life-and-death power over us, to be manhandled and punished as they pleased.

Inevitably, this scenario where prefects ran the residential houses with scant supervision by teachers made abuses a certainty. The prefects were a full generation older than the school's youngest students—they were strapping, hirsute young men of sixteen to eighteen compared to the diminutive boys aged ten or eleven, who had not even begun the growth spurts of male adolescence. They were, however, still immature, and their newfound sense of absolute power over others often went to their heads.

Endemic bullying was one egregious consequence. The novelist Vikram Seth, a decade my senior at Doon, said during a Founders' Day address at the school in 1992, twenty-plus years after he graduated, 'For days after I left, I thought of school as a kind of jungle, and looked back on it with a shudder ... I was teased and bullied by my classmates and my seniors because of my interest in studies and reading, because of my lack of interest at that time in games, because of my unwillingness to join gangs and groups.'

The bullying routinely escalated to physical as well as sexual abuse, and the thin line dividing them often vanished in this place where pubescent sex drives were such an overriding, coursing force. The perpetrators were not just the usual minority of cruel and psychopathic boys, but also, tragically, a number of innately decent boys whose sense of right and wrong had gone awry because of the savage atmosphere and often from years of being victimized themselves.

One of my sharpest memories is of an afternoon in the summer months of my third year there. A prefect in my residential house, an infamous sadist, had developed an inexplicable hatred for a roommate of mine, an awkward, harmless boy. The prefect was a powerful young man, his face marked by volcanic clumps of acne and a perenially enraged look. He started persecuting my hapless roommate by subjecting him to unending punishments through the day—waking up early, running several times around the playing fields, doing jackknives and press-ups, walking on all fours on the gravel until his knees bled, and squatting in the murga position for so long that he would fall over helplessly, at which point his tormentor would kick him brutally.

One afternoon, a few weeks into this persecution, my roommate had become so withdrawn and anxious that he looked visibly ill. The four of us who shared the room with him were worried to see him like this, but our awareness of being helpless ourselves kept us from trying to comfort him. We knew, without having to ask, that matters with his persecutor had taken a turn for the worse. We were all half-asleep in the summer heat when the prefect entered our room, yelling at us to get up, which the five of us did with alacrity, our hearts pounding.

He slapped our roommate hard across his face, then told him to remove his shorts and underwear, and bend over his bed. Weeping, our roommate followed his orders. Then his persecutor yelled at us to take one of the long bamboo poles used to hold up the mosquito nets and push it up our roommate's rectum.

We were stunned. By now, we had learnt to obey the prefects unquestioningly. But we still retained enough sense of what was right and wrong from our homes to know this was going too far. We hesitated. The prefect punched and slapped several of us, painfully hard.

With no choice but to obey, we all gripped the bamboo pole and placed its fist-thick end against our roommate's anus. He was weeping uncontrollably. We held the bamboo there, not applying any pressure.

The prefect hit us again, more violently this time. Terrified, we pushed the bamboo lightly. We were hit some more. The bamboo's gnarled end went in a bit. Our roommate screamed.

Somehow, eventually, the afternoon's horror ended. We helped our roommate dress. None of us said a word. We were all too terrified to even console him, let alone discuss whether we should collectively complain to our housemaster.

Astonishingly, none of us ever discussed this harrowing incident in our remaining years together at Doon. And that was one key reason why abuse continued to flourish there through the decades—both the abused and the witnesses learnt to hide it behind silence, suppressing any knowledge or memory of the brutal things we witnessed or underwent.

It was in this warped atmosphere of endless hierarchies and domination that I first became the target of male desire manifested as sexual abuse. Nothing in my short life had prepared me for dealing with the terror I felt during these episodes, or the shock at realizing that desire—the glorious thing I had instinctively responded to in reading Barbara Cartland romances—could take on as vile a form as predation and violence.

In my second year at Doon, a huge prefect called Nutty began tormenting me. He had looked at me with unsettling intensity ever since I had joined school, but now that he was in the senior-most batch, he felt emboldened to act as he wished. Nutty was notoriously crazy, hence his nickname. Even his classmates gave him a wide berth.

Though I did my utmost to avoid Nutty, there was no escaping him in the second half of the day, after classes ended and we returned to our common residential house. Unfailingly, several nights a week, instead of studying after dinner like my other classmates, I would do an unending series of somersaults on Nutty's orders.

One after another, I did the somersaults virtually in the same spot of a study room I shared with a dozen other students, as there was just enough space for me to do two somersaults before I banged into the wall or furniture. Nutty stood right by me, staring down with a strange mix of lust and hatred writ large on his face.

Each time I paused out of exhaustion, half hoping that he'd relent, he yelled, 'Who told you to stop, you pansy!' He's insane, I'd tell myself angrily and return to the somersaults, even though my head was burning from forehead to nape from chafing against the stone floor.

No one ever interceded. My classmates kept their eyes studiously trained on their homework, fearing that they would otherwise be made to share my predicament. The senior-most prefects charged with running our house would sometimes drop by to look at me somersaulting, crack a joke or two with Nutty, and then continue on their way. They did not intervene even when Nutty, a star hockey player, 'putted' me repeatedly with all his strength—transferring his frustrated lust into agonizing blows of the hockey stick on my upturned buttocks. (I never really expected any of the other prefects to intervene, as some of them occasionally partnered with Nutty in abusing me. They would together corner a terrified civet—a wild cat-like animal often found on Doon's verdant grounds—in one of the study rooms and begin beating it to a pulp with hockey sticks and cricket bats, stopping only to fondle and slap me around as I angrily tried to stop them from killing the hapless beast.)

I even gave up any hope of our housemaster putting an end to any of my torture. When on his evening rounds, he would simply pass by our study room with his gaze averted. Sometimes, he would stop to chat affably with the seniors, his golden Labrador staying obediently at heel.

Ever so often, Nutty would make an offer. If I did just one naked somersault in the privacy of his dressing room, he'd stop punishing me. I asked Bharat, whose watchful presence had kept me from being subjected to even worse treatment, if I should comply with his wishes. But he yelled at me, anxiety evident in his voice, saying that Nutty would rape me if he got such a chance. So, I kept silent whenever my tormentor made his offer.

The episodes I hated even more than the somersault sessions were when Nutty had me sent to him in the early evening, after we'd bathed and dressed for dinner, to the open square adjacent to our residential house. He would hold court here over a motley crew of hangers-on. I hated these sessions most because there was always a new addition to his gang to egg him on.

'Oaay, do you know what a pansy is?' Nutty once asked in his rough voice.

I kept my eyes down. 'Yes.'

'Are you a pansy?'

Everyone laughed.

I said softly but defiantly, 'No, I'm not a pansy.'

'You're a pansy, you madarchod, and you want me to chodo you,' Nutty yelled. 'You want to give me a blow job, you pansy! Here, come here, suck it!'

This time there were guffaws from his admiring audience.

I felt utter hatred for him. I wanted to kill him.

But I hid my feelings. I stood there silently. I forced my eyes downward. Whenever he or one of the others touched me, stroked my hair, or tried to put their arm around me, I just edged away.

*O*ne night about a year later, I was sleeping in a long dormitory that I shared with about a dozen others. My bed was in a corner, by one of the windows. Grey-white mosquito nets covered each of the beds.

Suddenly, I woke up to find that I was lying on my back and somebody's hand was on my groin. Another hand was holding up the mosquito netting. There was a large face pressed against the netting, staring down at me. Through the netting, the face seemed to be a featureless apparition, something from a horror movie.

I shut my eyes quickly. I wanted to scream for help, but I was frozen with terror.

The hand fondled me, moved from my penis to my testicles and then towards my butt. Even as the hand continued to fondle me, I just lay there with my eyes shut in dread.

The boy in the bed on my left turned and muttered loudly. The hand lifted off my groin, and I felt the netting fall. Lying there with my pajamas pulled down, I began to cry. I even peed, unable to control myself.

The lights came on. There was chaos. Someone said, 'It's Dube. Let's call his brother.'

Bharat came from a room nearby, and two of his friends were with him. I was still sobbing, eyes shut, lying where I was in a pool of pee. Comforting me, he led me to the bathroom to wash up.

When we got back to my dorm minutes later, Bharat was in a state of towering rage. He yelled, telling my roommates to get out of their beds, asking each of them if they had seen anyone enter the dormitory. One of my hapless peers who couldn't force himself awake at that early hour got a hard blow from Bharat.

The next morning, Bharat took me to our housemaster, the genial man with the obedient Labrador. He sat behind his large desk in the study attached to his house. Bharat and I told him about the events from the evening before. I could sense that the housemaster was getting irritated. At some point, my fear from the night gripped me afresh and I started crying. The housemaster brusquely told me to stop crying. 'These things happen,' he said. 'You need to become tougher.'

The only reason I escaped from even worse sexual assaults, such as being raped, in my most vulnerable years was because Bharat was such a strapping jock that even boys several years older than him were reluctant to take him on. But, like the housemaster who instructed me to adapt to abuse by becoming tougher, the school administration played no discernible role in protecting me in those early years.

Later, after Bharat graduated, I was protected to some degree by the mere fact that I was somewhat larger in size by then (I had crossed fourteen), and because I had a reputation of being a ferocious fighter if pushed. Later still, the worst excesses in my residential house began to wane under a new housemaster who, unlike his peers, began to curb the physical and sexual abuse that had flourished so far. This earned him the ire of the senior boys in our house, and there was considerable muttering about how he was an outsider who didn't understand 'how Doon worked'.

Nonetheless, though the intensity waned over the years, I continued to face sexual harassment until my final year at Doon. I came to think of it as an inevitable part of life there, an adjunct of the school's savage atmosphere, to be taken in my stride. Even so, every incident was inevitably traumatic—whether it was the lewd comments and leering by the occasional gang of students or the nerve-wracking experience of being cornered by one or more particularly aggressive seniors who would feel me up and try to make me touch their penises, threatening to punish me for refusing.

I was aware that there were many other boys who fared far worse than me, in large part because they did not have a protective elder brother like I did in Bharat. It was not just the markedly feminine ones like me who suffered. Virtually every pre-pubescent boy was androgynous and hairless, and consequently even those who later grew into masculine hulks often faced sexual abuse in their junior years.

Even in school, we had a clear idea about which of our classmates—at least the ones in our residential houses—were being sexually harassed or abused. Sometimes, in particularly vicious cases of abuse, we would come to know about abuse taking place in the other residential houses too. Day after day, the victims would keep emerging from the seniors' rooms in tears, or arriving late for dinner looking as if their spirit had been torn out of them.

If they were our close friends, the unwritten code was that we would never discuss this particular kind of trouble with them, neither immediately nor at any point later. We'd pretend to not have noticed.

They would keep up the act too, despite the terrified expressions and red eyes.

But they fared badly with those who weren't close to them. Our juvenile society was so rank with hypocrisy that victimized boys were endlessly stigmatized and gossiped about. They were called 'lenders', the Dosco slang for boys who played the passive role in sexual intercourse. They were portrayed as sluts who had encouraged their own abuse, and enjoyed being used sexually.

Forever tainted as the male equivalent of 'easy' women, they were made the target of even more sexual abuse. (I was accused of being a lender too, though with little conviction as no senior could reliably claim that he'd succeeded in having sex with me.) The stigma that these poor boys wore, at times endured even after they left school. All the while, the senior boys who abused them were admired for being macho, rather than criticized for being abusers.

This hypocrisy ran very deep. Thus, in 1976, the year that my brother, Bharat, was a house captain, his fellow prefects launched a school-wide witch-hunt to root out homosexuals. Tellingly, the hunt targeted only junior boys, the reviled 'lenders'—while among those leading the witch-hunt were the very seniors who were sexually abusing these younger boys.

Night after night, residential dorm by residential dorm, young boys accused of being actively homosexual were dragged out and beaten up by several senior students. (Tellingly, not one housemaster intervened, despite marauding gangs of prefects entering residential houses they didn't belong to.) I was spared by virtue of being Bharat's brother, but several of my classmates were among those beaten.

One of my close friends told me, years after passing out of Doon, about the savage beating inflicted on him. He said the ones who hit him most mercilessly were the very seniors who regularly forced themselves on him. The only senior who didn't hit him was Bharat, who knew he was a friend of mine. He said Bharat looked ashamed and stood to one side, averting his eyes.

Bharat, for his part, said those weeks of the witch-hunt were the most dispiriting point of his school years, cementing his strong dislike for Doon. Always upright and humane, he castigated himself for not having possessed the independent thinking and courage to refuse participation. It convinced him that teenage boys, even those on the verge of adulthood, were so prone to despotism and bloodlust that they should never be allowed any power over other children.

But so overpowering was the atmosphere of fear and so complete the lack of redressal mechanisms that, even though both physical and sexual abuse were widespread and flagrant, I can recall only three boys being even temporarily expelled for such abuses in all my years there. The lack of recognition by the school administration of the prevailing physical and sexual abuse also meant that there were no counseling services available for the victims, leaving them with deep traumas that were never addressed.

In my case, the abuse I faced left a lasting imprint of fear and suspicion of overtly macho men. For decades to come, I would get apprehensive whenever I encountered a group of rambunctious men, fearing that their group dynamics would somehow spill over into aggression against me. I was also left with a bleak awareness of the monstrous violence often displayed by men in lust—using violence to get sex or using it to hide their desire for taboo forms of sex.

Despite the harassment I faced, I had found a way of coping by my middle years at Doon. One means of doing this was to suspend thinking about what I was going through. I realized later that it was a common coping mechanism amongst us boys when faced with this bizarre world of regimentation, fear and compelled obedience. My childhood habit of daydreaming about safe refuges inhabited by protective animals continued, providing me with a much-needed escapist sanctuary.

Spending time on my own was also vital to my equilibrium. One of my favourite haunts was the swimming pool—I was happy every second of my time in the water, doing backstroke lengths effortlessly and incessantly, carving out a calm, impenetrable cocoon.

Another haunt was the library, where I must have pored over a vast majority of the books and magazines over the years, investigating everything from atlases to bound back-copies of *Life* and *Time* magazines. I went for solitary walks around the verdant campus, which had once been part of the colonial Forest Research Institute, and came to love nature even more deeply.

I lost myself in songs about love and passion, which I listened to on a boxy cassette player. The British singer Shirley Bassey, with her dramatic style, was a particular obsession of mine. Every lovelorn song of hers—from '*I who have nothing*' to '*Feelings*'—seemed to echo my own deep yearning for romantic love.

I was also sustained by close friends, a significant number of whom were also designated outcasts—the bookish, the artistic, the frail, the ones bad at sports, and the ones who just didn't care to fit in. I had good friends among them, and several of these friendships endured even after school.

I was too troubled to shine academically, barring English and the social sciences, for which I had a natural aptitude. Nonetheless, to my surprise (by then, I had a deadeningly poor opinion of myself), I managed to pull in decent first-class grades. I was also too awkward among other boys to do well in team sports. However, as I instinctively enjoyed exercise, I went riding at the nearby military stables, and became a star swimmer, eventually captaining the school swimming team.

To avoid attracting trouble, I tried to keep a low profile. I gave seniors and the more thuggish ones among my peers as wide a berth as possible. I kept my disagreements to myself, such as my feeling that the drummed-up enthusiasm for house, and school-spirit was just another means to making us conform.

But my efforts to be left alone were never particularly successful. Sexual harassment was one major reason. Whatever I did, there seemed to be no way I could escape the unwanted sexual attention of seniors. Another was the proud, defiant expression that I wore no matter how apprehensive or fearful I was, a mannerism I had adopted in my La Martinière days in an effort to hold on to some sense of dignity and self-worth. This air of self-assurance seemed to incite seniors into beating me down.

Admittedly, my affected behaviour was also to blame. Not only were my mannerisms particularly anglicized, I also showed off my family's affluence with Speedo swimming briefs, Puma running shoes and expensive watches, all enviable imports in that era of 'Licence Raj' austerity.

Yet another constant reason for not being left alone, as I had feared when I lost that decisive fight in my first weeks at Doon (ending my pretence at being a regular boy), were my feminine mannerisms. They made me a target of ridicule through the entire length of my time at school. At La Martinière, I had been told that I needed to behave like a boy, not a girl. At Doon, I was given the mixed message that I should be a boy, though they secretly preferred me as a girl. Consequently, I never knew whether this attribute of mine was going to spark condemnation or desire.

Even so, the animosity against my femininity surfaced only when several boys were together, as if spurred by some kind of atavistic pack mentality. One of my indelible memories of Doon is of an afternoon when I was fifteen or so. I'm in the changing room attached to our dorm with a group of my classmates. They are coaching me on how to be a man.

'Come on, Dube, you can walk without swaying your hips!' says one of my classmates.

'Try it like this ...,' says another. 'Keep your spine stiff. And move your arms like this ...'

I walk the length of the changing room again. All eyes are on me.

It's still girlish, they tell me.

I try it again. And again. And again.

I still fall short of the masculine ideal, they tell me. Each has advice on how I can correct the way I walk, talk, sit, stand, behave. Nonetheless, they are all amiable. We have become friends of sorts and I'm a willing participant, even though I'm aware of the undercurrent of scorn in their tones. Over the years of being ostracized, I have lost some portion of my will to fight back. I now envy their boyish camaraderie and long to share in it, even though it seems composed only of inane or weird things, including endless arguments over sporting competitions and a painful game called thols that has them bashing each other in the testicles.

'Dube, you should learn about Test cricket scores,' one of them says. 'Then we'll have something to talk about.'

I agree.

We go off for afternoon tea. For once, to my elation, I'm included in their gang.

Ironically, it was in the traumatizing environment of Doon that I first experienced intense, wondrous romances. They were the high point of my years there, hinting that this boys-only environment could have been a natural paradise for me if it was somehow shorn of the abuse and violence.

My first romance began, ironically, in the same year of my sexual harassment by Nutty. I never associated one with the other. While one was my first experience of mutual romantic love, the other was about violence—even hatred. Despite the fact that both the experiences were rooted in desire, they had nothing in common.

This first love was a jock in my class, with sinewy muscles, a wide mouth and a thatch of silky hair. His relentless joking around and playing to the gallery hid an enormously affectionate nature. Our romance started when we were aged twelve or so.

We'd sit next to each other in class so that we could secretly keep our legs pressed against each other. During movie nights, in the dark of the crowded auditorium, our embrace was so tight—our legs entwined, his lips pressed to my neck, his arm encircling me—that we were almost sitting one on the other. We disguised our erotic intentions by pretending to tickle each other under our shirts. Eventually, the tickling would give way to lingering caresses on the chest, nipples, stomach and back, expanses of my body that suddenly came alive with an almost unbearable sensitivity. In the Rose Bowl, a sprawling outdoor auditorium that allowed for great privacy during evening performances, we'd take turns to rest our head on each other's lap. When I did so, I could feel the burning heat of his large, distended penis through the flimsy fabric of his cotton kurta-pyjamas.

Every day, I could smell him on myself long after we parted at dinner, forced to return to our separate residential houses. He smelled clean, of Liril soap and sometimes of Old Spice cologne. I'd inhale his smell deeply and unfailingly feel comforted—his smell on me meant that I was loved.

Though we were mad about each other for two years, we didn't go beyond kissing and caressing each other. He often tried to. I knew that he had had sex with other boys—he seemed to have the skilful assurance of the experienced in the way he kissed, caressed my buttocks, or tried to undo my pyjamas. But, when at the brink, I always pulled myself back from acting on my desire. This, quite obviously, exasperated him.

After that first relationship faded out, I had several strong mutual attractions, all of them long-lasting and emotionally rich too. They were with pleasant, good-hearted boys of my age, or at most one grade senior or junior to me. However, it was in my last years at school that the great romance of my youth finally happened. It was of such all-consuming intensity that I was to remember it all through my life.

This boy was idolized as much for his sportsmanship as his movie-star looks and physique. Though we had known each other for years, our mutual attraction sparked one summer evening, every detail etching itself permanently into my memory. It was half an hour before dinner, when the sky was still bright. He walked over to where I was chatting with a friend at the corner of the main playing field, looking at me so intently—as if he had just recognized something about me—that my sentence trailed off. Something palpably passed between us at that moment, an acknowledgement of immense attraction or some kind of embryonic connection.

Within a few days, our attraction had turned into obsession. During classes, he'd walk slowly past my classroom several times a day just to catch a glimpse of me, his eyes intently locking on mine. I began to spend too much time with my eyes on the corridor, waiting for him to appear, rather than on my studies, which suffered.

The morning assembly was a precious extended time for us to be together. He would stand behind me in the choir section, our bodies pressed so tightly against each other that we could hear the other's heart hammering.

After sports hours, I'd sit in his private study with him, listening to '*Goodbye, yellow brick road*' on his cassette player. We'd just stare at each other full of desire, yet rooted to our chairs and unable to make a move towards each other. In its entire span of two years, our relationship remained essentially a wordless one, everything expressed through looks and subtle touch.

Inevitably, many of his classmates knew about our romance. To tease us, they'd call me across to his table in the dining hall. 'Dube, are you his? Do you love each other? Why don't you love me instead? Come on, aren't I handsomer? Okay, now sit on his lap. Listen to me, do it!' He never responded to their banter, but through it he'd smile at me in a steady, protective way that affirmed our feelings for each other. So, far from being an embarrassment, these episodes left me elated.

With this great love of mine, if he had pushed me even a little bit more I would have had sex with him. We came close to it on several occasions. But, my most cherished memory of this boy's character was the fact that he held back out of some kind of loving concern for me.

One night, to my surprise, he called me out of my study, and began to pace awkwardly up and down the length of the adjacent playing field. I walked by his side, casting sideways looks at him, filled with foreboding at his silence, fearing that he wanted to break up our relationship. Then, abruptly, he said, 'I don't want to spoil anything about you.'

I was flooded with relief. I knew he was referring to my being a virgin. Despite being vilified as a 'lender', everyone close to me knew that I'd not had sex with anyone in all these years, and the label was attached to me by frustrated senior boys bent on coercing me into sex.

But I ached so much to make love to him that I embarrassed myself by blurting out with transparent eagerness: 'What if I want to be spoiled, what if I don't care?'

He stopped and turned to look directly at me. I was elated by the emotions I could see on his face—this was love, no different to what I felt for him, this overpowering, almost painful mix of physical desire and appreciation for the good qualities we saw in each other. But even though I had now given him the go-ahead, and the perpetual awkwardness between us diminished greatly, we never had sex.

There was nothing singular about my romances. In a boarding school with five hundred boys speeding through adolescence into manhood, it was inevitable that romances between us would take centre stage. Very little effort, if at all, was made to hide these romances from others.

In our common rooms, boys would pair off romantically to The Eagles' '*One of these nights*' or Donna Summers's '*I love to love you baby*', holding each other around the waist or shoulders in transparent attraction. We routinely teased each other about the objects of our desire. No one insisted that they weren't attracted to some boy or the other.

How could we not desire each other? We were in the throes of becoming full-fledged sexual beings, our young bodies erupting with semen and lust. Our physiological sexual pressures were so intense that even masturbating several times a day only provided us momentary relief. Not only was this a world without girls, but every one of us looked better than we ever would again—our faces and bodies lean and fresh from exercise and good food, our shorts scrunched around strong thighs, bursting crotches and muscular buttocks. How could the campus not palpably course with desire?

And because many of us had never stopped aching for affection to fill the void of being away from our parents and home, our desire was often combined with emotional need, making these our first earth-shattering experiences of romantic love. Beyond the minor perils of jealousy, unrequited desire and even broken hearts, these romances caused no harm and indeed did us much good. These experiences of eros were probably the only aspect of Doon that kept alive our capacity for love and tenderness, otherwise damaged by the school's oppressive environment.

Our romances didn't always, or even usually, lead to sex. Doon's notoriety as a hothouse for homosexual love is exaggerated. (When AIDS hit India in the mid-1980s, a popular joke had it that the acronym stood for 'Acquired In Doon School'.) Every other all-male boarding school, in India or elsewhere, has probably seen as much romance and sex among its pupils as Doon. But, on the other hand, there is no doubt that a good number of my Doon peers had consensual sex with their schoolmates.

Oddly, I was one of those who didn't allow myself to have sex while at Doon, even with the boys I loved intensely. This is ironic because, as an adult, I proved to be one of the very few among my classmates who was avowedly gay. My only sexual experience in my Doon years was an unforgettable, endless night of deep-kissing and masturbation with a hot-mouthed, muscular friend, while out on a mid-term trekking expedition in my final year.

I came close to having sex on many occasions. But, again and again, though aflame with desire, I held back at the last moment—largely because my father had wrested a promise from my brothers and I that we would tell him before we ever had sex with another male.

I look back at that promise with incredulity. It almost defies credence that our father, despite being a Doon alumnus and remarkably frank about sexual matters, could have broached this matter with us in that conservative era. None of us now remember how exactly he had discussed the subject with us. In a *Rashomon*-like twist, we don't even agree on the particulars.

Bharat is convinced that our father said he would throw us out if we did it along with any of the other things on a short list of strictures, including drugs, cigarettes and alcohol. In contrast, Pratap and I believe that our father said we just needed to tell him first, and then we could proceed unhindered. (When we belatedly turned to our father for clarification, by which time all of us were middle-aged, he said that the interpretation held by Pratap and I was the right one. All he wanted was her us to be honest with him about doing anything that posed a risk, a claim that made sense given his personal mantra that honesty was key to living correctly, and was indeed the core part of our family's dharma.)

I can understand how my brothers' largely even-keeled relationship with our father helped them keep their commitment to him, despite the intense sexual temptations at school. What baffles me is why I also complied. Why did I not try to rebel against my father by going out and having as much sex as possible? It would have underscored my animosity towards him. Perhaps I held back because honesty was the cardinal virtue dinned into us by our father, and because—despite the resentment I still harboured—I desperately wished to have his love.

Whatever the confused mix of reasoning on my part, the upshot was that my sex life at Doon was ruefully non-existent. I enjoyed only a tantalizing taste of the pleasures that could have been mine if I had sensibly ignored my father's strictures.

Even though we treated our romances as unexceptional, our schoolboy views on homosexuality were convoluted and conflicted. Thus, tellingly, there was no acknowledgement of our romances being between two boys, and hence, *homosexual*. The unspoken construct that governed our thinking was that once we left Doon we'd be attracted to women, marry, and would then send our sons back to our alma mater.

Our views were also shot through with patent homophobia. There were the despised slurs of 'homo' and 'lender', condemning their failed masculinity as well as their guilt of true homosexual desire because they were giving blow jobs or being fucked, acts of servicing deemed demeaning to males. (Doon was my first inkling that homophobia and misogyny are almost always intertwined, both springing from the same set of arbitrary prejudices and taboos.) There was the absence of any stigma attached to being the penetrative partner, or the 'taker', who was seen as a masculine boy simply satisfying his sexual needs through a quasi-heterosexual act of penetration and ejaculation.

Strikingly, the homophobic views were largely voiced by the abusers, those who forced themselves on other boys instead of having consensual relationships. In contrast, the students who didn't hide their romantic feelings for other boys rarely voiced this homophobia, or did so only in a half-hearted way, just to keep up appearances. Nonetheless, the upshot was that the homophobia dominated our views about homosexuality, even for the many of us who had strong romantic feelings for other boys.

The reasons for this pervasive, learned homophobia were not difficult to untangle when I later reflected on it. Despite Doon's largely homo-social environment, the school's ethos was rigidly heterosexual. There was no hint of homosexual desire in the novels and poems assigned to us in literature classes—everything was about women and men, whether as star-crossed lovers or married couples. There was not even any mention in our biology textbooks about homosexual behavior among animals. This institutionalized, single-minded emphasis on heterosexuality, combined with the blanket pretending-away of the romances between us were the primary reasons why we all imbibed the view that heterosexuality was correct and same-sex desire deviant.

This feeling of homophobia solidified as the boys graduated from school. With rare exceptions, there was now a blanket denial of the attraction and feelings they had previously held for their classmates. The denial was so extreme that graduates from Doon—or similar boys-only schools like Mayo and St. Paul's—rarely behaved any better or more understandingly towards gay men and lesbians later in life. It was as if their experiences of same-sex eros had never occurred. The prejudice that same-sex desire was disgraceful had been so deeply internalized by everyone at Doon that, upon graduating, no one had the gumption to break free from this mentality. It was as if we had collectively vowed to keep our past strictly secret, an unmentionable boyhood folly.

Some months after my first romance began, at age thirteen and in class seven, I wrote a short story for our weekly English essay assignment about two boys falling in love with each other. The setting was not a boarding school, but a neighborhood more European than Indian, with the boys living next to each other in row houses. One of the boys was handsome, the other more femininely beautiful. Both were loving and decent. I clearly had myself in mind while writing the story, considering that the two characters also remained staunchly virginal despite their desire for each other.

Sadly, a few years into the boys' deepening love for each other, one set of parents decided to move away, turning an uncomprehending ear to the boys' protests that they could not bear to be separated. The boys were heartbroken.

I remember I left the future of their relationship unstated, giving no hint whether the boys managed to renew their relationship later in life, or whether they even met again. The story did not have the happily-ever-after finale of the Barbara Cartland romances that I had thrived on just a few years earlier. Had I somehow concluded, despite my inexperience of life, that same-sex love was a doomed venture, certain to end in tragedy? Or was it simply that my belief in happy endings had cracked from being too close a witness to the dissolving of my parents' marriage?

While writing the story, my words had flowed out effortlessly onto the ruled pages of the essay book. But upon completing it, I told myself that I should tear it up instead of handing it in. Vaguely and inchoately, I felt I was crossing a forbidden line. I was portraying romantic love between two boys.

By doing this, I was breaking with all that I had imbibed—from books, lyrics, movies, everything and everyone—that love was always between men and women, between boys and girls. Yet, in the impulsiveness of my youth, I handed in the essay to Krishna Kumar, a young teacher I as well as other English enthusiasts idolized in the short years he taught at Doon.

A few days later, I was gripped afresh with trepidation as Kumar began returning our essays to us, calling out the marks we had scored and, in his characteristically acerbic manner, adding a comment or two of stinging criticism or (far more rarely) faint praise. Though I was sitting in the front row of the class, my turn never seemed to come. I took this as proof that I had erred badly in submitting the essay. I burned with apprehension at the prospect of Kumar mocking me in front of all my classmates over this freakish love story between boys.

Kumar had just two or three essay books left when he turned to hand me my book, announcing, 'Seven on ten! That's the highest I've ever given anyone. Well done!'

Weak with relief, I barely registered my classmates hooting and calling out: 'Wow! Well done, Dube!'

That class session flew past for me in a haze of delight, as validation—let alone unstinting praise—from Kumar was a rarity. As I was leaving class, Kumar called me back to say that he wanted to publish my story in the *Doon School Weekly*, a campus paper largely featuring works by students. I was overjoyed. It would be my first article in the *Weekly*, an honour at that young age.

A few days later, Kumar asked me to stay back after class, and, looking distinctly awkward for once, told me that the teachers overseeing the *Weekly* had decided against running the essay. He didn't elaborate. Given the formal ethos of Doon, I didn't have the gumption to ask why or even express my disappointment, though my dejection was no doubt evident.

In my remaining years at Doon, I went on to have several articles published in the *Weekly*. Even so, I never quite forgot that rejected short story of gay love, with its inconclusive and possibly tragic ending. I felt it surpassed all my published articles in authenticity of personal feeling. It was only later in life, after facing up to my orientation in matters of desire and romantic love, that I realized what the story actually was—the first public statement of my orientation, despite its fictional form.

As it happened, decades after I graduated from Doon, Krishna Kumar and I became close friends in New York City. When I asked him about the essay and why the *Weekly* had turned it down, I was surprised that he remembered it readily. Kumar told me that he had been impressed with the candor and directness with which a 'difficult' matter had been handled, and this had led him to recommend it to the teachers on the *Weekly's* editorial staff. He said he had no doubt that while it opened their eyes in a very tangible way, they probably justified their decision to not publish it on the grounds that it would hurt the sensibilities of parents as well as the younger children.

And so I came to learn that I had been a young schoolboy when I first suffered censorship for daring to mention homosexuality, 'the love that dare not speak its name'.

3

The Real World

The early years of my adulthood became a piecemeal escape from the vicious cycle of persecution and self-loathing that my childhood had deteriorated into. This was made possible because I entered the real world, which was a less warped place than the boys-only worlds of Doon and La Martinière. Crucially, I was back again in a world populated with women, not just men.

Delhi University's St. Stephen's College, which I joined late in the summer of 1980, had begun to admit women a few years earlier, gradually relinquishing its Doon-like status of privileged male power. In my years there, the women were a small minority and were only allowed as day students. But even so, in a world with women, a natural world to be precise, my life began to change.

Within a few months of being at Stephen's, I had developed a close friendship with several women students. My relationship with them quickly revealed a lovingness and emotional intimacy that not even the closest of my Doon friendships or romantic relationships possessed. The difference, I realized later, stemmed from the simple fact that women retained a capacity for expressing affection while men had been taught to suppress and deny it. Any kind of tenderness was thought of as weakness that would keep us from being men, rational, authoritative and in control.

Adding to my joy was the realization that I was universally liked by the women in my class, a far cry from my outcast status at Doon. In the literature course in which I had enrolled, women far outnumbered male students. In our class of twenty-five or so, only half a dozen were men.

I became especially close with two women, Alka and Rosemary, who were already fast friends with each other. At first glance, they looked like an unlikely pair. Alka was light-skinned, kept her hair short, and wore demure *salwar-kameez* as well as unfashionably large spectacles. Rosie was dark, had a glorious mane of hair, and favoured tight jeans and fashionable tops that emphasized a siren's body. Alka was invariably gentle and giggly, while Rosie often seemed fiery, sometimes even brusque. Alka brought to my mind Winnie the Pooh; Rosie conjured up images of Brooke Shields. But, for all these outward differences, I soon realized how similar they were on fundamental matters, both being principled and loving.

I soon became an equal third in this friendship. The fact that this development didn't spark tension between any of us I can only put down to the great purity of affection we each came to feel for the other.

We were inseparable during college hours. Some of my loveliest memories of Stephen's are of the mornings, when they would arrive at college. On most days, barring the cold winter months, I rose at dawn to practise swimming with the rest of the college team at an off-campus pool. By nine, I would have returned to college, eaten breakfast, and showered. I would then restlessly look out of the window of my room, which faced one of the main gates. Sure enough, there would soon be female cries of 'Siddharth, Siddharth ... come on down! Hurry!' One voice would be reedy, punctuated by giggles. That was Alka! The other would carry a flirtatious tone. Rosie!

I would spot them somewhere in the crowd of day students, a

discovery that never failed to fill me with joy. I'd dash down to them. There would inevitably be several minutes in which, ignoring the shocked looks of other students (because it was sacrilege for women to be so familiar with men), they tousled my hair, messed up my clothes, and teased me for being too neat. And then, with one of them pulling me along by the shirt, I would be dragged off to class, where we would sit at neighbouring desks. Our heightened level of fun lasted through one class after another, all the way until it was time for them to depart for home in the early afternoon.

These long-unaccustomed feelings of happiness brought out the clownish side of my personality, something that had shone when I was a young child, both at home and at Miss Higgins's, but had been drowned out at La Martinière and Doon. I became the class joker. No matter how uninspired my quips would be, they would always find appreciative peals of laughter. I was thrilled.

Unfortunately, these daily disruptions earned me the ire of every professor—I earned the sorry distinction of becoming the one student

Teesta Verma

Happy days at St. Stephen's. I'm at the centre, with Alka and Rosie directly behind.

who was ejected from almost every class. But I didn't care, because once launched on this trajectory of fun and popularity, I was loathe to be serious again.

As it happened, my special status with women at Stephen's was cemented by an incident on the day before Holi in March 1981, when a rowdy group of men from neighbouring colleges—many of them visibly high on booze and bhang—invaded Stephen's, making a beeline for the women in the main academic building. (The relationship between Stephen's and the nearby colleges was always tense; the men there thought Stephanian men were elitist and arrogant, while Stephanians thought the others were uncouth goons.) Instantly, every male Stephanian disappeared into the library or their hostels. I was with Alka, Rosie, and a few others, and instinctively stayed put.

The marauding men began to daub the women's faces and bodies with dry colour. Despite the inviting vista of my white T-shirt, nobody seemed to even notice me. The daubing became suggestive touching, fondling, even caressing. The women began to protest, slapping away the hands. I stood in their midst, bristling and tense, like a small protective dog that knows that it is powerless to do anything besides growl.

For a while, it seemed as if things would turn even uglier. But luckily, the incident came to an end just as abruptly as it had begun. The outsiders left as raucously as they had come, looking satisfied that they had got their way with such impunity. I helped Alka, Rosie and some of the others, comforting them and removing as much colour as possible. They were shaken.

Extraordinarily, the incident turned me into a hero of sorts. Not only did all the women tell me that I was gutsy for standing up for them, especially when all the other Stephanian men had fled, but for days afterwards, women I had never spoken to before would stop me in the corridor to express their appreciation for my 'courage'. I was taken aback, because I had been calling myself an utter coward for not interceding when it was obvious that the men were assaulting them.

But eventually, I came to relish the thought that the women regarded me as a real man, despite not being conventionally masculine.

My friendships with women were unusual, because a gulf divided men and women at Stephen's in my time. It was a bizarre standoff, which spoke volumes about the dysfunctional disarray between the sexes in modern India, even in this privileged set of young people.

The two groups co-existed, sharing classrooms and roaming the same campus during the day, but they didn't integrate. Their interaction was largely restricted to banter in the classrooms or awkward conversations in the corridors or café. (While groups of men would leer covertly from the sidelines, there were no outright incidents of harassment.) Dating was rare, even though a large number of women appeared hip and westernized, wearing jeans and even smoking cigarettes in public. The unspoken but overriding expectation, persisting even in the 1980s, was that almost all the women would undergo arranged marriages of some sort. Only a small minority had the assurance that they could marry a man of their own liking.

As for sex, the prevailing dictum could be summed up thus: good girls didn't date, ever. Adventurous girls dated, held hands and, if sorely tempted, moved on to kissing and fondling. Only women who had decided to live dangerously had real sex.

The chances of friendship between men and women were also soured by the sexism that dominated the campus back then. Many men seemed unable to think of women in any other way but crude sexual terms, an attitude exemplified in the 'chick charts' published frequently on the college's official notice board, ranking women in accordance with their overall attractiveness as well as by individual body parts.

While at Stephen's, I didn't reflect on the ease with which I formed and sustained strong friendships with women. But I wondered about it later, for I had had little exposure to women until then—between not having sisters and languishing in a boys-only environment for much of my school life. It was evident that several of the women at Stephen's thought of me as a close friend, allowing me into intimate spaces and thoughts like they would do with their women friends. My being a man was not, in itself, a barrier to a real friendship.

For my part, I responded first to the fact that the women at Stephen's didn't seem to think I was a freak. I also liked the fact that their group dynamics did not amount to the superficial back-slapping ties that existed between men. I felt I fitted in with them, with the gentler, more tactile, more caring and more principled way they behaved towards each other as well as the world in general. And crucially, perhaps I also subconsciously realized that they too, like me, were inferiors in this man's world. Disadvantaged in myriad ways and forever at risk of facing violence and abuse by men, this overlap between our struggles made us natural allies.

The lack of sexual tension on my part undoubtedly contributed to the intimacy of our friendships. Though I found many of the women attractive, my anxiety about being essentially homosexual in orientation was becoming so troubling at that point that I denied any thoughts of my feelings indicating any desire beyond friendship. The Stephen's of our days was also such a non-sexual place—bereft of couples necking or even holding hands—that I never felt pressurized to prove that I was attracted to any woman. Similarly, as the women were constrained from showing that they were attracted to me, they didn't pick up on any of the hints that revealed I was gay.

As for my close women friends like Rosie, my first instinct later in life was to reductively explain their affection for me as stemming from the proverbial 'fag-hag' syndrome, the intimate friendships that often occur between gay men and sympathetic women. But Rosie disagreed vehemently, explaining that she and other women had never thought of me as the 'safe gay friend'. To my great surprise—as I had assumed that women too would condemn femininity in men—she said they had held me as an ideal for men, whether heterosexual or not, because 'we felt you saw the world in the same way as us. We were amazed that a non-sexist boy existed, a boy who saw each of us as a person, who was interested in us as friends for being funny, smart, intelligent, and who wasn't just into the obviously beautiful trophy girls.'

While my homosexuality was not an issue for my women friends at Stephen's, it was my own growing awareness of being gay that caused a crisis within me. Within just weeks of joining Stephen's, I realized that the men on the campus, including my peers who had been attracted to other boys at Doon, had now turned heterosexual.

There was no doubting their desire for women. They stared surreptitiously at the women in the corridors, talked incessantly about their crushes, boasted about how they had secured a date (nothing more than tea in the café), and told tall tales about how close they were to getting laid. Battered issues of *Playboy* and *Hustler* made the rounds of the campus. Pin-ups of Katy Mirza, a well-endowed Indian actress from those days, and busty blondes festooned their rooms. Several among the men went off to lose their virginity at the nearby brothels on G.B. Road or sneaked call girls into their rooms.

All this made me realize that they were not attracted to me or to other men. Yet, I remained attracted to a number of them. The singularity of my sexual and romantic orientation started becoming nakedly evident to myself—the fact that only I was a homo, and the rest were heterosexual.

I never had to confront this fact at Doon because, despite the pervasive homophobia, it was a homo-social space and same-sex orientation had been the norm. But here, it was clear to me that only two or three of the men I was attracted to displayed even the slightest hint of mutual attraction. This turnabout from Doon fueled my feeling that true homosexuals like me were inferior and abnormal, forever lusting furtively after people who obviously weren't attracted to us and indeed, would probably be enraged if they learnt that we desired them.

Compounding this new source of self-loathing was a constricting new fear—that people would discover my homosexuality. Once I realized that I was so fundamentally different from other men on this vital count, it followed logically that I had to hide the fact from everyone.

My apprehensions were confirmed when, within a month or so of joining Stephen's, the cover story in a student-run campus magazine portrayed the handful of us who had joined that year from Doon as effeminate homos. If I recall correctly, this unpleasant article was titled 'The Dosco Bird Bath'. It caricatured each of us ex-Doscos as feminine birds of one kind or another, mincing, chattering and splashing around an ornate bird bath. Alongside each sketch, there was a pseudo-scientific feminine bird name as well as some scornful annotation about our individual traits as bird species. The place of pride in this grouping had been given to me as well as a close friend of mine, who also had somewhat feminine mannerisms.

There was no doubt about the homophobic sentiments motivating the authors of the article. Cravenly, they had not signed their names, publishing it as an anonymous piece.

I didn't need any more evidence to realize that I needed to conceal my homosexuality at all costs. The dangers were very clear.

My immediate worry became that any signs of effeminacy—the stereotyped characteristic of homosexual men—would confirm people's suspicion that I was indeed homosexual. Once again, as when I joined Doon, I began to fret about how I could disguise my feminine traits. But the difference was that I now had two shameful secrets to hide—the original shame of being feminine, and the corrosive new one of being homosexual.

To look like other Indian men, I grew a moustache. It was sparse and patchy, and looked hideous above my wide mouth. But, at that time, it was a reassurance that I was passing myself off as just another 'normal' man. I was to learn later that I was not alone in this quandary in their desperate search for safety, gay men the world over have done everything possible to masquerade as straight men.

But I gradually realized, much to my surprise and relief, that nobody seemed to be remarking about my femininity anymore (beyond that one mocking article in the campus magazine). This turnaround was probably because I had passed the age where I looked my most androgynous. I had also learnt during my years at Doon to disguise or erase altogether the most overt of my feminine mannerisms. And I gradually realized that many of the men attending Stephen's who had not been to regimented, British-tradition schools like Doon, were less macho in their mannerisms. Given their habit of walking languidly, openly holding hands, and even cuddling each other, my own softness did not stand out so sharply.

So this original shame and fear, which had burdened me ever since I joined La Martinière, receded into the background. (But remaining unresolved and unaddressed, I was to find it inevitably re-emerged periodically, even late into my life.) Its place was taken by the new shame and fear about being homosexual.

My desperation to hide my homosexuality was intensified by the realization that it was also condemned by adults. When out with my parents, whether in Calcutta or Delhi, I found that the conversation often turned to prominent men who were rumoured or known to be homosexual—the unmarried editor of a Calcutta newspaper, an unmarried business magnate who reputedly had a young male lover in his staff, and a former nawab in Delhi, who was married and had children. I don't recall a single mention of women rumored to be lesbian; the conversations were all about men.

These men were spoken about in disparaging, hate-filled tones that I never heard in any other context, even when talking about the most vile politician or corporate swindler. Inevitably, someone would call them pansies, the insulting word triggering unpleasant memories of Nutty taunting me at Doon. Someone would pronounce that they should be sent off to England or Pakistan, as homosexuality was a vice peculiar only to English and Muslim men.

Far from contesting these comments, everyone seemed to be wholeheartedly amused. I shrank at seeing that my father was often an active participant in these discussions, adding prejudiced comments about these men, even though he knew several of them well. I was too unsure of myself then to dwell on the peculiarity that the class of Indians who were most sexually liberated—what with the strip-tease shows, affairs and divorces—reviled just one kind of sexuality so intensely, and that too a sexuality that was rarely seen in that era, in which there was not even a single avowed homosexual across the country. These repeated displays of homophobia convinced me that I would never get succor from anyone, not even my parents, if they discovered I was homosexual.

Capping all this, there was nothing in the India of the early 1980s to help a young man or woman deal with his or her homosexuality. There were no openly gay men or women visible to validate the way I felt, or for me to emulate, or turn to for advice and help. Homosexuality or gay issues were never talked of in Indian newspapers or magazines at that time, not even in popular 'agony aunt' columns. Homosexual themes were not portrayed in films or the nascent television programming of that time.

There was nothing positive or supportive that could have served as a lifeline, as an affirmation to help me cope with my fears and anxieties. There was just a nullifying silence, punctuated by instances of virulent homophobia. I began to feel there was no one else like me, no one else with this shameful, evil desire for people of the same sex.

I couldn't help but look into my future, and everything I saw was a source of despair. As an adult, the world was forcing me to define myself sexually, to place myself in the camp of normal, heterosexual men or that of the despised, deviant homosexuals. I would have to hide my homosexuality forever, or end up as one of those reviled men that everyone gossiped about. There was no happy ending possible. My distress increasingly took on a sense of hopelessness that I had never known before.

I even began to feel distanced from Alka and Rosie despite our enormous affection for each other. A wall of secrecy about my homosexuality had begun to divide me from them. We were sitting at a café when one of our women friends jokingly said that I should marry Alka—her parents were pressuring her to tie the knot, and wouldn't taking this step be the happiest possible solution?

Tears welled up in my eyes, and with obvious distress I said I couldn't marry anyone. I recall the look of consternation on all their faces. But despite my cryptic, bizarre response, they didn't probe further, probably because it was clear that I was holding myself back from sobbing.

So I kept my dark secret to myself, a subterranean source of anguish. My despair might eventually have mounted into some kind of breakdown, but I was spared this predicament because of my father's loving attentiveness. He and I had started to become close since my last years at Doon. Though I remained attached to my mother, with maturity I could see that I was wrong in taking sides in their conflicted relationship. Sensing that I was deeply troubled for a reason that I could not confide in him (he later told me that by now he had a sense that I was homosexual), my father urged me to move to the USA to complete college, ideally close to Bharat, who was an undergraduate at Harvard. He said the new setting would do me good.

He had looked intently at me while saying this, obviously hoping that this overture would give me the confidence to open up to him. But I had looked away evasively, because uppermost in my mind was the fear that he would despise and disown me if he came to know that I was homosexual.

4

In America

Heeding my father's suggestion, I left St. Stephen's after three semesters, and headed to the US, to Tufts University in suburban Boston. It was January 1982 and I was twenty years old.

I missed Alka and Rosie intensely—writing them long letters and phoning frequently, despite the prohibitive cost of international calls back then. But I also felt a huge sense of relief at being in a place where I was anonymous, with no one on the campus knowing anything about the stigmas I carried from my past. Even Bharat, at Harvard, was a twenty-minute bus ride away. It was a completely new start.

I desperately hoped that being in the US, a beacon of freedom and progress, would somehow help me deal with the anguish and fears raised by my homosexuality. But it proved to be an unrealistic hope. America was not the 'promised land' I had imagined it to be in the naiveté of a young man from a distant developing country. I soon found, astoundingly, that not only was homosexuality criminalized here, the hatred for it was immeasurably more real than in India.

My initial steps in confronting my homosexuality were so furtive and ridden with shame that while making them, I never imagined that they were steps forward—that they would cumulatively add up to emancipation for me. Thus, at the sprawling university library, praying with a pounding heart that no student I knew should chance upon me, I began to read the occasional articles in the *New York Times* and *Boston Globe* about homosexual issues. I would hold the newspaper in such a way that people sitting nearby could not see what I was reading, or I would make a great show of pretending to be engrossed in an unrelated article on a facing page. So, it was in this illicit, conflicted way that I first came to read and learn about homosexuality, about my homosexual self, the self of my intense yearnings, as well as of self-loathing and despair.

So absolute was my lack of formal knowledge about the issue that every article came as a revelation. Despite studying at India's leading school and college, I had never come across the slightest scientific information on homosexuality, not even in biology textbooks. The sum total of my reading on the subject had been a handful of sexual passages in Harold Robbins's potboilers and Gore Vidal's oddball *Myra Breckinridge*, along with milder allusions in Jacqueline Susann's books. The only other context it found mention was in the disparaging comments made by my peers at Doon and Stephen's, as well as my father and his friends. All my life, so far, I had been trapped in a prison of ignorance and prejudice constructed by others.

The articles that I read most attentively, almost greedily, were those reporting on the roots of individual sexual orientation, a matter of obvious personal relevance. I knew nothing at all about it. Indeed, until I read these articles, I had had no way of knowing that the study of sexuality, including sexual orientation, was an established field of research. In Europe, it had dated back a century to Richard von Krafft-Ebing's *Psychopathia Sexualis*, followed by the sympathetic work of Havelock Ellis, Magnus Hirschfeld and Sigmund Freud. Alfred Kinsey's research in the US in the late 1940s marked another watershed, like Freud pointing to how widespread same-sex attraction was between men and between women.

As it happened, the early 1980s saw major advances in research on sexual orientation, led not just by mental health specialists but also by a broad range of sex therapists and researchers. Hence, I was faced with a bewildering onslaught of information to digest. At that point, research began to show that sexual orientation, including homosexuality, had complex origins that included genetics and hormones as well as psychological dynamics within the family and society. The older and cruder ideas—that homosexuality was a mental illness or was caused by traumatic heterosexual experiences—were finally giving way to more sensible theories and understandings.

I was riveted by the arguments put forward for one set of causes or theories, as well as the rich counter evidence. Thus, at that time, results from several major studies suggested that gender non-conformity in childhood—'sissiness' in boys and 'tomboyish' behavior in girls—was a clear marker for homosexual orientation. This theory instinctively made sense to me, given the strength of my feminine traits as a child.

But I read that even this theory was hotly disputed, as other studies showed that gender non-conformity was not a necessary prelude to homosexuality because many homosexual men were masculine during their boyhoods and many lesbians feminine as girls. While I couldn't resolve these often-conflicting arguments, I felt enormous relief at seeing that homosexual attraction was discussed in reasoned, matter-of-fact terms, as part of a scientific effort to understand a complex human issue, instead of the prejudice that characterized every mention of it back in India.

I also remember my relief at realizing from these articles that the consensus among American psychotherapists and sexuality researchers was that same-sex attraction was not an abnormality or a mental illness but a normal variant of human behavior. This had been one of my strongest dreads—that my homosexual desires meant I was crazy or deviant. I read that nearly a decade earlier, in 1973, the American Psychiatric Association had removed homosexuality from its list of mental disorders in response to protests by homosexual men and women as well as to the wealth of research that found no difference between the happiness and well-adjusted nature of self-identified homosexual men and heterosexual men. I was equally relieved to find that most American mental health experts now felt that the goal of therapy with homosexuals should not be to convert them to heterosexuality, but to help them become happier with their orientation.

My other recollection about those articles on homosexuality is that, with a few exceptions, they were grim, both in subject matter and tenor. I read with disbelief the numerous articles about the hate and persecution faced by gay Americans. Everything I had absorbed in my teens from American and British novels, movies and even pop music—not just the sexy purring of Donna Summer and Barry White but also Baez's '*Love song to a stranger*' and Dylan's '*Love is just a four-letter word*'—had made me imagine that Westerners had wonderfully free sex lives, irrespective of the form it took, unburdened by notions of shame or by censure from others, let alone criminal prosecution by the government for such things as adultery, pre-marital sex or homosexuality.

Prominently in the news at that time were legal battles over US laws that criminalized homosexuality, and this was where I learned that homosexuality was a serious criminal offence in over half of the fifty American states, including Massachusetts (where I was studying then). Astonishingly, men were being arrested even in the privacy of their homes for having sex with their boyfriends or other men. Convictions could lead to jail terms of up to twenty years.

Other articles reported on how homosexual men and women lived in terror of being thrown out of their jobs and homes, and being socially destroyed if their sexual orientation was discovered. This forced them to lead double lives—outwardly 'straight', and 'gay' only to others like them—or move to urban ghettos to find a semblance of community and acceptance.

Somewhere, I read that US immigration law explicitly barred 'suspected or self-declared' foreign homosexuals from entering the country because they were 'afflicted with sexual deviation'. This meant that I would be unable to immigrate if my sexual orientation was discovered, and I would have to return to India, a prospect that now terrified me.

These chilling articles made me realize that my worst imagined fears about the persecution faced by homosexuals were a reality even in the US, though I had assumed it would be a safe haven, a modern democracy that had long guaranteed equality for every citizen, even those who were homosexual.

Another set of disturbing articles was about a mysterious killing disease among homosexual men, which had been discovered in the summer of 1981, just six months before I arrived in the US. The basic facts about this disease were still trickling in. Doctors in Los Angeles and San Francisco, and subsequently in New York and other major American cities, were finding that young and middle-aged homosexual men, ranging from twenty-five to forty-five years, were developing harrowingly severe forms of diseases, including extremely rare cancers, pneumonias and parasitic conditions that only affected people whose immune systems had been devastated. Many of them died rapidly, failing to respond to even the most powerful drugs available.

As early as mid-1982, experts feared that this deadly disease had reached epidemic proportions among America's homosexual men, with tens of thousands of them thought to be silently infected and certain to develop life-threatening ailments in a few years. Fear turned into panic among homosexual men because, at that early point, scientists still didn't know the cause or exact means of transmission. Theories abounded—some stated that it was caused by 'poppers' and other inhaled party, drugs, while others opined that it spread through the air by sneezing or coughing. It would be nearly another two years before it was known with certainty that the cause of the disorder was a virus that was primarily spread through sexual intercourse (whether homosexual or heterosexual), and that latex condoms were virtually fail-safe in checking its sexual transmission.

No one even knew what to call the terrifying new disease. Some derisively called it 'the gay plague'. Health experts first called it GRID, for gay-related immune deficiency, suggesting an inherent link between homosexuality and the syndrome. In mid-1982, a year after the first scientific reports describing the condition, the disorder was given the name by which it is now known—Acquired Immune Deficiency Syndrome or AIDS. But whatever it was called, the stigma against homosexual men in the West worsened because of their association with this burgeoning, frightening epidemic.

These bleak articles made me realize how unwelcoming the Tufts campus was to gay students. Rather like at St. Stephen's back in Delhi, the college felt entirely heterosexual, a universe of men and women attracted only to the opposite sex. This reality was concretely evident here because amorous desire was so visible everywhere, in their casual flirtation and necking. In contrast, gay men and women were invisible—thus, not even one couple was to be spotted romancing amongst the vast throngs of straight couples that filled the main lawns during the 'Spring-Fest' rock concerts. Out of the eight thousand students at Tufts, even by the time I graduated, I knew definitely of just two other gay men, and not even one avowedly lesbian woman.

I was not alone in my predicament. The overwhelming majority of gay students at Tufts in my time, whether American or foreign, did not join the Tufts Lesbian and Gay Community (TLGC), the student-run lesbian and gay group. Though the group was established several years before I joined Tufts, it was not a visible presence on campus, and in my years there, I did not even know of its existence. My own fears and the fact that I was a foreigner unfamiliar with this new setting kept me from actively seeking out the TLGC. However, it is telling that even the small number who did join the TLGC did so with great apprehension. Even in the mid-1980s, in their annual group photos, TLGC members wore bags over their heads to hide their identity.

There were sound reasons for not revealing one's sexual orientation at Tufts in those years. Even though gays were practically invisible, homophobia was rife on campus. A year before I joined Tufts, homophobic graffiti—Fags Must Die—had been spray painted across the Memorial Steps. In the dorms, men and women discovered to be gay were often ostracized. Sensing this, I soon moved to an off-campus apartment, despite the twenty-minute commute by bicycle through a grim neighborhood.

Not only did the university's administration make little effort to combat homophobia among students, it also displayed overt homophobia in its policies. Thus, the TLGC's application for official recognition as a student group—so it could receive funding from the university like the other student groups—kept getting rejected, year after year. Similarly, despite the many reported incidents of homophobia on campus, the university refused to add sexual orientation to its non-discrimination policy. By not handing out AIDS prevention information, the university also shirked responsibility for helping its students protect themselves against AIDS, even though the disease was by then known to be cutting a swathe through young gay men, many of whom were infected in their college-going years.

At that time, especially on days when I was feeling low for one reason or another, I would often feel dirty, like a sex-obsessed freak, for poring secretively through these news articles, or the gay sex ads and personals in the *Village Voice*, the bohemian newsweekly. However, I realized later that this exposure to gay issues had a liberating impact on me.

The regular mention of homosexuality was profoundly affirmative in itself. The realization that there were countless other men and women facing the same challenges and fears as me gradually helped break my apprehension that there was no one else in the world with my shameful affliction. This utter psychological isolation, the invisibility to even each other, was among the very harshest aspects of being gay. In one of the earliest articles on homosexuality that I had read upon reaching the US, a gay psychiatrist had commented that it was 'a miracle' if any homosexual could become a stable and happy individual, since 'unlike women and blacks who can at least identify with one another, gays have no one to counteract the negative societal assault on their egos'. I was so struck by this insight that I purchased this issue of the *New York Times* from the newsstand, storing it out of risk of discovery in a suitcase and keeping the entire day's paper so that the article would not stand out. And, at least in the liberal papers that I read, despite the primarily grim context of the articles, I found that the reportage was respectful of homosexual men and women. They were portrayed as normal people engaged in the universal search for fulfillment in life, seeking romantic love, family and community, acceptance and self-respect.

The usage of the word 'gay' instead of 'homosexual' in the *Village Voice* and by gay people themselves, itself reinforced this sense of respect. Both the *New York Times* and *Boston Globe* used homosexual in their own text, though the individuals they quoted often used 'gay'. Even in those early days, when my gay-related politics were yet to take root, I was intrigued by the word 'gay'. Though I didn't know why it had become a synonym for homosexual men (it being many years before the Internet made information readily available), I loved the joyous association, and also that it left us beguilingly undefined and, consequently, wholly human—rather than defining us reductively in sexual terms, as in homo*sexual or* in *sexual* orientation. Being gay was a matter of the heart's desires, not solely of sexual desires.

There were also articles that were inspiring. There were frequent reports on mobilization by gay men and women to pressure politicians to get rid of 'sodomy' laws, and prevent discrimination in employment and other aspects of life. Several men arrested under sodomy laws had taken the police to court. Many individuals and groups came to their help, not just gay activists, but also decent-minded straight people who simply believed that everyone, irrespective of their orientation, should be treated justly.

Some months after I had read about homosexuals being banned from immigrating to the US, I found out, to my delight, that an American judge had ruled that this law was unconstitutional. I noted the courage of a Congressman who fought back after his homosexuality came to light, and the outpouring of support provided by his constituents and well-wishers, who insisted that only his political ability mattered in public office, not his orientation. I read about the annual lesbian and gay 'pride' marches in Boston as well as other major cities.

All this was a huge affirmation compared to India, where it had seemed as if there was no one else openly struggling with these desires or the stigma against unconventional genders. Here, there was openness as well as struggle.

While the pace of change of dealing with my homosexuality was excruciatingly slow, giving me little succor at all, I found I was being rapidly transformed in other ways by being at Tufts and the US.

I realized that rather than lacking interest in academics, I relished every intellectual challenge, and was grateful just to have this chance to learn and prove myself. To my surprise, I soon found myself excelling in all my courses. I had done decently in India, apart from that one year when I played the class joker at St. Stephen's, but here I excelled as a result of my genuine interest in these subjects as well as the resulting diligence.

It would have been difficult for all but truly indifferent students to not be infected by the industrious mood. Teaching was taken seriously. Professors arrived on time in the vast, modern classrooms—which to me seemed like the plushest movie theatres in India—and had clearly prepared their lectures painstakingly, almost as if they had laid out in advance what they would say from minute to minute. Learning was taken seriously by almost every student—we unfailingly read each word of the lengthy texts assigned for every course, even though this often amounted to reading hundreds of pages in a single week. Even the course syllabi were impressive—the logical progression from one stage of learning to another, the carefully selected readings, the regular schedule of classroom exams and take-home essays, and the clear criteria by which one's work would be graded.

Perhaps the most thrilling aspect was to have broad, multidisciplinary coursework to choose from, rather than the British-Indian system of focusing on just one discipline. At St. Stephen's, I had found much of the assigned literature coursework fusty and irrelevant, comprising Chaucer, Dickens, Fielding and the Romantic poets, with only Shakespeare capturing my interest. But at Tufts, I realized that without conscious design on my part, I had been drawn to courses and reading that addressed injustice or marginalization of any kind, whether social or economic. This had become the unifying theme linking the diverse courses I was selecting, spanning modern India's political economy, Latin American history, communism and radical politics in developing countries, the global political economy of hunger, several courses in economics, and modern American fiction and poetry.

These readings helped me make sense of my own situation of exclusion. My reading about homosexuality had already made me realize that I was not entirely alone, that there were scores of men and women who were dealing with the very same anguish as me of their vilified same-sex desires. But these books about poverty, racism and subjugation of different kinds made me realize that the predicament of gay men and women was no different from that of countless other outcasts. Through them, I discovered that we were part of an even larger and more universal community of people—oddly, even a majority of the world—who had been marginalized by mainstream society, always on bogus grounds. It was a turning point for me, and I never forgot the handful of books that changed the way I looked at the world.

One was Mulk Raj Anand's *Untouchable*, written in the 1930s, which portrayed a day in the life of Bakha, a young man from an 'untouchable' caste. Like generations of his ancestors, he had no choice but to follow the caste occupation of cleaning latrines in the village of his birth—these being pit latrines from which faeces had to be scraped off with a broom and then hauled away in a basket, lumps of which inevitably spilled onto him. Could there be a more accursed occupation to be born to, to be condemned to for life?

The injustice was made even worse by Anand's account of how the better-off reviled Bakha for his work, paid him a pittance, and shrank from his touch even though each of them depended on him for maintaining community hygiene. And to my sharp discomfort, I realized that *Untouchable* depicted realities that persisted even in today's India, fifty years from the time Anand had written it. I recalled how the men and women employed as 'sweepers' at public places (including the schools I had attended) were always visibly small and shrunken from generations of deprivation. They themselves avoided touching or even looking at anyone, and everybody seemed to instinctively avoid touching them as if they carried some terrible, contagious disease.

Just as disquieting was *Native Son*, a novel by Richard Wright, a leading African-American writer from the 1940s. My stomach turned on reading its chilling opening lines, set in a tiny, dark ghetto room: 'A huge black rat squealed and leaped at Bigger's trouser-leg and snagged in his teeth, hanging on.' Those first pages of violence set the tone for the rest of the book. Twenty-year-old Bigger Thomas, an impoverished black man in 1930s Chicago, accidentally kills a white woman. Then, terrified that his black girlfriend will tell others about it, he rapes and murders her too. Bigger finds that this violence, for the first time, has given him a first sense of freedom in a life otherwise dominated by fear and racial oppression.

'In all of his life, these two murders were the most meaningful things that had ever happened to him,' Bigger thinks to himself. 'He was living, truly and deeply, no matter what others might think ... Never had his will been so free as in this night and day of fear and murder and flight.' Such anomie, Wright angrily showed, inevitably gripped many black Americans because of the extreme, dehumanizing racism they faced through their lives. (James Baldwin, another great African-American author, wrote, 'No American Negro exists who does not have his private Bigger Thomas living in his skull.')

The naked anger of Wright's writing was such that it made everything I had ever read so far seem tame and censored. His anger also shook me into realizing just how unjust a country even America was, and therefore made me conclude that perhaps all societies, even those claiming to be havens of liberty, were inherently cruel in how they treated large groups of people within or outside their borders. (This being many years before globalized television news made viewers intimately familiar with the problems of every part of the world, those of us from developing countries still naively harboured the colonial-era notion that the Western world—in particular Britain and the US—was perfect, while our own societies were congenitally and shamefully backward.) That realization was reinforced by Howard Zinn's *A People's History of the United States*.

I was stunned when Zinn laid bare the hidden savagery of the US's past and present—the merciless genocide of Native Americans in centuries past; the brutal slavery of millions of Africans; the shameful use of napalm, Agent Orange and nuclear bombs against civilians; and the chronic failure to tackle its massive domestic burdens of poverty and social problems. What a chasm there was between the glorified popular notion of America as the promised land of freedom and prosperity, and its true reality—this bleak, violence-torn country, some parts of which seemed more despairingly Third World than even the worst of India.

I had never read history like this before—accounts based on the views of women and men who had been dispossessed, excluded and kept disenfranchised rather than the elite, who wrote about the past from their own perspective. Hearing their voices speak from the book—Zinn had culled every possible source for written records of slaves, subjugated women, prisoners and other kinds of excluded people—filled me with an empathy for what they had been through as well as admiration for the ways in which they tried to emancipate themselves, despite the seeming hopelessness of their cause. It was through Zinn's book that I also began to understand that, while human societies were inevitably unjust and cruel in their treatment of vast numbers of people, the excluded always fought back. And it was these efforts of countless ordinary, wronged people—whether African-Americans fighting to be treated as humans, women fighting for equality, or workers fighting for labour rights—that fueled social progress, not the handiwork of altruistic leaders (as elite historians would have us believe). This was a truth that I was to often see played out in events that unfolded during my lifetime.

And then there was Frances Moore Lappé's *Diet for a Small Planet*. This simply written book jolted me awake to the world's astounding material inequities. More than a billion people went hungry every day, and millions starved outright every year, while a well-off minority around the world consumed far more than they needed and wasted enormous amounts. (Examples of over-consumption and waste were on display every day at the Tufts campus cafeterias, where a smorgasbord of food, drink and desserts—so unlike the Spartan fare of Doon and St. Stephen's—was inevitably left half-eaten or discarded by the students.)

Lappé showed that the massive scale of hunger prevalent on this planet was not caused by laziness on the part of the poor, population pressures, hostile climates or even an overall shortage of food, but because of exploitative relations both within and between its countries. Quite simply, a huge proportion of the world's people went hungry only because they were too poor to be able to buy enough food, or too powerless to ensure they too control a share of the world's vast food-producing resources. It didn't take much for me to realize that this was yet another manifestation of the exclusion of the powerless by the powerful.

Lappé's analysis forced me to confront just how much I was a part of the elite systems that perpetuated this suffering, and emboldened by her advice about the small steps each of us could take to help end this inequity, I eventually cancelled my campus 'meal plan', learning to cook simple meals in my off-campus apartment. I also turned vegetarian to free up for others the many kilograms of grain that would otherwise have gone into producing the meat I was consuming.

These books, awakening in me an understanding and empathy for all kinds of exclusion and injustice, inspired me to push my own boundaries of class and privilege, and attempt things that I would not have dreamt of earlier. To begin with, I took up various part-time jobs. I wanted to contribute as much as possible towards paying for my education, rather than letting my parents cover everything. I was impressed by the conscientiousness of many of my American peers, who juggled studies and part-time jobs while putting themselves through college. I felt this model was inherently more responsible than the custom among well-off families in India and Britain, where college-going children were not expected to take up part-time work.

In my second semester at Tufts, in the fall of 1982, I began working two afternoons a week at a small university office that dealt with foreign students. It was located in the basement of a quaint old house. My responsibilities consisted of sorting and distributing the mass of incoming mail, and handling the equally large volume of outgoing mail. I handled this routine work with such enthusiasm—even licking the stamps and labels with my tongue instead of wasting time on using the wet sponge—that the full-time clerical staff began to look at me with some distaste, undoubtedly because my naïve embracing of this work had heightened their awareness of its inherent drudgery. And though I was paid the federal minimum wage, roughly three or four dollars per hour, and my bi-monthly cheques were always for modest amounts, I was thrilled to receive them because they made me feel that I was being responsible and conscientious towards my parents as well as society in general.

Buoyed by this first experience of the dignity of labour, I decided to spend the winter of 1982 working full-time, rather than flying back to Calcutta for the one-month break as my parents had indulgently urged me to. In addition to Anand's *Untouchable*, I had been reading Mahatma Gandhi's autobiography, *My Experiments with Truth*. Inspired by the Mahatma's insistence on cleaning toilets himself, I decided to seek out work as a janitor. I was hired almost instantly, because very few people wished to work over the Christmas holidays. (Not for the first time, it struck me that without exception, all the janitorial staffers were black men, with a handful of white men acting as supervisors.) I was assigned to cleaning the cavernous main gym, including the showers and toilets.

But, to my shame, my dedication and enthusiasm vanished in my very first hours on the job. Faced with the prospect of scrubbing row after row of stained toilets, my strong repulsion to filth nearly overpowered me. It took all my self-control to keep from quitting on the very first day. Every weekday morning, I forced myself awake in the near-darkness of my college dorm, reported for work, donned my cleaning gloves, and somehow spent the entire day cleaning. I worked diligently at mopping and cleaning the sports areas. But I skipped the task of cleaning the bathrooms—cheating by splashing pails of water over the toilets instead of scrubbing the bowls with the toilet brush as I was expected to do.

Hence, rather than being a period of revelatory personal growth, it turned out to be just a depressing year-ending. When the new term began, I hastily refused an offer to stay on as a part-time janitor, and left, shamefaced but relieved! I had realized the limits to which I could follow my ideals. I was certainly not made of the stuff of Gandhi or his true followers.

It was back in India, when I was home for the long summer breaks, that my engagement with matters of exclusion and injustice set down deeper roots. In the summer of 1984, the year I graduated from Tufts, I volunteered with a charitable organization—the Lutheran World Service—which undertook projects in Calcutta's slums and jhuggi-jhopri shanty-towns. I had no practical skills to offer, no first-hand knowledge of poverty, and not even a working grasp of Bengali because of my anglicized upbringing and schooling at Doon. But the director of the charity's Calcutta office generously found a task for me, asking me to document and write what I saw, explaining that they had been struggling to report on their work.

I began to visit parts of Calcutta that I had not even heard of before, despite the city having been my home all my life—Ultadanga, Khudirampalli, Rajarhat and beyond. These were odd worlds, village and city at the same time, these illegal 'squatter' settlements that had mushroomed around ponds and canals. The tiny huts were no more than twenty feet by ten feet each, and were pieced together from mud, broken bricks, and scraps of thatch, plastic and tarpaulin. I was struck by the fact that the families who lived here had so few possessions—just bare mud floors, a calendar on one wall, a handful of cooking vessels in a corner, a few clothes hung on a line, a stainless steel trunk for storage, and no bed or chair.

There were no bathrooms, so everyone defecated in the open. Drinking water came from the few creaky hand-pumps in the area. Everyone bathed in the ponds and canals even though they were contaminated with waste and pollutants. There were no schools in the vicinity, and medical clinics and hospitals were miles away. There were no municipal services, not even electricity connections. In this context of want, anything that the Lutheran World Service did—whether it was the crèches and schools it built or the adult literacy efforts, health programmes and training classes for 'cottage' industries that it conducted—made a world of difference.

Everything I saw and learned over several weeks of visits to a bewildering number of programmes, I turned into a brief report for the charity organization as well as an article in the *Statesman*, at that point Bengal's pre-eminent English-language newspaper. The article was painfully earnest in its portrayal of the charity's noble work—which was probably why the sub-editors gave it the maudlin title of 'Light at Least a Candle'. But the good folk at the Lutheran World Service were delighted by the public attention it got for their work.

Later that summer, I volunteered at a grassroots group working in rural Bihar. I was an urban kid and every leg of the three-day journey by train, bus and cycle rickshaw took me further and further away from the things I knew. The grimy, industrial expanse of Calcutta gave way to the sleepy towns of Patna and Muzaffarpur, and then they gave way to villages, and the villages gave way to hamlets consisting of just a few mud huts grouped together.

Eventually, I arrived at Gokhula village, a short distance from the headquarters of the 'Paroo Parkhand Samagra Vikas Pariyojna', a rural development organization run by a progressive Christian priest. All in all, its premises consisted of a small brick office, about a dozen mud-and-thatch huts, and an acacia hedge circling the compound. As a visitor, I had been allotted an independent hut—a tiny room with a thatched roof and furnished with just a newar cot. (I was given a mosquito net the next day, after a first sleepless night fending off bugs and apprehensively listening to snakes pursue rats through the roof thatch.) There was no fan or lights; electricity was yet to reach anywhere near Gokhula village. There was no running water, just communal hand-pumps for bathing and drinking. If you wanted to go to the bathroom, the dry pit toilets were your best bet.

Despite the alien setting, I settled down readily. In the weeks that followed, the academic material on 'development' as well as the social novels of Anand and Markandaya that I had been studying at Tufts began to take on real meaning for the first time. I began to see that the bucolic sights of rural India—the mud huts, the paddies, the groves of leechi and mango, the buffaloes and children splashing in the Gandak river—disguised a great degree of exclusion and oppression. I began to understand what caste meant in practice—it kept the Chamars and Musahars, the impoverished communities that the Paroo group was working with, forever destitute, landless, illiterate, 'untouchable', and robbed of dignity. On the other hand, it placed me, born of Brahmin parents, at the very peak of these oppressive caste and feudal hierarchies.

From the tense stand-off between the Paroo group staff and the upper-caste landowners, I came to sense how violent much of rural India was. Fights between the landless lowest castes and the land-owning upper castes had already claimed hundreds of lives—disproportionately from the poor—in Muzaffarpur district over the past decade. The upper castes and the wealthy viewed change as a zero-sum game, and they fought ferociously against any attempts by the poor to emancipate themselves.

Haltingly, because it defied easy comprehension, I began to understand the real, human costs of chronic poverty and exclusion. For instance, children born to impoverished families would almost certainly remain impoverished themselves because government schools would not admit Dalit students, and these impoverished families anyway needed their children to work from as early an age as possible.

I began to realize how excluded women were in much of rural India—there were few of them to be seen anywhere in public, and even they had pallus pulled down to their chins. This was a world ruled by powerful men, and they forced women to be invisible.

I also began to realize that even though nearly forty years had passed since the country's birth as a democracy, the basics I took so much for granted—sufficient food, clean water, good housing, decent clothes and modern medicines—were far beyond the reach of a vast majority of Indians.

In those summers, while at home with my parents in Calcutta, I would also learn about poverty and exclusion on my own. Almost every evening, after dinner, I would change into a kurta-pyjama, drive alone to some poorer area, park the car on a side street, and begin to walk. In Calcutta, dire poverty was visible virtually everywhere, cheek by jowl with affluence. Hence, even from my parents' home in exclusive Ballygunje, I didn't have to go far—often just to the vicinity of Park Circus or CIT Road, a ten-minute drive at that time of night—to see how a majority of my compatriots lived.

I would walk aimlessly for hours, wherever my impulse or interest took me, hardly self-conscious because there were so few people awake.

While the daytime visits to Calcutta's slums did not usually trouble me, these nighttime forays were a source of intense disquiet. There was none of the daytime bustle, the appearance of life carrying on despite the poverty, nor the context implying that the Lutheran World Service's projects would soon start making some headway in resolving their economic and social issues. This was Calcutta in extremis—the Calcutta synonymous with Mother Teresa, the destitute and leprosy sufferers, the Calcutta that would soon be immortalized in Dominique Lapierre's *City of Joy*.

The suffering I saw sometimes made me question my life to such an extent that I felt it should end right there, at that very moment. I felt that I should become incapable of returning to my parents' luxurious home or the cosseted wealth of American private colleges, that I should become incapable of living normally or of taking up a conventional career that would assure me of a comfortable life.

In the yellow light and the silence, with the cratered pavements, the heaps of garbage, the threatening black maze of electric wires criss-crossing every street, the giant cockroaches swarming everywhere, the ficus and grass taking over walls and roofs, and the damp destroying bricks and plaster, some of the sights became indelible, remembered in living detail, as if experienced at this very moment.

At a corner step, three scrawny street children eat from discarded patthas of food that they have scavenged. They are barefoot, dressed in filthy ragged shorts and shirts. They look like siblings, the youngest being no more than three or four years old. No parent or home can be seen anywhere in the vicinity.

There is a white-haired, bent-over, bespectacled widow in a telltale white sari, rooting through a stinking expanse of garbage. It is almost meditative, the care with which she looks at things ferreted out from the rotting mess. She discards most of the stuff, placing a handful of select items in a thick plastic bag. Ever so often, she eats things she has found. The only other living beings visible near her, and also eating from the garbage, are a mangy dog with its skin peeling away, several white-and-black cats keeping a watchful eye on the dog, and many bow-legged rats that somehow look threatening, despite their furtive manner. While the cats and rats are well-fed and well-groomed, the old woman and the dog are in a heartbreaking condition.

On the pavements of almost every road are unending rows of people sleeping. I realize that in Calcutta there are homes without walls set right outside the homes that have walls, comprising a city more populous than the city proper. Under the lungis and thin sheets that they've covered themselves with, I can make out the shapes of adults and children holding each other tight in their sleep. All kinds of questions come flooding to my mind, practicalities that never struck me as a child. How do they sleep through the heat, noise, filth and mosquitoes? Where do they go to wash, to defecate? Where do they keep their belongings? Where do they have sex? Where do they give birth?

My most searing recollection is from an evening's walk near Park Circus. I spot a street dog, average in every way, from its size to the widespread skin infections, with the exception of a conical *something* sticking out of its anus. This protrusion is meaty, serrated, probably a part of its intestine or a massive growth of some kind. I stand stock-still, suppressing an urge to retch. Moments pass. The dog moves off.

What happens next seems as hallucinatory and unbelievable then as it seems when I recall it decades later. An impoverished man appears, dressed in a frayed lungi and shirt, and squats to pee beside a parked car, a few metres from where the dog had been. And there, protruding from his anus, is a horrific growth almost identical to that of the dog.

However traumatic these sights were—and however far these places and things were taking me from the life choices normal to young men of my privileged background—they were crucial to my personal development, radicalizing me so that my resolve to work on social justice issues eventually proved to be a lifelong commitment. My own suffering seemed less random and unfair now that I could see so many other people who had also been wrongfully cast out by society. Many of them had suffered far more than I had because of the terrible social failures that seemed to blight virtually every society—shamefully, even democracies with such vast potential as India and the US. (Because I began to view both these countries from the perspective of the excluded, my respect for their remarkable strengths was invariably eclipsed by disillusionment at their almost habitual indifference to the suffering of so many millions of their citizens.) And because my passion for social justice was genuine, my work on these matters made me feel that I was being an upright and good person, that I was living up to the very best aspects of my family's dharma. This gradually bolstered my nascent feelings of self-respect and self-worth.

5

Coming Out

About ten months after moving to the US, I couldn't keep myself from blurting out the truth to my closest friend from Doon. I was visiting him in New Haven over the Thanksgiving break, and had hoped that the joy of seeing him would ease the dispirited mood that I had been in for several days. The bleak skies of November, combined with the week-long break from studies, had brought my worries about being gay to a head. But, to my embarrassment—as our friendship had so far, always been uncomplicated and fun—my spirits had not lifted.

Early evening, we found ourselves sitting face to face in his tiny apartment, him lounging on the sofa bed and me sitting rigidly upright on the chair. He was looking at me expectantly, with an expression of obvious concern that I had not seen before in our decade of friendship, which had begun at age eleven. That look made me break down.

My confession erupted—haphazard and unformed, told through sobs.

I have little recollection of what I told him. I hadn't planned on ever telling him about it, or anyone else for that matter. I had hidden this foul secret about myself so anxiously and painstakingly for the past few years, beginning with my own recognition of it at St. Stephen's, that my fear of it being discovered had become a prison from which I could not plan an escape. A desperate, spontaneous jailbreak was the only way out of this prison, and that was indeed how it happened.

The only thing I recall doing is blurting out, at some point, 'I like men, I like men.'

I'm not sure how long it was before I stopped crying. But it was clear that he had been comforting me for a while before the sound of his voice broke into my consciousness.

I had braced myself for the worst. Instead, there was an outpouring of affection. At some point, as my tears subsided, I heard him say how proud he was to have me as a friend, that I was strong and brave to have faced all this on my own. From the tone of his voice alone, there was no doubting his care for me, as well as no doubting that the secret I had revealed to him had not lessened his affection for me.

For the first time ever, we talked about our Doon years. Despite his evident heterosexuality now, he told me about his romances at Doon, particularly the abiding, mutual love he had experienced in the greatest of those relationships. He was astonished that I had not had sex at Doon, and teased me about how much I had missed out on, given that I now realized I was gay.

Towards the end of my stay with him, he, in turn, disclosed the secrets that had been weighing him down—that in his early years at Doon he had been routinely sexually abused, and that during that terrible witch-hunt launched by the school's prefects in 1976 to weed out homosexuals, only Bharat had not joined in beating him up viciously. Our friendship became immeasurably stronger from that day, cemented by the trust we had placed in each other.

Buoyed by the supportive response to my disclosure, I resolved to confide in Bharat. We had remained deeply attached to each other over the years, and the fact that our days of education overlapped at Doon and then in Boston had only brought us closer. In all this time, from my toddler years to this point at the age of twenty-one, I had never hidden anything but my gay identity from him. Given the paramount importance our family placed on honesty, and now that I had confided in my closest friend, I began to feel that I had to tell Bharat the truth about myself.

Some months later, in the spring of 1983, Bharat developed pneumonia and I went to Duke University—where he was studying law—to look after him. On the evening I reached there, he had a high fever and looked visibly ill. But I forced myself to not latch onto this as an excuse to delay telling him. We had just turned off the lights in his bedroom—I was sleeping on a sofa-bed—when I said I had something important to tell him, something that would explain why I sometimes appeared sad. He sat up in bed and said he had wondered about this.

At this point, I lost every shred of self-control and began to shiver uncontrollably, faced afresh with the terror of being rejected and losing someone I loved so dearly. I began to cry. Bharat, no doubt shocked by this, began to painfully rise out of bed. So I forced myself to say, barely audibly and choked with sobs, 'Bharat, I like men, I'm gay.' (Even at that anguished moment, I felt a twinge of pride that I had identified myself as gay, and gone beyond the euphemism of 'liking men' that I had used with my friend in Philadelphia.)

To my utter surprise, Bharat burst out laughing, saying this was no great revelation—that he had arrived at this conclusion a few years ago. And then, obviously to put my mind at ease, he proceeded to tell me about all the pretty boys that he had been attracted to while at Doon, and about his cute friends at Duke at whom I should make a pass, just in case they were secretly gay too!

After this great leap forward, with my fears of rejection diminished, I gradually began to tell my closest friends. I realized that the intensity of my fears was diminishing with each successive confession, though I still remained tense and apprehensive.

I wrote to tell Alka and Rosie, in a letter addressed to them together. Several weeks passed before I heard from them—such was the slow speed of even airmail to India—but my intimacy with them was so special that I surmised, correctly, that all I would find in their letters would be an outpouring of love and affection for me.

I told Pratap, my eldest brother, when we next met. Looking uncomfortable, he abruptly said we didn't need to talk about such personal matters. With the matter swept aside, our relationship continued much as before. Only decades later did Pratap admit to me that he was so troubled by this revelation that he played his worst game of golf that afternoon.

My greatest surprise was when, on successive weekends while at Tufts, I confided in two dear friends, Rishi and Siddhartha, who were studying at nearby East Coast colleges. (Rishi and I had overlapped at Doon; Siddhartha and I had become close friends a few years back, when on holiday in Calcutta.) Both promptly told me that they were also gay, and had been struggling to decide whether they could safely tell me about it.

I was flooded with indescribable relief. The years of killing isolation had come to an end. I now knew other gay people in flesh and blood. And these were individuals whom I loved and admired, and who were patently not abnormal or sick. It bore testimony to the oppressive strength of the taboos against homosexuality that all three of us were prisoners in the same prison of lies, passing ourselves off as heterosexual and unable to reach out to each other until now, years later. But thankfully, we had broken free and found each other. I now had the company of steadfast friends in charting my life as a gay man.

Eventually, in the summer of 1984, after graduating from Tufts, a few months short of my twenty-third birthday, I resolved to tell my father that I was gay. I reached this decision on my own, without discussing the wisdom of this course with my brothers. I did not speak to my newfound gay friends about it either, as I knew that none of them—whether Indian or American—had told their parents. I had very personal reasons pushing me to tell my father, and they overcame my knowledge that he abhorred homosexuality.

Over my years abroad, my father and I had become ever closer. I was moved that he encouraged me to follow my passion on matters relating to social justice, whether this meant working in slums and villages or entering the poorly paid profession of journalism (which I had decided to pursue, getting a fellowship for an MA at the University of Minnesota's School of Journalism). Indeed, with my growing maturity, I had come to realize that he also genuinely cared about poverty and injustice, despite being a businessman and relishing the finer things in life. I had also come to admire his ability to uncomplainingly cope with whatever difficulties he faced, whether it was his mounting business problems or the inexorable unraveling of his marriage. I marveled that he unfailingly remained cheerful as well as generous to others, regardless of the stress he was enduring.

I didn't want to hide this vital aspect of my being from him, especially now that I had already told my brothers and several of my close friends. And, more than any other factor, there was the old imperative to be truthful with him because he had always put the highest stock on honesty, telling us children that anything could be forgiven if individuals remained unfailingly honest and trustworthy. (I didn't feel a comparable need to tell my mother because though we remained emotionally close, our relationship had not made the transition to an evolving, adult understanding.) If anything, I believed that I had lived up to the letter and spirit of my father's dictum that we must tell him first if we wanted to have homosexual sex. I knew it was only after being honest with him that I could go on to lead life as a gay man.

Though I was determined to tell the truth to my father, I became anxious about doing so once I reached Calcutta for the summer holidays. The scenario that kept repeating itself in my mind was that he would be so consumed by anger that he would throw me out of the house, and disown me. I steeled myself for this. In a feverish, half-fantastical way, I made plans about which friend I could stay with if that happened, and then how I would find the money for my flight back to the US.

I should have had more faith in my father's decency and affection for me. But, at that young age, and faced with this particularly intense fear, I lacked the capacity to think it through calmly, and hence was overcome by my worst fears.

The right time to tell him never seemed to come. Two weeks of my vacation ticked away. And then one evening, on the way to our regular game of badminton at the club, my father asked in a tone that was distinctly purposeful, 'Why didn't you bring along your woman friend to join us this evening?' My heart skipped a beat and then began to thud anxiously. This was not how I had wanted to start my confession, by discussing women.

I said, 'Dad, I don't want her to get the wrong notion—to think that she is my girlfriend.'

He was driving, but even so he turned momentarily to look at me.

After a few moments of silence, he asked, 'Son, is there something you want to tell me?'

Now that I had been given a clear opportunity, all I wanted to do was to avoid it, to delay, to pull back from this precipice. I said, 'Dad, there's really no point, because your knowing won't make either of us any happier.'

He pulled the car over to one side of the road, outside the luminescent, marble expanse of the Victoria Memorial. I was frozen with fear. He looked at me with an expression of sombreness and gentleness that I remember distinctly even today, and said, 'Don't worry. You can tell me anything.'

I buried my head in my arms, began to cry, and said 'Papa, I like men. I like men, not women!' (My courage had failed me, and I couldn't utter the word gay.) I waited, terrified, for the anger and the blows.

Instead, through my disorienting anxiety, I could feel my father hugging me tight, kissing me on my bowed head, saying over and over again that I was such a special child, that he loved me enormously, that everything would be fine. I could not have dreamt up a happier response.

But then I also heard him repeat, almost as if trying to convince himself with a mantra, 'Don't worry, son, we can fight this together. We can solve this.' Despite my gratitude for his loving response, I bristled inwardly. I knew he meant that I should go to a psychiatrist to change my orientation. My father was never the kind to give up on trying to fashion his life and that of his loved ones into exactly what he thought best. But, for the moment, I just gave myself over to the pleasure of being comforted by him, and the joy of hearing such deep love in his voice.

Of course, that discussion had left a lot unresolved. Over the next few days, I could tell from my father's unusual quietness and the intent way in which he looked at me that he was thinking about the discussion we had. Not knowing what to do, I kept silent and wished the matter away.

But then, a week or so later, over breakfast, my father suddenly erupted with uncharacteristic rudeness, calling me 'an unrealistic fool' and left the table—food barely eaten—slamming the dining room door on his way out. At first, I thought his comment had something to do with my plans to spend the summer working in violence-torn rural Bihar, which we had just been discussing and which he was opposed to. By the time it dawned on me that he was actually referring to my homosexuality, and my anger surged, he had already left for his office.

Commandeering my mother's car, I drove rapidly to his office on Shakespeare Sarani, incensed that he should think badly of me even though I had unswervingly followed his diktat to be utterly honest. He gave me a chilling look as I barged into his room without even knocking, but after seeing the anger on my face, asked his staff to leave us.

I erupted, 'Dad, I've never lied to you or done anything wrong, so if you're ever rude to me again about my being gay, I'm going to walk out and you won't see me again!'

My father parried this threat skilfully. 'How can you even be sure you're homosexual if you've never had sex with either a man or a woman?'

I said, 'Dad, trust me, I've always known that I'm attracted to men, not to women.'

True to his forceful nature, he continued to direct the conversation. His strategy worked. I began to feel foolish, standing there like an angry child opposite his imposing table, my back pressed against the wall to keep my knees from giving way.

He asked me to not tell anyone else, that I could at least agree to this wish of his. I said I would consider it, but then immediately became angry at my acquiescence, because I knew that he wanted me to keep this matter under wraps more because of the social shame of having a homosexual son than out of concern for me. To my surprise, I also felt a surge of satisfaction that my father was now paying the price for his own ugly homophobia. This would teach him a lesson, I thought to myself. He would learn never to hate and condemn needlessly. This was sweet, ironic revenge.

He pushed further, saying I should get married, that this is what all homosexual men did in India and even in England.

'There's no way I'll get married, Dad.' I was relieved to find some firmness in my voice once again.

Not one to quit, he said, 'You must promise to go to a good psychiatrist when you get back to America.'

I said 'no' firmly, adding that I didn't see how a psychiatrist could be of any use. My confidence began to return.

I went back to the point that I had been making at the beginning of our conversation, the point that was most important to me. This time, I spoke with a sense of calm and maturity that I never knew I possessed. 'Dad, you have to treat me with respect. I've never lied to you, so don't I deserve your respect?'

My comment must have hit at the nerve centre of his ideas of how homosexuality was innately degrading, because he lost control, shouting, 'I feel sick at the thought of a man giving you a—blow job!'

'Well, if it makes you feel any better, then just think of me giving him a blow job!' I said that without any forethought, equally out of control.

He looked stunned. I had won.

To the end of his life, twenty-six years later, my father and I never fought or even argued again about my being gay, or my decision to be increasingly open about this matter. Though I was aware that he struggled to accept my decisions for many years, he kept his feelings to himself, never once voicing them for fear that it would mar our relationship. And characteristically, whatever his inner ambivalence, he was also my most unwavering supporter through the many crises I was to face in India because of homophobic discrimination.

6

First Steps

Telling my father about my homosexuality was a turning point in coming to terms with my orientation in matters of the heart and desire. My lack of honesty so far with the person whose acceptance most mattered to me had kept me from acting on my longings, through not just the years at Doon but also as an adult. Given the stress my family placed on honesty, if I had had gay sex secretly I would have been consumed by shame, not only regarding my dishonesty but also from having lacked the courage to confront the consequences of my actions.

But now I felt I could allow myself to open up to relationships and sex, rather than constantly denying myself these essential human needs. I decided to enjoy my newfound psychological freedom as well as my financial independence at the University of Minnesota. Suddenly, my life felt unimaginably different from the morass I had been stuck in just thirty months earlier at St. Stephen's, before I left for the USA.

Just a few months after moving to Minneapolis, I summoned up the courage to go to a gay bar—something I had never done during my three years in the US. In the local weekly magazine, the Twin

Cities' equivalent of the *Village Voice,* I had spotted ads for two gay bars. I picked the Saloon, imagining it to be filled with rugged, laconic cowboys in sexy leather chaps, Clint Eastwood or Montgomery Clift look-alikes.

On a Saturday night, I dressed myself in a white kurta-pyjama (which I had washed, starched and ironed to crisp perfection), certain that this stark Indian minimalism highlighted my exotic good looks. I put on an alluring dash of Dior's *Eau Sauvage,* and set off downtown by bus. I knew where the Saloon was housed because I had figured out the directions earlier that week, so that I would be able to find it at night without having to ask for directions. The neighborhood was deserted and looked even seedier than it did in the day.

I finally found myself outside the Saloon. It was a dangerous-looking windowless expanse, whose walls were pulsating with loud music. There was only a dark door leading in, with a small neon sign on top. I was riven with contradictory emotions—sexual excitement mixed with an apprehension so intense that it bordered on anxiousness. Thus, I had a raging hard-on despite the fact that my entire body shook with nervousness.

When I walked in, I was sure to find countless virile men locked in copulation and blow jobs, the handsomest of whom would immediately turn their amorous attentions to me. This was the pleasurable fate that had befallen all, the virginal young men in the few gay porn movies I had seen. What would I do? How should I respond? What about AIDS? What if they wanted to have rough sex?

I walked into a large, dimly lit room, rancid with trapped cigarette smoke, a long bar on one side and a wooden dance floor on the other. There were certainly men everywhere, but barring one or two who were kissing or hugging each other, the others were merely talking, dancing or standing alone along the walls. This was no Dionysian orgy.

My spirits plummeted upon realizing that no one had paid the slightest attention to my entrance. They sank further still when I noticed that the dress code was blue jeans, plaid shirts and boots, a uniform worn by almost every man there, whatever their age, size or looks. In my kurta-pyjama and delicate Kolhapuri slippers, I seemed like a Hare Krishna monk who had stumbled into a lumberjack camp.

I edged my way to the bar and asked the bartender for a beer. Even this was a first for me, my first alcoholic drink. But rather than feeling happy about my brave foray into gay life, I felt like an idiot. Faced with the incontrovertible fact that my attire was odd beyond belief in this setting and not a single man had shown even the slightest interest in me so far, I stood crestfallen by the bar for a long while. I was too dispirited to even savour the novel experience of watching men dancing freely together and sometimes kissing and fondling, the sexiness of some of the men in their rough attire, or the campy histrionics of a particularly ebullient group.

It must have been at least half an hour later that, summoning up all my courage, I pushed myself away from the bar towards a man leaning all by himself against a nearby wall. He was not attractive, so I reasoned that my overture was a safe bet. He glanced at me as I came up, but as I said 'hi' and proffered my hand, he turned away deliberately and walked off, not saying a word. My face aflame with embarrassment, I quickly took his place against the wall, praying that no one had witnessed this humiliating rejection.

An hour passed. It was either my innate courage returning or the unaccustomed effects of the beer, but I finally decided I would dance and try to enjoy myself, even if this meant dancing alone in my odd white clothes. So that's what I did. As much as possible, I kept my eyes shut tight as a way to reduce the indignity of knowing that everyone else on the dance floor had a partner. After a while, I succeeded in relaxing somewhat, losing myself in the music. Madonna's voice seeped into my mind, singing '*You must be my lucky star*' in her trademark devil-may-care twang. Forever after, I thought of '*Lucky star*' as a gay anthem, though it was no such thing.

I skulked out of the Saloon later, my mood very different from the one I had entered with. On the bus back to my apartment, it took every ounce of my strength to prevent myself from bursting into tears. Oh, what an awful evening this was, and I had made such an ass of myself!

Though it was midnight when I reached home, I was so upset that I couldn't keep myself from phoning my friend Rishi in Boston. Rishi was leagues ahead of me as far as integrating into gay life was concerned, and so I was sure he could help me make sense of what had gone wrong. Despite the late hour, Rishi heard me out most sympathetically, tut-tutting when he heard that no one had expressed any interest in me, and sounding appropriately outraged upon learning that the one man I had approached turned away so rudely.

Provided by author

In Minneapolis, 1986, in my quasi-Gandhian attire

And then, with a note of suspicion evident in his voice, he suddenly asked, 'Siddharth, what were you wearing?' (By now, I was infamous among my friends for the Gandhian khaddar kurtas I had adopted during my senior year at Tufts, the most visible expression of my embrace of Indianness.) On hearing my shame-faced admission that I had worn my best kurta-pyjama to the Saloon, he chortled with laughter, mirth driving out all the sympathy from his tone.

Over my two years in Minneapolis, I took huge steps forward in actually leading the life of a gay man. Towards the end of 1984, some months after my disastrous first visit to the gay bar, I went to a meeting of a gay students group, known as the University Gay Community. From flyers on notice boards and announcements in the campus newspaper, the *Minnesota Daily*, I had been aware of the group's existence since my arrival at the university. I had never seen such announcements at Tufts. The meeting was being held late in the week after the late-afternoon classes got over, at the Coffman Union, one of the main buildings near the river.

While searching for the room through its labyrinthine corridors, I realized, to my own surprise, that I was feeling furtive and anxious. Being part of this group was an irrevocable statement on coming out—from now on, it would be difficult for me to control and limit just who all knew that I was gay. I hated the feeling that I still had these worries about being 'exposed' when, intellectually, I knew there was nothing wrong with me, nothing that I needed to hide.

My doubts faded when, upon entering, I noticed that the group of twenty or so men were regular, mainstream students. When we introduced ourselves, I realized that most of them were graduate students, besides a handful of senior undergraduates who—being particularly politicized—led the meeting as officers of the group. The meeting proved to be unexciting, with seemingly no agenda and purpose beyond that of getting together, but I relished it nonetheless.

Barring the visit to the gay bar, it was my first time in a group of other avowedly gay men.

I became a regular participant at the meetings thereafter. My feelings of furtiveness lifted. The meetings were never particularly interesting, always remaining somehow stiff and lifeless, but I still enjoyed the interaction. I hoped too that being part of this group would lead to a relationship, which I ached for intensely. But though I was attracted to several among them, nothing concrete came of it. This was my introduction to the discordant laws of adult attraction—those to whom you are attracted are not attracted back; those you're not attracted to inevitably desire you; and only rarely are the attractions both mutual and simultaneous.

Anyhow, it was no surprise that I was not really sought after. I was awkward and shy in large groups, and these traits were intensified in this context. I was also relentlessly serious, preoccupied with spiritual searching as well as activism, while the rest of the men in the group were far more mainstream, interested in the more normal, fun things of life, such as clothes and television shows. My intense personality was writ large in my semi-Gandhian dressing style, which, even in the biting cold of the Minnesota winters, inevitably included a kurta and khadi jacket topped off by thick, woolly sweaters from South America that were all the rage with US activists back then. Only someone with a taste for peculiarly dressed foreigners would fall for me.

Despite the lack of romance, a great outcome of being a part of this group was that through some of its more bookish members, I was introduced to the pioneering works of gay and lesbian writing, many of them published in the past few years alone. I read them, one after another, in rapt succession: Baldwin's *Giovanni's Room*, Boswell's *Christianity and Homosexuality*, Brown's *Rubyfruit Jungle*, D'Emilio's *Sexual Politics*, Forster's *Maurice*, Foucault's *History of Sexuality*, Genet's *Querelle*, Isherwood's *A Single Man*, Rechy's *Sexual Outlaw*, Renault's *The Persian Boy* and White's *Nocturnes for the King of Naples*.

What a welcome relief it was to discover this vast history of men and women who, like me, desired and loved those of the same sex. It was a relief to know that many others had felt the same things I did—the unstoppable urge for love, intimacy and sex; the shame and self-loathing generated by the prejudice we saw all around us; and the courage it took to act on what we felt, even if we did so in secret. However tortured this history, however tragic the outcome for individual after individual because of the intolerance they faced, it was still validation that I belonged to a community that had heroically endured across eons, despite terrible persecution.

It was a joy to learn that many famous historical figures were also attracted exclusively—or in part—to the same sex. What a roll-call of distinction they were, including Plato, Alexander the Great, Julius Caesar, the Roman emperors Trajan and Hadrian, all the way to Leonardo da Vinci, Michelangelo, Lord Byron, Oscar Wilde, Walt Whitman, Marcel Proust, Leo Tolstoy, Federico Garcia Lorca, John Maynard Keynes, Virginia Woolf, Marguerite Yourcenar and Gabriela Mistral. I hungrily latched on to every one of these examples because they were proof that one could have same-sex desires and yet be an extraordinary individual.

Equally, I latched on to the evidence that at least in a few societies, same-sex desires had been widely accepted. Indeed, the societies that the Western world considered as its birthplace, ancient Greece and Rome, had celebrated same-sex desire between men. (Less was known then about these societies' attitude to same-sex desires between women.)

I read that almost every male Greek god, from Zeus to Apollo and Dionysus, had same-sex passions and exploits attributed to them, as did other celebrated figures in Greek mythology and literature, such as Achilles and Hercules. The great Plato lionized love between men to such an extent that in the Symposium, he argued for an army to be comprised of same-sex lovers. (Thebes did form such a regiment of amorous couples, the Sacred Band, who were renowned for their valour in battle.) In Boswell's ground breaking work, *Christianity, Social Tolerance, and Homosexuality*, I read the affirmation that 'many Greeks represented gay love as the only form of eroticism which could be lasting, pure, and truly spiritual.'

I was startled to find that these societies had treated same-sex desire simply as a matter of taste or preference, often varying over the course of an individual's life. The gender of one's beloved was essentially irrelevant, with personal attributes of character and beauty explaining erotic attraction towards a particular individual. This was in direct contrast to the way same-sex desire was now portrayed—as a fixed, life-long dichotomy between 'heterosexual' and 'homosexual', amounting to an exclusive sexual-emotional attraction to either the opposite or the same gender, with only a tiny minority of 'bisexuals' who were attracted to others irrespective of their gender.

My joy at discovering this history was leavened with outrage that all of it had been so thoroughly suppressed that I was only now, at the age of twenty-three, becoming aware of it. Thus, even in my literature courses at Tufts, from what I or several of my peers could remember, the fact that Oscar Wilde, Walt Whitman, Thomas Mann, Garcia Lorca and E.M. Forster desired men was never explicitly mentioned by professors.

The refusal to acknowledge the same-sex desires of these writers as being relevant to a true understanding of their body of work, let alone to the great works in which they directly address same-sex desires—such as Whitman's Calamus poems, Mann's *Death in Venice*, Lorca's 'Ode to Walt Whitman', Forster's *Maurice*, and much of Cavafy's oeuvre—resulted because this matter was too stigmatized to be mentioned even in the elite circles of Western academia. The times were so absurd that in addition to not dealing with same-sex orientation in literary scholarship, feminism was also dismissed as an irrational demand that would harm the field.

It was only now, building on the gay rights movement that had gathered strength from the 1970s, that an explosion of both novels and scholarship on same-sex desires was underway. It was led by gay men and women themselves, rather than sexologists, psychologists and other presumed experts. Even this efflorescence was restricted to Western Europe, North America and Australia. It would be many more years before the history of same-sex desire in other regions, including India, and amongst indigenous people in the Americas or Australasia, began to be researched and written about, revealing astonishingly wide differences to 'white' societies in terms of greater traditional tolerance of same-sex desires as well as alternative genders.

I found that the existence of homosexuality had not only been suppressed for centuries, a war had also been waged against it. Since my days at St. Stephen's, when I confronted my own orientation and became keenly aware that many people held a pathological hatred for homosexuals, I had assumed that men and women like me had faced stigma and persecution everywhere and always. But even so, what I read now, a chronology of brutality and injustice through almost the entire course of Western history, with one hateful falsehood or the other employed to target men and women attracted to those of the same sex, far outstripped my worst imaginings, each outrage becoming etched into my memory.

The atrocities began in the late-Roman Empire, when 'effeminate' men—those who were penetrated—were castrated or burnt to death. In the innumerable witch-hunts, inquisitions and pogroms launched by the Church as well as secular authorities across Europe from the 12th to 18th centuries, 'sodomites' were hunted down along with witches, blasphemers, Jews and Muslims, blamed for every commonplace hardship suffered by these societies, from bad weather and crop failure to plagues and wars.

Thousands of men were executed for sodomy in these centuries—hung, burnt at the stake, garrotted or drowned, while huge crowds jeered and mocked at them, revelling in their suffering. Even larger numbers of first-time offenders were whipped, castrated, blinded or had their hands and feet severed. Scores of women were executed too for lesbian acts, usually charged with oral sex, a sex crime just one level lower than sodomy.

In England, even more than elsewhere in Europe, persecution of 'sodomites' became a defining national mania from 1534—the year that Henry VIII made 'the detestable and abominable Vice of Buggery' punishable by hanging. The animus set such deep roots that, though most mainland European countries decriminalized victimless sexual acts such as consensual sodomy between adults or sharply reduced the penalty in the late 18th and early 19th centuries, (affected by Enlightenment-inspired thought and the revolutionary Napoleonic Code), Britain continued to execute male homosexuals until 1861. Lesbianism was never expressly punished in British law, the logic being that as women cannot penetrate each other, they were not having real sex.

Inevitably, Britain exported its paranoia about 'buggery' and 'sodomy' to its vast colonial possessions, part and parcel of the imperial notion that it was the white man's burden to civilise heathen natives by replacing promiscuous, sexually-perverse traditions with Christian values. By the end of the 19th century, male same-sex relations had been outlawed across much of Africa, the Americas, Asia and Australasia. (The main exceptions were Dutch, French and Spanish colonies, whose legal systems were primarily based on the Napoleonic Code, and the handful of countries that escaped direct colonialism.) State-mandated persecution of same-sex relations became a universal fact, rather than being a phenomenon exclusive to Christian Europe.

The demonization and persecution persisted. Even at the turn of the 20th century, the lives of Oscar Wilde and other prominent men in both Britain and Germany—including several of the Kaiser's top military counselors—were ruined by legal and social persecution for homosexual relations. Under the Nazis, thousands of men convicted of homosexuality were sent to concentration camps, where most died. Lesbians were made to work in camp brothels, and subjected to systematic rape to cure them.

In the wake of the World Wars, homophobic persecution worsened in many parts of the English-speaking world. The anti-communist paranoia in North America, Western Europe, Australia and New Zealand saw gays being accused of posing a risk to national security, on the grounds that Soviet agents could blackmail them. A similar paranoia about sex crimes saw gays being vilified as perverts who were threats to children.

In Britain, police arrests and court cases involving charges of sodomy, gross indecency and indecent assault outdid even the rate of prosecutions in the nineteenth century. Over a thousand gay men were in prison in 1954, the year that Alan Turing, the British mathematical and computer genius, committed suicide after undergoing court-mandated chemical castration following his conviction on homosexuality charges.

In the USA, McCarthyist campaigns led to thousands of men and women suspected or known to be homosexual getting expelled from the military, and hundreds more fired from government jobs and schools. The medical establishment bolstered the vilification, with the American Psychiatric Association listing homosexuality as a 'Sociopathic Personality Disturbance' in its guidelines in 1952, including it with 'pathologic behaviours such as ... paedophilia, fetishism and sexual sadism (including rape, sexual assault, mutilation).' A sodomy conviction—or sometimes just a mere accusation—typically led to psychiatric examination, and often incarceration in a mental hospital, where a large but unknown number of men and women were forced to undergo sterilization, lobotomies and other devastating procedures. Police vice squads began using decoys to entrap gay men, and gay bars and clubs – and even people's homes – were aggressively raided. (In New York City alone, by 1966 over a hundred men were arrested every week on average as a result of vice raids.) Countless gay men and women were publicly humiliated, imprisoned or incarcerated in mental institutions. Several states required those convicted of sodomy to register as sex offenders.

And then, in the 1980s, AIDS became the excuse to further demonize gay men. Almost all the progress Western gay activists had won since the 1960s—from challenging discrimination at work, to occasionally winning public office, to convincing courts and legislatures to overturn sodomy laws—was quickly imperiled or reversed outright. In the US, Reaganite Christians and other bigots accused gay men of being responsible for the epidemic, and violence against suspected homosexual men mounted across the country. Openly gay men—especially those visibly showing symptoms of AIDS—were thrown out of their homes and fired from jobs. Sodomy-law arrests were always in the news. In 1986, in a confirmation of the increasingly dangerous times, the US Supreme Court ruled that state sodomy laws were not unconstitutional and could remain in place, on the basis of 'millennia of moral teaching'. As a consequence, even private homosexual acts remained a criminal offence in more than two dozen US states.

Reading all this, I often felt that there was no safe place in the world for gay individuals, where we were not criminalized, where we could live without constantly feeling fear, where we could hope to lead open, full lives like everyone else. At most times and places, even in societies that boasted of being beacons of civilization, men and women with same-sex desires had been barbarically persecuted.

And though I searched hard to understand the root cause for gays being singled out across the centuries, I could never find a convincing rational answer. The truth was simply the depressing one that in many societies the powerful men who dominated religion or politics maliciously targeted homosexuals as scapegoats, just as they picked on witches or heretics. Fundamentalist readings of fanciful, obscured myths—such as that of Sodom and Gomorrah—were used as justification. It was easy to fuel such demonization as most societies treated anything to do with romantic or sexual desire—even mainstream, heterosexual desire—with pathological anxiety. This irrational hatred was then dinned into everyone, to be passed down from generation to generation so that it became an unexamined truth, a tenet of religion and culture, bred into the bone. This realization left me forever distrustful of every kind of establishment leader and institution, all those who made and enforced the rules. It seemed almost in their nature to stoke the most inhumane inclinations in people.

Fortunately, as a graduate student on the University of Minnesota campus, these threats also seemed worlds away. For the first time ever, I felt safe, and not worried about being gay. This was in great part because the University of Minnesota was a progressive place and the several gay students' groups that sprang up over the years had already secured remarkable gains, far in advance of Tufts and other elite East Coast colleges.

Not only was the university home to the country's first gay student group—founded back in 1969, a few weeks before the Stonewall Revolution (the contemporary gay-rights movement of assertive 'gay pride' is often dated back to this spontaneous revolt that erupted after a brutal police raid on a New York City transgender and gay bar)—but the university administration had also been admirably supportive, recognizing it as an official campus organization within a year. The original gay group was called FREE, Fight Repression of Erotic Expression, and its radical goal was 'to free people from outdated, damaging moral restrictions' and 'abolish any law or prejudice that prohibits sexual activity between consenting persons.' In 1972, two officers of the group had the distinction of becoming the first same-sex couple to receive a marriage licence in the United States, a decision quickly overturned by a court.

In 1986, the year I graduated, the university amended its anti-discrimination statement to include sexual orientation. This was, in large part, because of the efforts of the gay students' group (of which I was a member) and the University Lesbians. By 1993, far in advance of its comparators, the university had established the Gay Lesbian Bisexual Transgender Programs Office to implement anti-discriminatory policies and integrate queer studies into the curriculum.

Most striking was how largely unafraid we were, those of us who had crossed the harrowing first hurdles of coming out. In contrast to Tufts, gay life on this campus went on in the open with a semblance of normality—if not total visibility. With Rishi, who had also moved to the university for graduate studies, as well as several men from the gay group, I went out for dinner and to the two gay bars in town.

At the bars—including the Saloon, the scene of my disastrous first foray into gay life—the atmosphere was relaxed, with the men enjoying themselves with no apparent sense of threat. None of us, whether Americans or foreigners, seemed to care about the existence of Minnesota's sodomy law, that this would result in police raids or other forms of persecution I had read about in various American states. (Inexplicably, given the state's long history of liberal politics, its sodomy law remained in force until 2001, when it was struck down by the courts.)

In my off-campus apartment building, I cared little about discrimination. Of course, I realized that as a graduate student at a progressive university, I was enjoying a fleeting moment of peace—homophobic discrimination would surely re-emerge when I entered the job market, even with media organizations or in academia.

Encouraged by this blessed feeling of safety, I became increasingly open about being gay. By the winter of 1985, I had revealed the truth about my orientation to dozens of people, even though it was just three years since my first terrified confession.

Thus, within a month or so of striking up a new friendship that was becoming increasingly close, I would inevitably broach a discussion about my being gay. Though I was no longer worried that my confession would provoke an adverse reaction, it still took great effort on my part to initiate the discussion. Subconsciously, it was still highly stressful. Consequently, each and every telling became a formal, portentous event, in which I would tell the friend that I had something to discuss with them and we would then go for a walk or a coffee where I would state the matter seriously, saying, 'I wanted to tell you that I'm gay.'

Everyone reacted differently, but always well. I was struck that not one of the male friends I confided in, whether an American or a foreign student, had ever known an openly gay person. This was a telling commentary about how guarded gay people had to be, and how terribly isolated this made us. But my honesty in this matter imbued these friendships with a special closeness in the years to come, taking them beyond the superficiality that is characteristic of male interaction.

In contrast, many of my new women friends said they already knew lesbian women and gay men. More strikingly, several immediately told me that they'd had romantic relationships with other women, beginning in their teens and continuing right till now, even though sexually they were more strongly attracted to men and hence, did not think of themselves as lesbian. This opened up a fascinating world of fluid possibilities in romance and sex. Though it was a realm I was incapable of making much sense of at that time, I was nonetheless intrigued by their honesty. Very few of the men I knew admitted to ever being attracted to other men, even as teenagers or in some experimental phase of their lives.

My openness about my orientation began to seep into the work environment. At some point, the two teaching assistants with whom I shared our large office room were talking about their girlfriends. One of them, a rather macho, mustachioed American, who looked like a sports reporter but was specializing in mass communication theory in reality, was getting married soon. When they turned their attention to me and there was a distinctly interrogative pause, I said in my most natural tone that I was gay and single.

There was a long silence. One of them then made a polite but meaningless comment that had nothing to do with my disclosure. We all turned to our work, an awkwardness settling over us. I had felt a pang of apprehension in being candid, especially as I hadn't thought this through at all. I remained tense and nervous through the rest of the day. But later, on my bicycle ride home, the discomfort was replaced by a sense of enormous relief when I realized that I no longer had to evade, dissemble or lie like before.

My intense need to disclose this fact about my orientation to people I was close to, and eventually to others who broached questions about my personal life, sprang from the paramount importance my family placed on honesty. It was also of a piece with my fighting spirit, which had now developed into an activist political engagement with social justice issues. And most of all, keeping such a major secret about myself was in itself a killing burden that I wanted to free myself of. Secrets spawn the fear of being found out—and 'fear eats the soul', as an unforgettable Arab proverb puts it.

Thus, my every act of honesty was a blow toward destroying the prison of shame and fear that I had long been caged in. Only by not hiding could I be truly free of fear. Only by not hiding could I bring an end to accepting the harm done to me by other people's bigotry, of viewing myself as shameful and deviant, of agreeing to be cast out and isolated. But, of course, I wished that my orientation had not been made a matter necessitating such anguish to begin with, that—like heterosexuals—I could take for granted that I was 'normal' and have nothing to do with either concealing or disclosing.

Unexpectedly, and with a romantic start worthy of the Mills & Boon novels I had devoured as a child, my first real relationship began. It was the fall of 1985, shortly after my twenty-fourth birthday. While waiting for a play to begin at the Walker Art Center in downtown Minneapolis, I noticed a man looking at me, half-smiling but with a confident gaze. A black polo-neck accentuated big muscles, fine features, thin blond hair and stark white skin. I smiled back. The man came over, said that he'd noticed me several times on the university campus where he worked, and upon waking that morning, he had inexplicably felt that we would meet. And so it began, love and romance, someone to call my own, someone to have every intimacy with—things I had craved for since I was a young child.

I saw M every day after his work got over. I longed for my first daily glimpse of him, the delight of once again feeling my affection for him as well as the thrill of erotic attraction. We'd embrace on the street, pulling each other close for a moment. Once in a while, we would even sneak in a kiss on the cheek. I would draw in his faint body smell, so mild and scrubbed that it almost seemed disinfected.

We spent most of our evenings at my apartment, as it was nearby. Within seconds of closing the door behind us, we'd be kissing wildly. M's lips felt cool and thin, but his tongue felt like a sexual object, thick, probing, with a will of its own. Dinner would be forgotten. Darkness would fall. Hours would be spent feverishly necking on the carpet of my living room or on my bed.

But despite being tremendously turned on by M, it took me several weeks to start overcoming my hang-ups about sex, which had mounted over the many years from Doon to now. Despite coming out to my father, friends and to others, I had so far denied myself sex.

Indeed, from my undergraduate years onwards, I had sought to suppress my sexual desires as part of a larger embrace of other-worldly living—turning vegetarian, shunning alcohol and smoking, practising yoga and meditation daily, and intently reading the philosopher Jiddu Krishnamurti (whose insistence 'to be your own teacher and your own disciple' had encouraged me to think through matters of right and wrong for myself, particularly the prejudices about femininity and homosexuality that I had so deeply internalized).

I had found support for this blanket denial of desire, carnal as well as material, in the Bhagavad Gita and, in vivid terms, Mahatma Gandhi's autobiography, *My Experiments with Truth*. (I was struck that Gandhi seemed just as intensely tortured about his sexual desires as I was, even though the desires he anguished over were heterosexual.) My subconscious motives became clear to me only much later, when I realized that—to me—being celibate meant remaining moral and good, a Gandhi acolyte who was overcoming his earthly desires for sex or for luxury. In contrast, being actively gay—as in having sex—

would mean that I had embraced a lifestyle that I still latently felt was evil and sinful, and would therefore cause me to forfeit any claim to goodness. So I insisted, to M's evident frustration, that we keep our jeans on even while necking, so as to ensure that we didn't end up having real sex.

When we finally progressed beyond necking and M stripped completely for the first time, I was awed by the beauty of his musculature, the heavy pectorals, the curving, thick thighs and the full buttocks, all so different from the light-boned physique of Indian men. Out of his marble-white, hairless body jutted a hefty penis.

But, almost immediately after we crossed this frontier from necking into having sex, our relationship began to come apart. My fears about contracting AIDS were to blame. From what I had read about the AIDS epidemic among gay American men, M perfectly fitted the demographic as he was already in his mid-thirties and had previous sexual experience. My fears were so intense that I held myself back. As I had never had sex and was still emerging from the closet, everything about AIDS seemed like a blind fog of confusion and uncharted terror. However bizarre this sounds, I was too nervous to have sex that could have satisfied M.

My apprehensions could easily have been solved had there been accessible resources—such as counseling services to provide advice on safe sex—at hand. I don't recall noticing any such service on the campus at that point; the university health services certainly did not make a noticeable effort to provide their gay or bisexual students (or straight students, for that matter) with such information. Nor was there any guidance provided by the students' gay group. I had never come across a guide to safe sex.

With no source of expert advice to help me out, I gleaned whatever I could about the risks of AIDS transmission and the particulars of safe sex from articles in the *Village Voice*, gay magazines, and—to a lesser extent—the science section of the *New York Times*. Despite reading all this with great attention, I never felt confident that my understanding was correct and foolproof, in large part because even this information was not explicit enough and was also hedged with 'ifs' and 'buts'. The most exasperating of these qualifications was, one, that there was a risk that condoms could break or fail, and two, that this advice amounted not to 'safe sex' but only to 'safer sex', a critical qualification that implied that there was still an untold risk of contracting HIV.

Thus, correctly or incorrectly, my conclusions at that time were the following: always assume that your partner is infected. Hence, always have safe sex. Fucking without condoms is clearly unsafe. Fucking even with a condom might be unsafe, because of a risk of the condom tearing. And giving a blow job without using a condom is probably also unsafe. The only safe sex acts were non-penetrative, notably kissing (but even deep kissing possibly carried a slight risk), mutual masturbation, getting a blow job (even this might have a small risk), and giving a blow job only along the penis shaft.

Was it any wonder then, that the only thing I allowed myself to do with M was the limited and unsatisfying repertoire of kissing, masturbation and oral sex where I scrupulously avoided putting his penis head in my mouth?

Eventually, M and I barely had any sex in the remaining four months of our relationship. The high point of our sex together, spread over these months, amounted to a dozen oh-so-pleasurable blow jobs by M. My blow jobs were obviously nowhere on a par with his, not just because I lacked M's expertise, but also owing to my fears of contracting AIDS. They just could not satisfy M. Consequently, I would simply masturbate him to ejaculation.

The problem posed by my fears was compounded by the fact that we were unable to openly discuss the practical matter of how to have satisfying safe sex, or at least to ensure that the lack of good sex didn't destroy our relationship. We barely broached the topic. Never having discussed these issues before, and also feeling awkward because only M was the object of worry about AIDS (given that I had been a virgin till now), I lacked the skills to open up. I'm not sure what kept him from leading the discussion, but he held back.

Our awkwardness was so severe that M and I never talked about putting my fears to rest by getting tested. A commercial test for the antibodies to the AIDS virus—the term HIV was still to be adopted—had became available some months earlier in 1985. People were encouraged to be tested. But there were enormous fears about testing, given the feeling of hopelessness that would follow a positive result.

By now, 1985, there was every reason for my extreme caution and worry. Gay men across the US were living in terror of AIDS, the newspaper coverage of Rock Hudson's losing struggle against the disease making it known everywhere. Many gay men became members of the Hemlock Society, which provided advice about suicide, or convinced friends or sympathetic doctors to agree to help them commit suicide if they fell direly ill.

While it was clear by now that the epidemic was not confined to the US—with every region of the world reporting AIDS cases—it still seemed to be affected more severely than any other country. American health experts already ranked AIDS as one of the most serious epidemics in modern times. One doctor wrote of America's city hospitals at that time: 'The whole era had a medieval feel, with visceral suffering and human decimation all around. Death was vivid, brutal and omnipresent. Every third admission seemed to be a patient in his mid-twenties who looked as if he'd arrived from Dachau or Biafra.'

I knew instinctively, even at that inexperienced age, that my relationship with M would have worked and lasted happily under better circumstances, free of the dread of AIDS. M and I were strongly attracted to each other, and we were both serious-minded people looking for a lasting relationship. But despite M's enormous patience, my worries about AIDS were so crippling that our relationship ground to a halt in a matter of months.

I castigated myself for this at that time. It was only much later in life that I realized that our problem was a commonplace one among gay men, unused to intimate romantic relationships and unskilled in these kinds of sensitive negotiations.

A few months after my relationship with M ended, I began to rapidly lose weight—from my already skinny 65 kg—and was constantly tired. The fear and shame that I may have contracted AIDS from M kept me from seeking medical advice or even mentioning my anxiety to Bharat. But, eventually, finding it difficult to attend classes or cope with everyday chores, I had no choice but to go to the university medical services.

After describing my symptoms to the attending doctor, I said I was from a high-risk group for AIDS. It was the first time I had ever made this admission, and I burned with embarrassment at saying it.

I was very fortunate, because the doctor was thoroughly professional. Ignoring my embarrassment, he simply asked me which high-risk group I came under. I said I was gay. I hastily added, almost involuntarily, that I had barely ever had sex, as if this qualification would reduce the opprobrium attached to being homosexual.

My blood was drawn for testing for the AIDS virus and several other possible causes. The results would take three days to come in, the doctor told me. However, given that my lymph glands were not swollen and I didn't have night-sweats, it seemed unlikely that I had AIDS, he added. I went limp with relief.

Three days later, I was back in his office. My nerves were in tatters—what if his confidence had been misplaced? The doctor walked in, instantly picked up the report—no doubt aware how nervous I was—and told me that the AIDS test had come back negative. He kept up his clinical demeanour but, even so, I could sense that he was pleased to be able to give good news. All I had was a severe case of hypothyroidism, which could be easily solved. This was my first encounter with the terror of testing for AIDS.

I spent another year in the US but there were no more romantic developments in my life. Though what I wanted desperately was a steady and loving relationship, I felt incapable of negotiating and sustaining one, given the mess I had made with M.

I slipped back into a dead-end pattern of burying myself in my work and my ascetic, disciplined lifestyle, besides pining for several men who were unquestionably heterosexual. The latter tendency was, of course, a subconscious strategy to actually avoid sex or romantic entanglements. Though I wrote passionate poems for these men, I had the good sense to never give these lovelorn compositions to them.

I was such a mess, full of emotional yearning and desire but incapable of acting on them, that I once again bolted from any men who showed any signs of being attracted to me. In New York City, where I spent the latter half of 1986 as an intern with a leftist magazine, I met a glorious Brazilian man at a literary party—velvety chocolate skin set off by a shirt of cream linen, with curly locks and an immense mouth—who, ignoring my protests, dragged me onto the makeshift dance-floor, gyrating with his crotch flush against mine. He bit me on the neck and kissed me on the mouth. His exuberance was infectious. I forgot my shyness and self-consciousness for some hours—as I didn't drink alcohol or take drugs, those means of unwinding were not open to me—dancing wildly and kissing him with passion. But when the party wound down, I refused his invitation to spend the night at his nearby apartment. And when he called the next morning, and for several days after that, leaving messages on my answering machine in a plaintive voice, I didn't return his calls.

Beyond that one evening, the sum total of my gay adventures in New York consisted of walking furtively a few times through Christopher Street, picking my way cautiously past the mustachioed gay men in denim and leather, lacking the courage to enter the smoke-filled gay bars or the porn stores. I quickly glanced away if anyone looked at me with interest. In this desolate city of drugs, violence and the neglected homeless, an epicenter of the AIDS epidemic, I was not going to have sex.

Of course, my paranoid sexual abstinence probably saved me from contracting HIV at that early point in my life. By the late 1980s, every third or second homosexual man in New York City was infected with HIV. The marauding epidemic of AIDS consumed my generation of gay men in New York as well as the ones that came immediately before and after it. Nobody—whether rich or poor, white or black, American or foreigner—was spared.

In the winter of 1986, a few months after my twenty-fifth birthday, I left New York City and moved back to India. I had decided against settling in the US even though my five years there had been transformative. The university scholarships and other plaudits I had won in the US gave me a certain degree of self-confidence. My passion for social justice causes now imbued my life with direction and meaning. While I was still not free of every psychological burden relating to my homosexuality, my family and friends had accepted—and often enough, even embraced—my orientation. At least intellectually, I was certain that there was nothing disgraceful or inferior about this matter. And I no longer felt I had to desperately conceal this central part of my being.

Yet, despite all that I had gained in the US, in one of those odd twists of life, I felt that to fulfill myself at this juncture, I needed to return to India, the place I had been so desperate to escape from just years earlier. My work interests seemed hugely more important to me than my personal life or the fact that I was gay. I was aching to work on the issues of poverty and social justice back in my own country. I thought that I could be of real use in impoverished, underdeveloped India, whereas wealthy America had no real need for me.

But, in part, the primacy I gave to my work also flowed from an effort to stave off my fears about the bleak likely course of my love life, which stretched out ahead terrifyingly bare and alone. I had

had just one relationship in all of my years in the US, and that had been disastrously short-lived too. None of my handful of gay Indian friends there were in relationships or even dating seriously. Of all the gay or lesbian Americans I knew, only one was in a live-in, long-term relationship. The few men I had met in the US through gay personal ads, some a generation or more older than me, seemed to have searched fruitlessly for love year after year. Gay men and women everywhere seemed doomed to living lives without lasting romantic love. Societies were so bitterly opposed to our partaking of this joy that they had criminalized us outright.

Only heterosexuals seemed destined to have fulfilling, happy personal lives. My brothers and my heterosexual friends, women and men alike, were almost all in steady relationships with marriage and children on the horizon, following the conventional, time-honored milestones of human society.

The one compelling reason to stay on in the US was the knowledge that living in India as an openly gay man was sure to be even more difficult, and possibly dangerous. I knew that homosexuality was a serious criminal offence in India, proscribed under Section 377 of the Penal Code, which had come into force 101 years before my birth—one of many of Lord Macaulay's legacies still profoundly affecting my life. (I had not yet read the text of the Indian law, but knew that it was similar to the US sodomy laws, all being derived from the medieval English 'buggery' law.) From the months I had spent working in India each summer, I realized that well-off urban Indians, the social class I belonged to, continued to hold bigoted Victorian views on homosexuality. My inkling that attitudes to male same-sex relationships were possibly less hostile in rural India didn't seem of direct relevance because it was an alien world that I could not possibly fit into.

My awareness of the possible dangers ahead was magnified by my father's vehement opposition to my returning. He told me frankly that he feared I would be ostracized and persecuted for being gay. He urged me to settle in the US and to forget about India.

Yet, I eventually set aside my own anxieties as well as my father's warnings. It was not that I was being foolishly headstrong; I had mulled over the matter closely, sometimes even anxiously. The key factor in helping me decide to return was that I didn't expect to lead a 'gay' life in India and there would probably be no scope for a romantic relationship, given that even my half-decade in America had been effectively barren in terms of love and sex.

As it turned out, I had utterly underestimated India's potential for both happiness and trauma, erring on both counts.

7

Love and Fear

I had known that India would not be a welcoming place for a gay man who wished to live openly. But within months of moving to Delhi, where I began to cover economic development and social justice issues for *Business India*, I realized that there had been no discernible progress in how Indian society treated gay issues since my days at St. Stephen's.

Neither the naked homophobia nor the nullifying public silence on gay matters had eased in this half decade. Indeed, in some ways, they were even more widespread and entrenched than I had imagined as a young college student. Five years was an epoch in my short life then, and while I had changed profoundly in how I dealt with my orientation in these matters of the heart and body, India seemed frozen in time.

At *Business India,* I found that several among the senior staff openly used homophobic slurs. Their target, because of some festering office intrigue, was a senior editor, a mild-mannered man from Calcutta in his late thirties, who spoke with a marked British accent and habitually chugged on an unlit pipe. When he was out of earshot, they called him 'pansy' and, bizarrely, an 'effete Bengali homosexual'.

The comments burned especially deep because they were so similar to the ones I had heard from my father and his friends during my St. Stephen's days. And, just like before, no one challenged them either. (In all fairness, I sensed that the magazine's editor-in-chief, Rusi Engineer, was unimpeachably fair-minded, and hence, would not have discriminated against any one for any reason.)

Consequently, from my very first months of employment in India, I retreated from the candour about my gay orientation that I had so come to relish in my last few years in the US. I rebuffed efforts by my colleagues at *Business India*—and then at the *Washington Post*'s South Asia bureau, which I joined in 1988—to know anything about my personal life or develop friendships. I decided against joining clubs such as the Delhi Gymkhana or the India International Centre, concerned that any rumors about my homosexuality would lead to my application being rejected or cause subsequent problems. I avoided Doon School's alumni events too.

I felt unpleasantly furtive as a consequence. I was no longer used to evasion. All this hiding also contradicted my openness around my friends and family members. I soon realized that I was once again living a double life, constantly wary, just like the years before I came out of the closet. My frustration at being forced back into this unpleasant state would have been sharper still if I had not realized that this was not the solitary imprisonment of the past, where I had absolutely no one to confide in, but a halfway house that I could tolerate.

However, despite curbing my candour and isolating myself to a large degree, there still proved to be no way to escape the pervasive prejudices in Delhi against gays. It was present everywhere, at every class level. I witnessed this hostility in the company of my beloved friend, Siddhartha Gautam, who had also moved to Delhi in 1986 to do a law degree at Delhi University after completing his MPhil in development studies at Cambridge.

There was a palpable intensity to my friendship with Siddhartha, evident in the amount of time we spent alone with each other, how we constantly touched and embraced, and how protective I was of him in my unaccustomed role of responsible elder brother protecting a madcap, vulnerable younger sibling. (To boast of our affection for each other, we proudly called ourselves 'Tiddarth and Tiddartha', *a la* the indistinguishable detectives Thomson and Thompson in the *Tintin* comic books. It didn't matter to either of us that we didn't look alike. We had everything else in common—our first names, our Calcutta childhoods, and our shared passion for social justice issues.)

My exceptional protectiveness had to do with the fact that Siddhartha had been diagnosed with Hodgkin's cancer at age fifteen. Though extended treatment had brought the cancer into remission, the threat remained, never spoken about, but ever-present and ever-dangerous.

Perhaps because he sensed that he had only a short lease on life, Siddhartha lived it at the most breakneck speed and with the most exceptional intensity. Being in his vicinity was a sure recipe for getting entangled in adventures and scrapes.

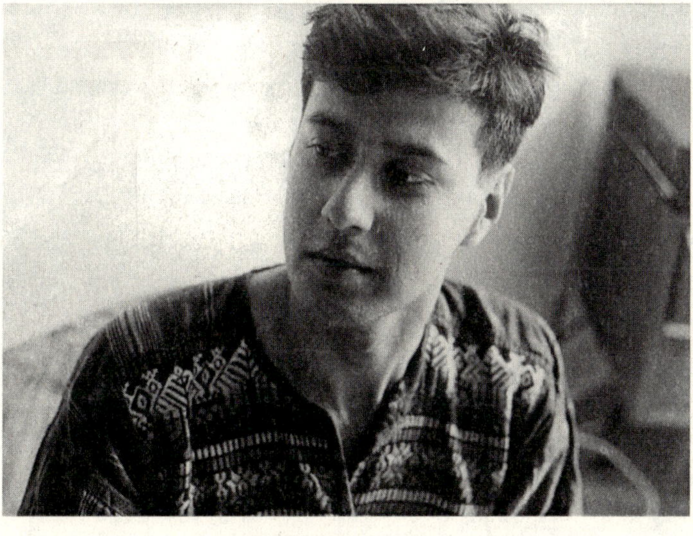

Provided by author

Siddhartha Gautam

As both he and I loved to dance, we overcame our shared dislike for plush hotels and decided to go to the discotheque at the Taj Mansingh, located just below the hotel's ornate marble staircase. The manager greeted us effusively, no doubt because we looked affluent. Though the disco music was largely unmemorable, Siddhartha and I had a wonderful time dancing together for hours. We always felt invincible when we were together, and so we laughed off the alarmed stares from several couples and the way they edged away from us. At some point, I noticed the manager staring at us from behind the bar, a hostile look on his face, but I ignored this too.

By our third visit, some weeks later, the manager's warmth was nowhere in sight. He was polite, but didn't seem happy to see us back. Siddhartha and I had just started dancing when one of the staff interrupted us, and said that men weren't allowed to dance together. Siddhartha and I retorted that we had danced here together before, and that we weren't touching each other or doing anything inappropriate. I looked around to speak to the manager, but he had mysteriously disappeared. Eventually, because so many people were staring at us, we decided to dance separately. After a while, we left, offended and fuming.

Siddhartha and I decided to go back the following weekend, having resolved that we wouldn't stop dancing with each other. So, when a similar request was made of us this time, we said no. This time the manager appeared, and told us grimly that we would have to leave the dance floor. Over the din of the music, Siddhartha and I took pains to politely explain that it was only fair to let us dance together, given that we were not hurting anyone. When it was clear that he was not going to agree, we went back to dancing—leaving the manager standing stone-faced in the crowd.

Not more than a minute had passed before the music was abruptly turned off and the lights switched on, a shock after all that darkness. Over the speakers, a male voice said, 'There's no stag-dancing allowed. Will the two gentlemen dancing together please leave the dance floor?'

Everyone turned to look at Siddhartha and me. We stared back defiantly. Minutes dragged past. The music stayed off. Couples began to whisper, their eyes trained on us. Siddhartha and I now pretended to be lost in some compelling conversation. We didn't move. This impasse must have lasted several minutes before the lights were turned off once again and the music resumed. Siddhartha and I started dancing again, nervous but victorious.

A few minutes later, the music went dead once more, the lights came on, and the loudspeaker announced again that stag dancing was forbidden. Near the entrance, I saw that the manager had been joined by another officious-looking man, probably a more senior colleague, who was also staring at us. Quite a few of the couples, giving us baleful looks, went and sat down by the bar. Siddhartha and I stood our ground. Many minutes later, finding that we were the only people left on the dance floor—everyone else was sitting down in a semi-circle, staring at us with hostility—we left the discotheque, ignoring the managers as we passed them.

Siddhartha and I should have been distraught at this public humiliation. But we were indomitable when together, even possessing the alchemy to turn our humiliation into victory. On the drive to my brother's home in Panchsheel Park, where I was living back then, our bleak mood vanished, replaced with fits of loud laughter as we regaled each other with our best moments of the evening. We recalled how we had bravely stood up to the manager's silly homophobia, and laughed at the idiocy of a world that could feel threatened by the sight of two men dancing together.

We yelled out to the empty streets, 'Beware! We are the leaders of a tribe of homos! We'll soon conquer all of Delhi! No one is safe! We're a tribe of homos!'

When we were together, Siddhartha and I could cope with whatever homophobia we encountered in the genteel neighborhoods to which we were accustomed. But we soon came to realize that outside these settings, any disclosure of our being gay could have far more harmful consequences—consequences that threatened to override our civil rights, notwithstanding our families' influence.

Ever since he moved to Delhi, Siddhartha had lived in a series of rented apartments in the cheaper sections of Defence Colony, Lajpat Nagar and Jangpura. Siddhartha's flawless Hindi and his angelic looks always enchanted his landlords initially. But, in just a few weeks, they would inevitably turn hostile.

They disapproved of the unending stream of bohemians visiting Siddhartha—kothi feminine men (some with tweezed eyebrows and a hint of kaajal), rough and macho men, obviously single women (based on their arriving and leaving without male companions), and even one flagrant cross-dresser who sometimes arrived decked out in the shiny slips he favored. Singly or in a group, they all disappeared into Siddhartha's apartment.

The curtains were then pulled tight. Whatever the hour, there was music and loud laughter, sometimes broken by suspiciously long silences. Impromptu parties took place at odd times, occasionally even in the afternoon. The sound of ghungroos and male voices singing '*In ankhon ki masti ke, mastaane hazaron hain*' would drift down. Siddhartha's voice, excited and giggling at a peculiarly high, feminine pitch, would float above the din.

Soon enough, the landlords would insist that Siddhartha move out, saying that his lifestyle was unacceptable in neighborhoods with 'good families'. Though they strongly suspected that he was gay, a gaandu or sodomite, it was never brought up. (They had no firm proof, and the large number of women visitors to his home must also have confused them.) Delhi being the lawless city that it is, the landlords would typically refuse to return Siddhartha's rental deposit. Or, without giving Siddhartha due notice, they would insist that he leave immediately or prepare to be thrown out forcibly.

Because I had long taken on the role of being Siddhartha's responsible older brother, I would inevitably get involved in the crisis too. But try as we may, matters would deteriorate. On one occasion, I came to blows with a landlord and his adult sons. Luckily, my years at Doon had made me a tough opponent, and they backed off after we traded a few punches.

Very often, Siddhartha and I—and occasionally, some of our other friends—would arrive at the local police station to file a complaint against the landlord. There, facing a bunch of dismissive, rough-mannered policemen, we took pains to present ourselves as unimpeachably respectable, upper-class young men, not the peculiar bohemians that the landlords insisted we were.

At these times, both Siddhartha and I felt intensely fearful of being identified as homosexuals. While he and I never came to discuss the particulars of our fears, his were doubtless very similar to mine. My fear sprang from knowing that the police would automatically brand me a low-life criminal because Section 377 of the Indian Penal Code specified that homosexual men needed to be jailed as punishment for their depraved ways. And, because my criminality was defined by sex, the police would view me in the same way as they viewed prostitutes—a sex-crazed person deserving of their scorn and abuse.

Given this intense and pervasive hostility, it was not surprising that the overwhelming majority of gay men and women, almost irrespective of their class, were closeted. In Delhi, through Siddhartha, I met a small group of gay men and women, all middle to upper-income professionals, and most a decade or more older than me. Numbering about two dozen, with the men in a majority, we were drawn together into friendship because of our shared secret orientation. Many of these men and women were candid about this matter only with their close friends and select relatives, but had not come out in their work places or broadly in society.

In fact, the bulk of them were not out in any real sense at all; only their sexual partners and this small group of people knew about their orientation. Thus, the most flamboyant man among our group of friends, a senior bureaucrat then in his forties, was married and had teenage children—a pretence that allowed him to lead an active sexual life with other men despite the visibility of being a bureaucrat.

I came to find that many gay men entered into such sham marriages in a desperate attempt to keep their orientation from becoming known. The threat of blackmail and violence by the police and thugs was an everyday reality, because most gay men had no place to meet, socialize or have sex beyond public areas like parks and toilets. This was many years before gay support groups and gay-friendly bars were opened in Delhi, let alone the smaller towns and cities of India.

It was no doubt because of the strains and obstacles raised by secrecy and fear that so few among them were in relationships. There were only two or three long-term couples, all lesbian, amongst our group of friends. But even these women were guarded about their relationships outside the circle of family and friends. They passed themselves off simply as close friends sharing a flat. None of the gay men in our group were in a long standing or live-in relationship. In all of Delhi, I knew of only two gay male couples, both part of the select world of design and fashion. But even so, both were painstakingly discreet about their relationships and orientation.

The only time everyone let down their guard was when we hosted parties at one of our homes. Invitation was only through a network of friends. In these evenings together, there was an unfailing feeling of security, of having a safe space where the world's hatred could not intrude. There was no censure, so we could just be ourselves. The men could be as extravagantly camp and limp-wristed as they liked, and the women as butch.

There would often be standing-room-only, because these parties were fun and inclusive. These were the only ones I knew of in Delhi where everyone was welcome, irrespective of orientation or class or any other difference. The city's one cross-dresser and a handful of working-class kothis, some of whom sold sex to men, would join us. So would the three gay men from Western European embassies, the two openly gay fashion designers, and some of the metro sexual party-boys who always hung around them.

Someone would begin to sing a Hindi film song, accompanied by someone inventively using a tin can as a dholak. Right away, Siddhartha or some other flamboyant character would swan into the centre of the room, copying a Bollywood dance or a traditional mujra. The more camp the performance, the greater the praise.

Apart from these unguarded moments, the extent of fear that even the most privileged of gay men lived in was evident from the fact that not one of us, anywhere in India, allowed our real names to be used in the first major article in the Indian press on gay men, published in 1988. This was a cover story in the then widely read but now defunct *Sunday*, a liberal weekly for which I often wrote at that time. Titled 'The Love that Dare not Speak its Name', the article described us as 'the country's most silent and secretive minority'. It was an accurate description. The only gay man who spoke on the record, using his full name, was British theatre director Barry John, a foreigner who had settled in Delhi. There was still no prominent gay Indian man or woman in the public eye who could start rolling back homophobic stereotypes and assumptions, and become a role model for others like them.

The first year of my return to India also marked my first adult sexual experience here. This happened on a visit to Bombay, where I was staying with a close friend from Doon and his wonderful wife. One of their favorite past-times was to tease me about my ascetic life—my insistence on doing yoga every morning, my absolute lack of interest in alcohol or cigarettes, and, most glaringly, my monk-like sexual abstinence. (I was still a virgin by any yardstick, my only sexual experience being the limited things I did with M a few years back and that one night of sexual pleasure at Doon, nearly a decade ago.) One evening, they energetically ganged up on me, insisting that I get out of their house and not return until I got laid!

I gave in to their bullying readily, relieved to be forced to do what I ached to do anyway. Here, a place where HIV was not yet as widespread as it was in the US, I was much more open to the possibilities.

Of course, neither they nor I knew even one avowedly gay man in Bombay, so going out on a date was ruled out. There were no gay bars in the city in 1987. The possibility of finding dates through the Internet was still many years away. But, I had heard from Siddhartha, always a reliable guide on matters of the flesh, that men cruised for sex near Flora Fountain. So I walked the short distance there from my friends' Colaba home.

As the ornate fountain came in sight, my heart began to hammer so uncontrollably that I stopped for a few minutes, worried that I'd be incoherent even if I met someone. On entering the small park circling the fountain, I detected several men's forms in the poor light. I noticed a handsome Nepali-looking man staring at me, dressed simply but neatly in a light shirt and dark pants. He came up, and spoke to me in Hindi. We must have exchanged names, but my wits deserted me in a rush of nerves and the next thing I remember was following him into a rundown office building on a side street.

We climbed three flights of creaking wooden stairs, tiptoeing past sleeping forms at the landings. He stopped on the top landing, lit by a weak bare bulb and street-light filtering in through the grimy windows, and—to my shock—started unbuttoning his shirt. I realized then that this small space was his home. I was about to baulk at having sex in this open space, but then desire overcame my fears.

He laid out a thin mattress and turned off the light. Casually, with his back to me, he peeled off his clothes. I watched breathlessly, my heart hammering. He turned to face me. He was beautiful naked—a David-like figure gleaming in the smoggy light, small penis jutting out hard and high. He grinned upon seeing my rapt admiration, came up to me, caught my hand and placed it squarely over his penis, making me envelop it in my palm. His confidence was aphrodisiacal.

He kissed me. His lips felt thin and foreign, and his mouth tasted unpleasantly of onion and fried food. Naked and so close, I also smelt a dark odour emanating from his armpits. But my aversion lasted just for a second, lust took over.

I began to kiss him back. Then, pulling him tight against me, I groped at his body and instinctively reached down to caress his testicles and the silky skin of his inner thighs. I was slightly shocked at my own complete loss of control.

He drew away and began to undress me, tugging at my T-shirt and pants. I realized, feeling gauche and inexperienced, that I was still fully dressed—I had not undone even my belt or a button in all this while. I was touched to see that, even though we were both standing there naked, sporting erections, he folded my clothes with great care, placing them with his own on a suitcase under the stairwell.

He pulled me down on the mattress, immediately laying himself atop me. For a moment, it felt odd to have a body and a penis rubbing so wildly against mine, someone's lips suctioning at my mouth and neck, hands touching every part of my body. But I soon lost control again, kissing him back feverishly, biting his neck and small erect nipples with such force that I was afraid I would draw blood, running my hands without restraint over every part of his body.

At some point, I'm not sure how much later, he asked me in a whisper to take his penis in my mouth—or did I want him below, in my ass? In my state of desire, I wanted everything. I whispered back, suddenly aware again of the people sleeping on the landing just below, to ask if he had a Nirodh. (As Nirodh was the only condom brand available in India for decades, the word had become synonymous with condoms.)

'Nirodh? Why a Nirodh?' He was clearly perplexed. I realized he had no concerns about AIDS; for him, condoms were solely a contraceptive barrier. Cursing myself for forgetting to bring a condom along, I told him that I couldn't do anything much without one.

I didn't explain to him why we needed to use a condom—that HIV had by now been detected in several Indian cities, and it was a disease that was spread through unprotected sexual intercourse of any kind, heterosexual or gay. He must have doubtless found my behaviour highly peculiar—after all, why would a man insist on a condom being used when he didn't have to worry about getting pregnant? Nevertheless, he said nothing.

He just spat in his hand and, reaching down, slathered the saliva generously over our penises—the cool liquid a welcome comfort. Then he went back to kissing and rubbing against me, his body excitingly hard against mine, and the pleasure making me forget about everything from condoms to the people sleeping nearby.

He came very soon—far too soon for me—his semen bursting out all the way to my chest. Then he lay still on me, his face buried in my shoulder, his breath coming fast. Lying there, despite suddenly becoming aware of the sweat and sticky mess all over my body, I felt a rush of satisfaction from giving him such pleasure.

After a while, he roused himself and began to masturbate me. I stopped him, whispering that I didn't want to come. He kissed me on the mouth gently, again and again. I was astonished by how affectionate he was. Like me, he was aching for love and companionship just as much as for sex.

When I said I had to get home, he wiped his semen off me carefully with a towel and handed my clothes to me one by one. Once I had dressed, he embraced me for a long while, caressing my hair and whispering that I was extraordinarily beautiful. I could tell that he didn't want me to leave. And so it was that I had my first adult experience of sex in India, encapsulating all the paradoxes of gay life here. This was a country where the only connections possible were brief sexual encounters with complete strangers—furtive and yet offering pleasure with the possibility of real tenderness.

But then, one morning in February 1988, over a year after my return, I finished an early walk through Delhi's Lodhi Gardens—its pearl-like tombs and great trees ethereally beautiful in the mist—and exited onto Lodhi Road, where my car was parked. Here, I ran into a man, a stranger who became one of the greatest loves of my adult life, and with whom I eventually spent several years. It was a lucky accident, so fortuitous that it would not have happened if either of us had taken a few seconds more in reaching that pavement where our paths crossed, where we looked at each other, where we struck up that first conversation.

He was a mystery man. He was a Frenchman from Paris, though of Tamil and Vietnamese ancestry. He was a Bharatanatyam dancer. I had never heard a name like his—Tandavan. I had never seen anyone who looked like him, a dark Nureyev, breathtakingly sexy, yet incredibly gentle. Tandavan was a decade older than me, but he looked ageless.

I fell in love with the man instantly, not bothered by the fact that we hardly even knew each other. He fell instantly in love with me too. This was not the fantasy of a love-starved twenty-six-year-old—I knew it as a certainty, in an unfathomable way, in a way that I had never known before. Baez's '*Love song to a stranger*' played inside me, that ode to 'passionate strangers who rescue each other from a lifetime of care'.

A month later, Tandavan gave up his Paris apartment and returned to Delhi to stay with me in a small rented flat in Jor Bagh, a minute's walk from the spot where we met. We weren't strangers anymore.

With a partner less loving and less self-assured than him, my accumulated burdens and fears would have wrecked any relationship. But Tandavan brushed aside all my problems as if they were trivial matters. Often, through the years of our relationship, I thought to myself that he was like a loving parent who was patiently teaching a child all the skills of life.

With my romantic life practically barren since Doon, I needed to love and be loved without restraint. This is what I did with Tandavan. We gave ourselves almost desperately to each other, as if we couldn't believe we had found each other and wanted to make the most of this blessed good fortune, before life—with its capriciousness—decided to snatch it away.

Tandavan was still emerging from a life-changing loss—his boyfriend of thirteen years had committed suicide back in Paris, and though over two years had passed, he was still drifting along, unable to live in Paris, but unable to leave either. That had changed once we met.

My desperation sprang from years of yearning for romantic love as well as from fearing that, as a gay man, I was doomed to a life without it. We promised to be with each other forever.

Tandavan had a gift for making everything sensually intense. Overnight, my world turned into a veritable explosion of colour, smells, tastes and senses that I didn't even know about until then. He fed me, by hand, from small turquoise-blue bowls as iridescent, fragile and perfectly formed as birds' eggs. He called me nai-kutti—the Tamil diminutive for puppy—his tone making it a synonym for all the love he felt for me.

He dressed me in his chalk-white cotton lungis, with thin borders of gold, red and blue. He bought hand-woven papers to draw and paint on, making me stroke them with my eyes closed to feel their concentrated mix of nubby grain and silk. I fell under the thrall of Maharajapuram Santhanam and M.S. Subbulakshmi in the mornings, and Maria Callas in the evenings. Under this assault of sensory delight, my tightly wound sense of asceticism began to fall away, the only remaining element being my unfailing adherence to morning yoga.

Of all these pleasures, the most sublime was watching Tandavan practise Bharatanatyam, every morning in the small patio outside our flat. There was the rhythmic, syllabic music. There was the strength and geometric sharpness of his arm movements. There was the resounding force with which his bare feet hit the ground. There was his beauty—his antelope-like musculature, neither distinctly male nor female, the expressiveness of his eyes, and the sheen of sweat on his brown skin. Shiva-Nataraj must have looked like this.

Then there was the physical everyday intimacy. I just couldn't get enough of that. My Brahmanical obsession with personal hygiene fell away, and I started kissing Tandavan passionately without even

Olivier Föllmi

Tandavan, at Delhi's Jantar Mantar

waiting to brush our teeth. I showered with him. We soaped every part of each other's bodies. I wore Tandavan's shirts to work and his kurtas at home, inhaling his distinctive chocolatey smell from them. I licked every inch of him. These tastes of the most intimate, personal parts of his body were the richest nourishment to me, starved of such intimacy through my adult life.

And then there was the sex, lovemaking. It was beyond anything I had ever imagined. Every inch of Tandavan's body seemed to be an erogenous zone, alive to pleasure, so much in contrast to mine, deadened by hang-ups. Tandavan gradually taught me to forget myself and surrender to pleasure. A giant dam of desire, pent up since my adolescent days at Doon, broke inside me. I just couldn't get enough of sex.

So we had sex all the time, many times a day. There were hour-long sessions as well as quickies. Sex when I was burning with fever; sex when he was unwell. We were insatiable.

There was physical pleasure beyond my comprehension, and there was communion in the sex. We had to possess each other and ejaculate inside each other for our union to strengthen, to be fertilized.

I turned my back on celibacy without any regrets, never to consider it again but with a flood of distaste. There had been nothing enlightening about it, this destructive struggle against an integral human longing, this twisted obsession with excising a need as natural and essential as air, water, food or love. Gandhi and the saints were welcome to wage their endless wars against the pleasures of the flesh, but I doubted very much if it would help them find peace or wisdom. For my part, I wanted to make up for lost time in getting my share of eros and carnality, these most wondrous of human pleasures.

In the first month or so, Tandavan and I used condoms. But later I threw caution to the winds, and began to have unprotected sex.

I knew well that I was placing myself at risk. Tandavan had come of age at a point when AIDS was exploding unnoticed in Paris, and there was little knowledge of the virus or the ways in which to protect oneself. So the odds were high that Tandavan might have contracted HIV. We didn't know either way, because he had never taken an HIV test. Though there was no place to test for the virus in complete confidentiality in India back then, without the risk of the results being leaked, I could have asked Tandavan to have himself tested on one of his frequent visits to France. But I didn't. My acceptance of the risks, after years of protecting myself to an extreme of safety, was an unspoken affirmation that our lives and futures were bound together forever.

Over the months, our life settled into a full, happy routine. Tandavan taught dance and art at the French School on the nearby Aurangzeb Road, going off on his bicycle every morning. He then went on to dance practice at his music accompanist's home. Even after our honeymoon period had long expired, we ached to see each other, and so I would leave work as early as I could, driving my little Fiat home as fast as possible. (Within some months of our meeting, I left *Business India* to join the *Washington Post*'s South Asia bureau as a stringer-reporter.)

Delhi was still verdant and orderly, and we lived in its most idyllic part. At the adjacent Lodhi Gardens, there were glorious trees and bird life to wonder at—amaltas, gulmohar, semul and sisham; parakeets, owls, hornbills, sunbirds, and even the occasional cormorant. In the evenings, between the India International Centre and various cultural venues at embassies, there was a constant supply of films, dance recitals and talks.

At home, Tandavan made fresh salads, casseroles that were a fusion of France and Pondicherry, and banana flambé. We inevitably had company. Many of my closest friends had moved to Delhi after studying abroad around the same time as me. And Tandavan, free-spirited and exotically beautiful, was a magnet. Perhaps too often for my taste, our one-bedroom flat would be bursting at the seams with an eclectic assortment of guests—Indian, French and innumerable other nationalities—for impromptu dinners.

This turning point in my life, my first long-term relationship, also marked the beginning of my embrace of sex and its pleasures. One outcome of this blossoming was that I now longed to taste everything that I had denied myself so far—and so, a few months into our relationship, Tandavan and I began having a sexually open relationship.

It began as threesomes with some of the attractive young Frenchmen posted in Delhi for their mandatory year of 'military' service. We then branched out on our own. Beyond occasional bouts of acute jealousy—mostly on my part because Tandavan was the mature one—none of this caused any real stress in our relationship. Our hearts belonged to each other. This casual sex amounted to just extra heapings of sensate pleasures. (These trysts, I was to eventually realize, also proved to be milestones in my developing a rational, uncomplicated attitude towards sexuality, free of commonplace anxieties and hypocrisy.)

I started off by rediscovering the myriad cruising areas in Delhi that Siddhartha had shown me in my days of abstinence. At the vast Nehru Park, as the sun began to set, the atmosphere would suddenly become tense with lust as scores of men would start making sexual overtures to each other. They would eye each other hotly, striking up flirtations, and then—as darkness fell—disappear into the park's numerous groves and rock outcrops for a few moments of pleasure.

At the busy Dhaula Kuan bus stop, where the nearby expanses of open land and parks provided privacy for sex, the numerous cruisers included fit, horny jawans from the adjacent army base. Even in the congested, brightly-lit Connaught Circle, I could see dozens of men cruising each other (and the occasional transwoman), usually going off to cheap hotels or homes for sex. But sometimes, you could even catch a glimpse of them furtively enjoying hand jobs or blow jobs at Central Park above Pallika Bazaar.

Everywhere in India that I traveled as a journalist, I came to find that there was a rip-roaring same-sex life amongst Indian men. India revealed herself as an unending playground for male homosexual sex. Whether in Ahmedabad or Imphal, Cochin or Srinagar, even in small-town Ranchi or tiny Jagdalpur, the one common fact—just as much as in Delhi and Bombay—was that men were desperately seeking each other out for sex in parks, public toilets, railway sidings or any secluded spot the minute the sun began to dip, their numbers multiplying in direct proportion to the intensity of darkness.

Many would travel long distances to get to their favourite cruising spots, driven by that primal, gut-deep need for sex. In some of these areas, such as Delhi's Nehru Park, it often felt like a frenzied sex party, with entire crowds of men dissolving off into pairs or even small orgiastic groups. It was thrilling to witness and participate in all this.

Even more astonishing than the massive scale of night-time cruising was finding, once I grew attuned to it, that men were picking each other up almost everywhere and at every hour—during any routine interaction in the day, in shops, while walking down a street, or waiting at the bus stop. The flirtation had its own secret lingo. It worked through gestures and innuendos known only to those already initiated into this sexual network but invisible to all others: a deep stare and an inviting smile, a handshake held for far too long, a hand dropping suggestively to the crotch, or the otherwise inexplicable offer of 'Aur kuch sewa kar saktha hoon?' ('Can I serve you in any other way?')

Given the lack of privacy in India, these connections usually led to assignations at night. But sometimes the goal was immediate sex, and ardent men tried to beguile me into a quickie in the corner of a shop or a galli, which somehow proved to be magically shielded from the pressing crowds in a way that was fully in sight yet invisible for the moment. I was left profoundly impressed with Indian ingenuity when it came to finding places for sex.

Participating in this sexual network were a vast range of men, almost anyone who mixed in public spaces rather than stayed in the isolation of elite privacy. They could be college students, taxi drivers, policemen, soldiers, and the myriad people employed in the informal sector (from manual labourers to shopkeepers), besides a smattering of white-collar professionals and a handful of foreigners. (Though prostitution by men as well as transwomen—the sub-continent's traditional 'third gender' communities [commonly known as hijra or kinnar]—was common in urban areas, it was dwarfed by the vast extent of sex that took place without payment.) I soon came to agree with what Siddhartha had long been telling me from his own experiences: virtually every youngish Indian male, barring those with westernized backgrounds like us—who were burdened with a Victorian-era paranoia about homosexuality—was up for sex with other men.

As to whether these men were gay or bisexual by orientation, or were having sex with men only as a fallback because women would rarely have sex outside of marriage or prostitution, was a conundrum that Siddhartha and I argued over. This matter was further complicated by the fact that though an overwhelming majority of men were married—or would eventually be married, given the social norm of arranged marriage—they saw their wives infrequently. Usually, the women stayed back in their native villages and towns, while the men moved to cities to find work.

Obviously, there was no doubt that all these men were strongly attracted to other men. They experienced sexual pleasure and release with male partners, after which they continued seeking them out for more. Just what this meant in terms of primary or preferred sexual orientation was less clear.

Even less clear was the related, overarching matter that Siddhartha and I often also argued over—whether traditional Indians were qualitatively more accepting of same-sex love and sex than those of us who were 'Macaulay's Children', the anglicized Indian elite who had been raised with Victorian British values. Siddhartha, who had been raised in a more Indian setting than I—a sprawling extended family sharing a large Calcutta house—took the view that traditional Indians were far more accepting of same-sex desire than anglicized Indians, whether it concerned men or women.

I had mixed views on this matter. On the one hand, from what I saw and experienced firsthand, many non-elite Indian men treated same-sex desire as routine and acceptable to an astonishing degree, qualitatively different to the overt homophobia displayed by anglicized Indians. I found this was true in both urban and rural settings. The naturalness with which they expressed their desire was such that I was often taken aback.

The handsome man I had met at Bombay's Flora Fountain in 1986, with whom I had that unforgettable experience of making love on a staircase landing, had displayed no discomfort at all with our bodies or what we did together. In a Jat village not far from Delhi, where I was reporting an article on agriculture, two young brothers—barely out of their teens, their kurta-pyjamas brown with dust from the fields—pleaded with me to spend the night at their rustic family home, rather than drive back to Delhi, their voices thick with desire, each gripping one of my hands, ardent co-conspirators and bitter rivals at the same time.

In rural Bihar, where I was volunteering with a grassroots organization, one smitten man would serenade me with amorous Hindi film songs as we bathed at the communal hand-pump every evening. This was the zenith of his ceaseless day-long advances. Our co-workers, all male, egged him on as if they were family members trying to facilitate a suitable marriage.

Outside Benares' Ramnagar fort, two handsome young policemen sprawled out on a charpai ogled me. Winking, they patted their bed invitingly and called out to me to join them, paying no heed to the crowds of Indian tourists passing by.

The head of security at a Madras hotel, a Tamil man with Tarzan-like physique and a torn underwear that resembled the ape man's loincloth, spent hours through the night making tender love to me. Innumerable incidents such as these left me with a feeling of certainty that same-sex desire was both individually and socially acceptable amongst many quintessentially *Indian* Indians, even if it almost unfailingly ignited Victorian anti-gay bigotry amongst its anglicized population.

Hence, it was ironic that even many men who routinely had sex with other men had ambivalent and even strongly homophobic feelings. While having sex, these men would vociferously insist on playing only the penetrating 'male' role. They would reject any intimacy or gentleness such as kissing. They would painstakingly avoid touching my genitals, sometimes even asking me to hide them from sight. They would show no reciprocity in terms of sexual acts.

Once they had ejaculated, their efforts to establish that they were heterosexual would intensify, often to laughable lengths. Some would promptly ask if I had women friends I could introduce them to. Others would begin to earnestly ask me why I was attracted to men, and then assert that they did it only because there were no women available.

These men with homophobic views, unlike the relaxed ones, displayed all the depressing, warped twists of Indian male sexuality—the frustrated, endless preoccupation with sex as well as the intense attendant feelings of shame. One of their common obsessions was that they had wasted energy by ejaculating. Looking rueful and tired, they would, in numbing detail, recount the belief that forty drops of blood had gone into producing each drop of semen. Of course, this regret was always voiced only after ejaculation. They would continue to sit there weakly, as if expecting devoted mothers or wives to considerately appear with glasses of full-cream milk and heaps of tandoori chicken with which to replenish their spent masculine vigour.

I had little patience with boors of this kind, even if they were physically attractive, and soon began to cut off flirtations as soon as I spotted tell-tale signs of homophobia. Friends told me that some of these homophobic men would even get threatening and violent once they had ejaculated—demanding money, hitting them, or directing other men to their homes for forced sex. I never really experienced this extreme behaviour, probably because I would snuff out any threat of abuse with the upper-class, authoritative manner I put on.

Strikingly, in my experience, the vast majority of the homophobic and abusive men were policemen, with a smaller number comprised of boastful young thugs. In contrast, men from the army or other defence services almost never displayed homophobia, just enjoying sex wholeheartedly.

The attitude of policemen made me conclude that, in India, even a little bit of power corrupts absolutely, because there are innumerable defenceless people to oppress. The police made many of the cruising sites dangerously unsafe for the men there, to the point that fear was almost as palpable an emotion as lust. Even though the policemen who took part in this exploitation were not on duty or in uniform, they would use their police IDs and power to extort sex or money. The hapless victim would have to give in to their demands, faced with the even more terrifying threat of being hauled off to the police station.

I noticed that they would always pick on the feminine men—slapping, beating and terrorizing them into emptying their wallets and providing sexual favours to them or others in the group they roamed with. Astonishingly, they would typically let the 'top' men—the 'penetrator' in homosexual sex—go, treating them as if they were part of the same brotherhood. Just like the abusers at Doon, they believed it was okay for a man to have sex with another man because of a pressing need for release, but that genuinely homosexual males—in their view meaning only those who were penetrated or gave oral sex—deserved to be abused because they were despicably unmanly.

I would inevitably intervene if I saw any harassment taking place, drawing out my Government-issued press card and barking at the offenders in my most authoritative manner. It always had the desired effect. After some grumbling, the policemen would leave, having reached some face-saving compromise for themselves, such as delivering a tedious, moralistic lecture to their victims or warning me that I would be held responsible if they misbehaved again.

In time, after my travels across India, I concluded that both macho behaviour and concomitant homophobia were strongest in the north, getting steadily milder as one headed towards its southern or eastern parts. I was not sure if this had something to do with the greater dominance of elite or land-owning castes in the northern region, the extreme misogyny of these areas, or if there were other factors at play.

I was particularly struck that the homophobia was most intensely expressed towards feminine men, or anyone known to play a feminine or servicing role in sex. Through Siddhartha, I came to know several kothis—the Hindi term for feminine men, as opposed to hijras who are men who consciously change their gender to female. The kothis led desperate lives. Almost all of them had been cast out as children or teenagers by their families or communities, and struggled with depression and poor self-esteem. Unable to find regular employment because of the scorn attached to feminine men, most resorted to prostitution. I was to find through my later research that hijras typically suffered the same fate as kothis, with poverty and social ostracism leaving them with prostitution as the only option.

I eventually concluded that the world of same-sex relations in India was remarkably similar to that of Doon. Even though homosexual behaviour was ubiquitous, the attitudes to it were convoluted, with the many signs of acceptance clashing with equally great evidence of prejudice, hate and violence. All in all, despite the widespread homosociability, the astounding extent of male-on-male sex, and even the vivid examples of ease with same-sex desire among average Indian men, I didn't think the outcome was, in the balance, a happy one.

And though I eventually came around to Siddhartha's argument that pre-colonial India was significantly more tolerant of same-sex desire, I also felt that India had been changed too much due to British rule, particularly because of its homophobic laws and policing systems, for this legacy to have a measurable impact any longer on the level of lived realities. Having same-sex desires in today's India amounted only to having limitless opportunities for sex. There was little scope for building a meaningful romantic connection.

I pitied the men attracted to other men who were seeking an emotional connection. Now that I was in a happy relationship with Tandavan, I became even more keenly aware of what other men were being denied due to the oppressive circumstances and fear they lived in.

Consequently, I came to feel that the homo-sociability and silence did not add up to providing a haven for same-sex desire. On the contrary, it provided only a dark space for us criminalized people to hide in, afraid and ashamed. The men had sex with each other furtively in the dark, hidden from sight—and they had to live in precisely this way, hiding the nature of their desire, hiding who they fundamentally were. This was not freedom—this amounted to being an outcast and an outlaw.

Despite all the unexpected joy that I had found in India with Tandavan, there was no escaping the burdens of secrecy and fear that came with being gay in the India of that era. Once I began to live with him in a rented flat, rather than at my brother's home, these myriad apprehensions intensified into a constant low-level fear, much like a chronic fever. This was so even though Jor Bagh is one of the few areas of Delhi that's inhabited by numerous foreigners, where Tandavan and I did not stick out as sorely as we would have elsewhere.

But by being together constantly—in our car, on the verandah of our flat, walking and biking together, going shopping—we drew the attention of some of our neighbours as well as of the domestic help and private guards in the area. From their comments and stares, I realized that Tandavan and I were the subject of a lot of discussion, some of it patently suspicious and unfriendly. Tandavan remained relaxed and unguarded, but this was not surprising as he was—for all intents and purposes—a foreigner to India and oblivious to many of its realities.

My tensions would cross into fear whenever Tandavan and I were being intimate with each other—whether it was kissing, having sex, or just cuddling together. I was aware that we were violating India's criminal laws—even if it was in the privacy of our flat—and we could be arrested and imprisoned as a consequence.

And then, less than a year after I started living with Tandavan, I found that my apprehensions were well-founded.

8

Prisons

On that dreadful night in the winter of 1988, I had ample time to castigate myself for my folly in moving back to India, my folly in not heeding my father's warnings.

It was about 7 p.m. when Tandavan and I entered the police station, an unremarkable single-storey building, located at a quiet crossroads near Jor Bagh. A few policemen sat in the hallway, desultorily talking to each other. They glanced at us but didn't stir. The bare bulbs emitted a faint, depressing light. The place felt like just another outpost of India's apathetic, callous bureaucracy, rather than a station serving one of Delhi's most elite neighbourhoods.

Eventually, one of the policemen led us to the station officer's room, and after he had checked with the officer, we were told to enter. I walked through the swing doors with Tandavan following me, only to realize that I had made a terrible mistake coming here.

The man sitting behind the desk looked at me with such an aggressive expression of loathing that I thought, momentarily, that he had mistaken me for someone else. He was short and powerfully built, with a clipped moustache. Possibly a decade older than me, he was wearing the muddy brown uniform of the Delhi police. Looking only at me, not at Tandavan, he burst out angrily, almost as if in a rage: 'Mr Dube, I know all about you. I have received enough complaints about you. You are a homo! You have naked men dancing at your house, exposing themselves. Go back to America! If you want to live here, you will live as an Indian, not like an American!'

Breathless with shock, I just stood there.

The officer must have misinterpreted my silence. Or perhaps he had already lost whatever self-control he possessed. Banging his fist on the table, he shouted, 'Watch it, I will come and arrest you! I will arrest you tonight! I will arrest you wherever I like, from the street or even from your house!'

My heart was pounding by now in a mix of rage and apprehension. I looked at this obnoxious man who hated me simply because I was gay, and suppressed an urge to punch him really hard. Instead, I collected myself and said, steadily but with anger in my voice, 'Just try and arrest me and see what happens.'

All hell broke loose. The officer sprang up from his chair and charged around his desk towards us, his fists clenched as if he meant to hit me. Changing his mind abruptly, he pressed a bell on his desk. 'Lock up these gaandus!' he yelled in Hindi at the two policemen who came rushing in. Then he approached me and stood practically nose to nose, his face apoplectic. I didn't budge. I could see the effort it was taking for him to keep himself from hitting me, the way he pushed back his shoulders and then locked his hands behind his back. By now, Tandavan had grabbed my arm, no doubt worried that I would hit back if the officer struck me. (He had stood in shocked silence through these sudden developments, clearly having difficulty keeping up with the Hindi and even with the officer's heavily accented English.)

The next thing we knew, Tandavan and I were being marched towards the back of the station. I presumed this was where the cells were, but the officer came to the door of his office and yelled that we should be locked up in the constables' duty room. The sole constable working there was taken aback when his colleagues told him that we were to be locked up here; clearly this was not normal procedure. I felt a slight feeling of relief—the officer was obviously restraining himself from doing what he longed to do because of his fear that I was well-connected.

The policemen left. We heard the door being bolted. Through a large window near the door, I saw that one of the policemen had seated himself on a nearby stool to keep guard. Tandavan and I sat down on the benches kept in the corner of the room. We were too shaken to speak to each other. It had all escalated too fast for us to even comprehend what was happening.

It took me a while to get a grip on myself. I forced myself to breathe deeply, so my heartbeat could slow down and I could think more clearly. I put my hand on Tandavan's. I was filled with love for him—he always stood by me unquestioningly, even in the most fraught circumstances. I tried to comfort him, saying that everything will be fine, and the officer knew better than to hit or jail us. The guy had held himself back because he realized that he would eventually get into trouble with his superiors for threatening me needlessly, I told Tandavan.

It made me wonder about the hate-filled threats the officer had spewed at us. Why and how did he know I was a 'homo'? Where did he get those bizarre ideas about naked men dancing in our Jor Bagh flat? Who on earth could have brought the fact that Tandavan and I lived together to his notice? (To that last question, at least, I had a probable answer—our landlord's unpleasant daughter-in-law had developed some kind of a twisted crush on Tandavan and me.)

As we sat there, my head swirled with angry recriminations. In that tense silence, there was infinite time to castigate myself for all my errors of judgment. Why had I foolishly listened to the officer on the phone that morning, when he casually suggested that I drop by to discuss my neighbours' complaints? I should have realized from his dismissive tone, and his refusal to specify what the complaints were about, that there was trouble in the offing.

Why had I assumed that being an accredited foreign correspondent would give me enough leverage to handle anything? Why didn't I have the basic common sense to inform Pratap, my brother, before coming here? He knew how to deal with India sensibly.

Or I should have left a note for Siddhartha, who was staying with us that weekend, saying that we had gone to the police station. He would have been able to do something. Why, why, why hadn't I behaved like a competent adult?

An hour passed. I knocked on the door, and when the guard opened it, I told him politely that I was entitled to speak to a lawyer, and wanted to exercise this right. He said he would ask the officer. He came back to say that the station's public phone wasn't working. I told him that I'd spotted a policeman chatting on it on our way to the lock-up, but he ignored me.

It was now 9 p.m., well past the time for Tandavan to have his evening dose of insulin. He had juvenile-onset diabetes, and needed shots of insulin morning and night. Tandavan said he was worried about his injection getting delayed for much longer. My heart sank as I saw tell-tale beads of cold sweat on his face, and the nervousness indicating that his sugar levels were plummeting.

I knocked urgently on the door and asked the guard to check if they could free Tandavan. I told him that Tandavan was not to blame in any way, because the neighbours' complaints were against me and that Tandavan had not talked back to the officer. In any case, he was a French citizen, not Indian, and this was a medical emergency.

The guard returned a few minutes later to say that the officer wanted to see Tandavan. It was 10 p.m. by now. Tandavan was sweating profusely, even though I had turned the ceiling fan to its highest speed. He was clearly in medical distress, but before he followed the guard out, he tousled my hair and told me not to worry. That was not possible; he was all I worried for now.

He returned a while later, looking ashen. The officer had said that he would be released only if he signed a statement saying that he had witnessed me insulting and threatening the officer. Tandavan had refused to sign. The officer had badgered him relentlessly. He was utterly drunk, Tandavan said, so much so that he wasn't even trying to hide the bottle of alcohol he was drinking straight from.

The next hour was the very worst of my life—even my most fearful moments at Doon paled in comparison to this. I pleaded with the guard to get a doctor for Tandavan. He was clearly sympathetic, because it had now become obvious even to the untrained eye that Tandavan was ill. He went off once again, but returned in a bit to say that the doctor would be called only if Tandavan signed the statement exonerating the officer.

Helplessly, I sat there watching my boyfriend, my love, tossing restlessly on the bench. I scolded myself. Why the hell had I brought Tandavan with me to the station? Was I so weak that I needed his support? Why had I answered back to the officer's threats? Couldn't I have kept my cool and figured a way out of there, and dealt with the officer once we were out of harm's way? Why had I stupidly moved back to India? Why hadn't I listened to my father's warnings? My beloved boyfriend was dying, and it was my fault.

It was nearly midnight when the door opened and four policemen came in, all carrying their wooden laathis. They said they would take Tandavan to our house to have his injection, and then bring him back here. By this time, Tandavan was pallid and shivering uncontrollably. As he couldn't walk, the policemen said that they would take him pillion on one of their bicycles. I quickly told Tandavan to phone Pratap, and inform him that we were being held at the Jor Bagh police station.

About half an hour after Tandavan had left, the policeman guarding the room unbolted the door and said in a deferential tone that I was free to go. Looking at me with awe, he said that one of Delhi's senior-most police officials had just phoned the station officer.

I had to keep myself from running out of the police station to my car.

It was past midnight by the time I reached home. Siddhartha was waiting up for me, his face gray with worry. Exhausted and sick, Tandavan was already asleep. Siddhartha didn't ask me to explain the events of the evening—and I said nothing, desperate to put them as far behind me as possible.

I called Pratap to let him know that I'd reached safely. I could tell that the only thing holding him back from scolding me was concern.

Minutes later, the phone rang. It was my father, calling from Calcutta. His voice was grim—his worst fears about my returning to India had come true. He told me that I should meet his close friend K.F. Rustamji, India's most distinguished police official, in the morning to get his advice on the abusive officer. Though Rustamji had retired recently, he was still closely involved in matters pertaining to national security.

I called my office at the *Washington Post* bureau the next morning to say that I was unwell, and wouldn't be coming to work. I then went to see Mr Rustamji at his home in Safdarjung Enclave. I had known him and his kindly wife, Naju Aunty, for as long as I could remember, and thought of them much like a third set of grandparents. On moving back to India, I had nervously told them that I was gay, but, if anything, this confession had made them become even more loving towards me. When I arrived, I saw both of them looking at me closely, as if to ensure that I had not been beaten.

Mr Rustamji took me to his study. He remained tight-lipped while I recounted what had happened at the police station the night before. After hearing me out, he told me that severe action was already being taken against the station officer. I said I hoped the officer would be dismissed and prosecuted. My heart missed a beat in surprise when Mr Rustamji said this happened only in cases of custodial death. I immediately replied that I'd take my fight to court. Mr Rustamji cut me off.

There was a look akin to sadness on his face. He said I should drop all thoughts of taking legal action against the officer, because this would only provoke others in the police force to act against me.

They would drag into court the fact that I was gay and lived with my boyfriend, and the damage that revelation would do just wouldn't be worth the battle.

Driving back home from Mr Rustamji's, I resolved that Tandavan and I must leave India. Though it was in India that I had found my first great adult love and relationship, I was sick of feeling fearful every day just because I lived with him, sick of feeling that I was a criminal just for being gay.

And now the worst of those fears—that of being imprisoned, of being deprived of my freedom, of my ability to fight back or even to flee—had become a reality. It left me with a terrifying new awareness of what it meant to be criminalized—it meant I could be summarily imprisoned to suffer the corruption and capriciousness of India's rotten policing and judicial systems.

The only reason things hadn't ended disastrously at the police station was because the homophobic officer had taken cognizance of my social status and held himself back from doing worse. From all that I had seen during my years in India, I knew that if I had been just an average gay man, Tandavan and I would have probably been beaten, raped, held indefinitely, and then blackmailed—our lives ruined, with no scope for recourse because we were criminals under the law.

A few mornings later, my phone at the *Washington Post*'s bureau rang. At the other end was the officer from the Jor Bagh police station, his voice slurred, clearly from drinking too much. He said something incomprehensible and then started crying. I kept silent because I was shivering uncontrollably, from both fear and hatred.

Eventually, I realized that he was pleading, saying that he had been transferred to a military area on the outskirts of Delhi—a hardship posting because the armed forces held sway here. He asked me if I could forgive him, and get him back his treasured posting at Jor Bagh. At some point, I heard him say plaintively that he had meant me no harm.

Filled with revulsion, I hung up without saying a word.

And then, just two or three months after our traumatic night at the police station, Tandavan and I learnt from Siddhartha that a young gay man in Goa, whose HIV status had become known to the police and health authorities, had been arrested and was being held in isolation under armed guard. Siddhartha, I, and other friends among our group feared that this was the first salvo in a campaign against gays, triggered by an AIDS scare that was intensifying, with a growing number of Indians being diagnosed with HIV.

We had long dreaded that hysteria about the disease would further demonize us, as had happened in the West since the early1980s because of the notion that AIDS was a 'gay plague' spread by promiscuity. We feared it would result in the systematic persecution of men known or even suspected of being homosexual, that we would become subjected to forced testing, quarantining, and other abuses. 'AIDS is the last thing the Indian homosexual needed,' the *Sunday* cover story on gay men had sympathetically noted in 1988. 'Proscribed by law, ostracized by society, he now faces the prospect of being held responsible for a scourge that is not of his making.'

I learned, with horror, of the details of the Goa man's ordeal, and it only took on a sharper edge because of my own recent hardships.

On Tuesday, 14 February 1989, in Parra, a rural parish of northern Goa, Dominic D'Souza had breakfast with his widowed mother and aunt like he always did. They left home before him and, hence, didn't meet the lone policeman who arrived a short while later. The policeman asked Dominic to come to the police station in Mapusa, northern Goa's major town, as soon as possible, but offered no further explanation.

Dominic was surprised, but Goa was a tranquil place then and his was a respectable, upper-strata Catholic family. So, having phoned his boss at the Panjim branch of the World Wildlife Fund to say that he had been delayed unexpectedly, he confidently started off for the police station on his motorbike. It didn't cross his mind to leave an explanatory note for his mother and aunt, informing them that he was going to the police station.

From the moment Dominic arrived at the police station—a series of innocuous Portuguese-era buildings—his life changed irrevocably. Without being given any explanation, he was driven in a police van to the nearby Asilo Hospital. He knew the hospital well because he went there regularly to donate blood. Suddenly, several doctors appeared and began to look closely at him, almost as if they wanted to conduct a medical examination without touching him. They badgered him with questions—asking if he frequented prostitutes, was homosexual, or injected drugs, or had had sex on his recent holiday in Germany—but not one would answer his increasingly anxious questions.

Dominic's fears turned into terror when he spotted a register with 'AIDS' printed across its cover, and one of the doctors entering his name into it. The trauma of realizing that he was infected with HIV was such that Dominic did not protest when he was handcuffed and driven to an unused tuberculosis sanatorium a short distance from Mapusa. The handcuffs were removed there, and Dominic was locked, alone, in a vast room littered with rat and pigeon droppings, bare but for broken-down metal beds. '(I) was left all alone with my helplessness and fright,' Dominic wrote later of this unnerving moment. Armed police personnel were stationed at every possible exit.

Dominic had begun the morning as a respectable, happily employed young man. In the space of a few hours, his life had been transformed so completely that the authorities now viewed him as a dangerous criminal. He wrote later, '(M)y arrest and isolation were the most traumatic and terrifying experiences of my life ... (they) seem almost like the acts of a sadist.'

Dominic's family and friends—led by his mother, Lucy D'Souza (a retired nurse), and Isabel de Santa Rita Vaz, a well-known professor of literature, whose amateur theatre company Dominic had been a part of—immediately came to his defence. D'Souza and Vaz pleaded with Goa's health secretary, legislators, the chief minister and the governor to release Dominic. They cited World Health Organization guidelines, which specified that people with HIV should not be incarcerated or quarantined. They emphasized that Dominic posed no threat to anyone, and they would guarantee that he stayed put at home.

Even a month later, they had made little headway. Dominic remained incarcerated. Officials and politicians, however sympathetic their tone, said they were constrained by the law. In 1987, Goa's legislators, concerned that Goa was particularly vulnerable to an HIV epidemic because of the thousands of foreigners who were attracted to its unspoiled beaches and its fame as a drug-and-sex hippie haven, had approved punitive anti-AIDS measures that effectively turned HIV-affected people into criminals.

Health officials were empowered to demand HIV tests of anyone they suspected of being infected. Those who refused could be arrested, even without a court warrant. Doctors were required to notify the authorities if they learnt that someone had HIV, rather than protect the patient's confidentiality. While infected foreigners were to be deported, Indians were to be imprisoned indefinitely in isolation. Dominic was the first Goan found to be HIV-positive, but nearly a dozen foreigners had already been deported by then.

In late March, Lucy D'Souza filed a case in the High Court, challenging her son's imprisonment on the grounds that it violated the Indian Constitution as well as the World Health Organisation's guidelines on HIV that the government had endorsed. Simultaneously, she and Vaz rallied public support for Dominic's cause.

The Parra panchayat passed a resolution demanding that the authorities release Dominic, and let him return home to his village. In tiny Goa, with its population of just 1 million, this was a powerful statement by his community to the government. On the day before D'Souza's writ petition was entered in court, she and Vaz led a massive demonstration through Panjim to seek Dominic's release as well as the repeal of Goa's draconian anti-AIDS law. They were joined by neighbours, women's groups, and local activist organizations. D'Souza herself carried a placard saying, 'I have AIDS, please hug me', to emphasize that her HIV-positive son warranted love and support, not imprisonment and ostracism.

The support for Dominic was so strong that the *Times of India* commented, 'It appears that the government [of Goa] has been taken aback at the barrage of protests and outrage from citizens, organizations and the medical community from within and outside the state over Dominic's incarceration.' It showed that at least in Goa, with its educated populace, the over-reaction to AIDS could not be blamed on public sentiment. Rather, it sprang from the paranoid attitude of government officials and the judiciary.

Eventually, on 18 April 1989, more than two months after Dominic's ordeal had begun, the court passed an interim order freeing him from his solitary, dirty prison at the sanatorium, and instead placed him under house arrest, with a police constable to stand guard. The court gratuitously instructed Dominic to 'refrain from having sexual intercourse with any person', and not donate blood or act in 'any manner so that the dreaded disease is communicated to others', yet

Positive People

Dominic D'Souza

again displaying its prejudice that people who have contracted HIV could not be trusted to behave responsibly.

That evening, Dominic's closest friends arrived at the TB sanatorium to escort him back home, bringing to an end this first harrowing chapter in Dominic's life as a nationally known figure of shame and notoriety.

Yet, to the surprise of Siddhartha and I, even after Dominic's widely reported saga, there was no punitive campaign by the government against homosexuals as part of its AIDS-control measures. In fact, remarkably, the government as well as the media treated his case without making a single reference to his orientation, with no one even referring to what Siddhartha, I and our other friends knew for a fact—that Dominic was gay. His assertion that he had contracted HIV while donating blood, via contaminated equipment, was accepted unquestioningly, even though such a scenario was highly improbable. The Indian peculiarity of accepting even the dramatically impossible when an appeal is made based on noble selflessness had provided a tailor-made escape for him.

When I look back at that time, it is fascinating to see what saved us. Here we were, gay men who felt so nakedly visible and threatened, certain that the hostile government—probably some department of the police or home ministry—was keeping close tabs on us. What we didn't realize, until years later, was that we had done such a good job of hiding ourselves that we truly were invisible, individually and as a group.

Consequently, policymakers—given their intense homophobic prejudices—could easily deny our existence and assert that India had no homosexuals, or very few of them, that homosexuality was a Western import with no real roots in India. Thus, in an interview with Siddhartha in 1989, the head of the Indian Council of Medical Research, Dr A.S. Paintal, insisted that homosexuality didn't exist in India simply because it was banned. However absurd this argument was, Dr Paintal and other policymakers genuinely seemed to believe it. And so it was that in those early years of the epidemic—when the government's draconian approach to combating it could well have led to targeting us—the spread of the disease was not blamed on gay men. Gay men, myself included, who could see that gay and bisexual Indian men were contracting HIV in large numbers, kept quiet about the trend, knowing that drawing attention would do us more harm than good.

But, there was a second, pivotal reason why we were spared the blame—another criminalized and reviled set of sexual outlaws, female prostitutes, was made the scapegoat for the spread of AIDS.

In April 1986, a few months before I had returned to India from New York, I had read reports in Indian newspapers about six prostitutes in a Madras reformatory who had been found to be infected with HIV, marking the first scientific confirmation that the virus was spreading domestically within India. In other words, it had spread between individuals who had contracted the virus within the country rather than abroad.

I was not surprised to learn that the epidemic had spread to India—it was, after all, five years since the first known cases of AIDS had come to light in the US, and two years since Asia's first cases in Thailand. I thought with dread that India's abysmal public health system, its largely illiterate population of 750 million, and the cultural prohibitions on discussing sexual matters would make it impossible to contain the epidemic, given the scant progress made in coping with even age-old infectious diseases such as tuberculosis and cholera.

As this was many years before the Internet made it possible for us to keep abreast of far-flung events, I gave little thought to the fate of the six unfortunate prostitutes at the Madras reformatory. By the time I began to research their lives many years later, there was only one among the six about whom anything much was known—Selvi.

Like many Indians, she used only her given name. She was the only one of the six with a traceable history, photographs, and even surviving friends and family. The other five women had vanished without a record, their lives and history obliterated by the fact that they were mere specks among India's impoverished masses of millions.

Even with Selvi, only a little is known of her early years, the years that ended with imprisonment at the reformatory. She was from a destitute Tamil family of landless laborers, educated through class five. She had left her abusive husband and was fending for her toddler son by working as a street prostitute. Sometime in March 1986, this small, dark-complexioned woman, aged twenty-three or so, was arrested for prostitution in or near Madras.

The police took her to the Madras Vigilance Home, a government-run reformatory for women in the city's Mylapore neighbourhood. Selvi should have been produced in a local court within a day or two, and this being her first arrest for prostitution, she should have been released after paying a fine of about fifty rupees. The whole saga, however harrowing, should have lasted no more than a week or so.

But the morning after Selvi's arrest, a syringeful of her blood—and those of the other prostitutes rounded up the night before—was drawn by a young medical researcher, S. Nirmala. None of the prostitutes dared to question or refuse the earnest researcher, given the enormous chasms of class and caste as well as the trauma of their imprisonment.

The next day, Dr Nirmala carried these vials of blood, along with another hundred drawn over the past two months from other prostitutes, to the Christian Medical College in Vellore, a three-hour journey by bus. That evening, she urgently called her senior collaborator in Madras, Dr Suniti Solomon, a microbiologist, to say that six samples had tested positive for HIV.

For Selvi, those results were to disastrously change the course of her life. While the other prostitutes at the home were produced in court and subsequently either released or sentenced to long terms at the reformatory, the six who tested positive—including Selvi—were not taken to court. The warden did not give them any explanation. Adding to their apprehension, a day or two later, Dr Solomon and Dr Nirmala arrived at the reformatory to interview them. Dr Solomon had been asked by the Director-General of the Indian Council of Medical Research to find out if these prostitutes were having sex with foreigners or Indians, to learn if HIV was beginning to spread domestically. All the six said they only had Indians as clients.

With only a handful of top officials in the government's health system informed about the worrisome positive results, the six blood samples were secretly flown to the US for confirmatory testing at the National Institutes of Health in Maryland, a process that was to take several weeks. Selvi and the other women were told nothing of this, and the reformatory authorities did not seek permission from the courts to continue holding them either. They were simply kept imprisoned.

Selvi's parents, who knew that their daughter had been working as a prostitute after leaving her husband, somehow tracked her to the reformatory from their home in Ulundurpettai, a nondescript town 50 km away. Though they were allowed to meet Selvi, the warden curtly told them that she could not be released because she had a 'blood infection' that required treatment. They did not argue. They were impoverished, illiterate and lived in a hovel, while the warden—the ruler of this jail with its imposing buildings and high walls—embodied the unchallengeable power of the government.

At the very end of April, the US National Institutes of Health informed the Indian Council of Medical Research that all the six women were definitely HIV-positive. The next morning, on 29 April, India's health minister announced in Parliament that six women with 'promiscuous heterosexual behaviour'—an elliptical but unmistakable reference to prostitutes—had been found to be infected with HIV in Tamil Nadu. There was pandemonium in the vast hall of the Lok Sabha. The health minister reassured her colleagues that officials were closely monitoring the situation.

But press reports—which inaccurately suggested that the women were suffering from AIDS (they were still asymptomatic)—fed a public frenzy. The panic was most intense in Madras when a south Indian newspaper, The *Hindu*, ran a front-page article on 30 April reporting that the AIDS cases had been traced to a vigilance home—the reformatory—in the city. The next day it reported in another front-page article that the state's health minister had 'assured the State Assembly that the government was keeping a strict vigil over the cases of AIDS in the state', and that the six infected women 'were under strict surveillance and follow-up action was being taken to see that the virus did not spread'.

Selvi and the other five women paid the price for the panic. They were immediately separated from the other prostitutes, and imprisoned in a small, barred room some distance from the main building. Selvi later described it to a friend as being 'like an isolated cell for the condemned'.

Food was pushed in through a small window. The women were forced to do everything in that small room—eat, sleep, go to the toilet, wash their clothes. Despite their anguish, they were not given any counseling about this unknown disease they were suffering from—an affliction so fearsome that they had to be kept in isolation.

But, within weeks, the focus of panic shifted to the scores of other prostitutes and individuals across India now being found to be HIV-positive. Selvi and the five other HIV-positive women in the reformatory were entirely forgotten. Years followed years, but they remained imprisoned.

Neither Indian nor international women's groups, human rights organizations or the medical establishment, including Dr Solomon and Dr Nirmala, challenged their imprisonment and the terrible, punitive conditions they were being held in. Not one of them protested that Selvi and the other prostitutes had been imprisoned without trial, and the state government continued to summarily imprison every prostitute found to be HIV-positive. When I later pieced together Selvi's history, what struck me most forcefully was how the downtrodden in India could be jailed without due process for years, despite the country being a democracy with a functional judiciary.

Forever after in India, AIDS was thought of as a disease pertaining to women prostitutes, merely because the first indigenous cases were detected amongst them. Prostitutes were accused of spreading this sexual infection to hapless men, and then onto their innocent wives and babies.

They had always faced persecution, but now it intensified to an unprecedented scale. Unlike us gay men, they were easy to locate in brothels or on particular street corners . They were impoverished. And they were 'sexual' women, that last fact making them prey to particular scorn and abuse in India, where misogyny is at its worst with women regarded as sexually immoral. The traumatic experience Tandavan and I faced at the police station was nothing compared to the ordeals that Dominic had to go through, and his suffering, in turn, paled in comparison to the calamities heaped on Selvi and countless other prostitutes as the epidemic worsened across India.

9

The Pandemic and Sexual Outlaws

It was not surprising that the AIDS pandemic became my most abiding and passionate concern.

I had come of age as a gay man precisely in the years that AIDS emerged as a killer of us gay men, and forever afterwards, sex was loaded with the threat of death, a harrowing spectre looming over every one of my relationships and sexual encounters. And the virulence of the anti-gay hatred exposed by the epidemic—embodied in the gloating that this terrible plague was punishment by a wrathful God for our depravity—enraged me. In the most intimate and profound ways this was a disease about me—this virus that was intertwined with sex, with society's irrational taboos and bigotry, with being outlawed and persecuted.

Beyond the personal reasons, my interests in policy matters had made me realize that this was no routine epidemic that would run a short, bloody course and then peter out. In 1987, less than six years since the first AIDS cases were identified, I had read a *New York Times* op-ed in which the eminent evolutionary biologist Stephen Jay Gould warned that the AIDS pandemic was 'the greatest danger of our era ... potentially, the greatest natural tragedy in human history'. Those were unforgettable words, given Gould's expertise.

And though of course I couldn't see this in those early years, the pandemic was to forever alter everything for us sexual outlaws, whether gay men or prostitutes. Its depredations would soon force us to fight for our very survival. This, in turn, would force the world to pay attention to us, leading to some recognition of the harshness of our lives and the many wrongs done to us, this killing disease being only the latest. Ultimately, the pandemic would even prove to be the rallying cause for our welfare, convincing decent-minded people that we deserved fundamental human rights protection no less than any other marginalized, disadvantaged individuals.

So, when I joined the Harvard School of Public Health to get a master's degree in the fall of 1990, on the cusp of my twenty-ninth birthday, I made AIDS my special focus. (Tandavan was going to be in Paris for the nine months that I needed to complete the degree; we were then going to figure out some way of living together in the US or France, a matter imperilled by immigration policies that did not recognize same-sex relationships.)

I was immensely fortunate that Jonathan Mann, the architect of the international response to the pandemic, who had resigned just a few months earlier from leading the World Health Organisation's Global Programme on AIDS, had joined the faculty of the public health school. Mann was already a legend in the world of health policy.

He had taken a disease that bureaucrats and political leaders inevitably sought to ignore because of its roots in sex and drug use, and turned it into an international health priority in just the four years between 1986 and 1990. There was no better person from whom I could learn about the pandemic. Mann agreed to be one of my academic advisors. In my second semester, I enrolled in his seminar course on AIDS.

Mann's course was held in a small room at a modern high-rise in the busy, downtown portion of Boston that housed Harvard's medical campus, including the public health school. Around two dozen students, drawn from every part of the globe, sat in rows that rose up on one side of the room. At the far bottom of the room were a table and a lectern for Mann. But Mann—an odd yet compelling figure, frizzy hair standing atop an unending forehead, inevitably dressed in a plaid coat and bow-tie—never sat at the desk. Instead, he would launch on his lectures as soon as he entered, almost as if he couldn't hold himself back, pacing the breadth of the room and stopping only when he wanted to challenge one of us in debate. There was no doubting that this epidemic had become his raison d'être.

Mann gave us students a privileged insight into the available knowledge about the epidemic, the first cases of which had been recognized exactly a decade earlier. An epidemiologist by training, one of Mann's first efforts at WHO's newly established Global Programme on AIDS was to collate accurate worldwide data on the epidemic. Country health officials, not wanting their nations to be identified with a sordid sexually-transmitted disease, were unwilling to collect or provide figures on AIDS and HIV cases. However, Mann and his team pushed them to do so, with the promise of funding as a lure. The methodologies for estimating the numbers infected, always many orders of magnitude larger than the reported cases of HIV, were improved.

The results showed that AIDS was spreading exponentially—an astounding 12 million people across the globe had contracted HIV by 1991, WHO estimated, of whom 2.5 million had died. The number of people cumulatively infected was likely to soar to 30–40 million by the year 2000, less than a decade away, the organization projected.

Though these estimates were disparaged at that time for being alarmist, they eventually proved to fall far short of actuality. It was astounding: a disease that had come to scientific attention as a killer of five gay men in San Francisco had—by its tenth anniversary—

morphed into a worldwide epidemic of millions of men and women, a vast majority of them heterosexual.

Strikingly, the data now showed that the epidemic was growing far more rapidly in developing countries than in the wealthy Western nations where it had first drawn attention. Soon, 90 per cent of all people infected were expected to be in developing countries. The 'gay plague' was now also the 'poor man's plague'.

For yet unexplained reasons, the epidemic was now taking its greatest toll amongst men and women in sub-Saharan Africa. African leaders had so far dismissed AIDS as a Western affliction caused by promiscuity, saying that their traditional societies were immune to such a disease. But by now, in some parts of central Africa, where HIV had probably begun to spread unnoticed since the 1970s or even earlier, as many as one in three of all urban adults were estimated to be HIV-positive, in comparison to an estimated one in thirty-five adults in New York City, the worst-affected American city. Wholescale depopulation was beginning in these towns, and only somewhat more slowly in adjacent rural areas. Tens of thousands had died, leaving behind orphans, ghost towns, and untended fields. Africa's development was beginning to haemorrhage with this massive loss of productive adults.

The crisis in Africa was a warning of things to come in other developing regions, which seemed merely to have been given a grace period. Asia, with more than half the world's population, was emerging as a new epicenter of HIV, Mann told us, because of a similarly incendiary mix of poverty and illiteracy, youthful populations, the inability of women to negotiate as equals in sexual relations, and high rates of the ulcerative sexually transmitted infections that enhance the spread of HIV. India was especially worrying.

This painstakingly gathered evidence served its purpose, convincing all but the most irresponsible government leaders that the world faced an 'unprecedented global crisis'. They agreed to make the pandemic's control a global priority. By the time Mann resigned from WHO in early 1990—after clashes with the body's autocratic new Director-General, Hiroshi Nakajima—almost every developing country had begun national AIDS programmes, nearly a billion dollars had been mobilized to finance their efforts, and the United Nations General Assembly had discussed the epidemic several times, the first instance of a disease being taken up for consideration by that body.

If anything, Mann's other historic achievement at WHO was even more impressive. This was to push governments into agreeing to AIDS-control strategies that respected human rights rather than relied on compulsion. The odds were heavily against him.

So far, health officials the world over had sought to control the spread of AIDS by using the punitive approach traditionally employed with other sexually-transmitted infections such as syphilis and gonorrhoea—involving compulsory examination and testing, 'contact' tracing (of the sexual partners of infected individuals), and enforced treatment, hospitalization or quarantine for any length of time. Their reliance on such harsh measures was even stronger with AIDS because of the wild hysteria about the disease, which cast it as a demonic force rather than an unusual viral disease.

Mann's usual passion intensified visibly when he started explaining why a diametrically different approach was needed to control AIDS, one that protected every individual's human rights. He took great pains to illustrate how AIDS was intertwined with human rights matters in a way that no other major existing disease was.

It began with basic civil liberties because, virtually everywhere, the disease epidemic was followed by an epidemic of human rights abuses—with everybody from families, neighbours and employers to government authorities turning on people with AIDS or sections of society blamed for spreading the disease. The abuses intensified once tests to detect HIV infection were developed in 1985. Governments authorized public health authorities—often working in tandem with the police—to carry out compulsory tests on groups presumed to be at high risk and to detain or isolate infected people without taking cognizance of their basic human rights. By the close of the epidemic's first decade, over a hundred countries had passed special AIDS-related legislation, most of which violated the civil liberties of particular groups.

But the inter-linkages extended all the way to the broad sets of rights that are essential for human well-being, said Mann. These rights are enshrined in the iconic human rights agreements that voice the aspirations of the post-World War II world, particularly the Universal Declaration of Human Rights; the International Covenant on Economic, Social and Cultural Rights; and the International Covenant on Civil and Political Rights. Mann pointed out that AIDS was disproportionately concentrated amongst populations whose human rights were least fulfilled.

He explained this evocatively, saying, 'In each society, those people who, before HIV/AIDS arrived, were marginalized, stigmatized, and discriminated against become those at highest risk of HIV infection ... HIV is now becoming a problem mainly for les exclus, the "excluded ones" living at the margins of society.'

Citing the practical complications presented by the disease's epidemiology, Mann insisted that the traditional, coercive public health approach was doomed to fail with AIDS. One crucial difference posed by HIV was that people remained asymptomatic and healthy for typically six to eight years from the time of initial infection, meaning that they could unwittingly pass on the virus to their sexual partners during this period.

Also, as there was no treatment or cure for AIDS, even resorting to mass testing to detect people with HIV offered no solution—short of the impossible one of quarantining millions till their eventual death. So, besides being bound to fail, Mann said that the use of coercive measures would worsen the already intense public hysteria about AIDS and drive individuals who are infected or at risk underground, away from health services.

Mann's insistence about the centrality of human rights to AIDS automatically made sense to me from my personal experiences as a gay man. From my earliest days in the US in the 1980s, as the epidemic swelled, I had witnessed the irrational hysteria and the abuses that had followed—the demonization of gay men, drug users and other groups popularly associated with the disease, followed by persecution and violence against them and anyone even suspected of being ill with AIDS or infected with HIV. And the activism of gay American men, in response, had rightfully cast AIDS as a civil rights matter—battling against being thrown out of their jobs and homes, or being denied medical care even when mortally sick. (That advocacy had eventually made the federal government include people with AIDS, and even 'someone perceived as having AIDS', under the protection of US disability laws, which explicitly prohibit discrimination in almost every sphere of life.)

In the years since, I had seen the Indian government and scores of others, rich and poor alike, adopt draconian policies for controlling HIV. They forcibly tested and locked away HIV-positive prostitutes, like Selvi, and others found to be infected, like Dominic D'Souza, attempting to treat this epidemic as a law and order problem that could be solved through harsh policing. I recognized that it was imperative that civil liberties not be violated in a government's efforts to prevent the spread of HIV.

I also knew from personal experience that criminalization and marginalization had made gay and bisexual men, as a group, more vulnerable to this epidemic. However, it was only now—from Mann's course—that I could begin to frame it in the formal human rights language of the 'systematic unfulfillment of broader civil, political, economic, social and cultural rights'.

The pathways were innumerable: by preventing us from having healthy, open relationships like our straight peers; by forcing us away from mainstream society as well as our families; by giving us no option but to have furtive, unsafe sex in parks and toilets; by keeping us from openly seeking information about safe-sex methods, from buying condoms and lubricants, or getting tested to know our HIV status. I began to realize that the marginalized were always far more vulnerable to virtually every threat—whether it was a natural disease or man-made violence—and AIDS was just the latest and most deadly of the injustices that had beset us.

But most of my classmates were mid-career health officials or practising doctors. Almost irrespective of whether they had trained in the West or in developing countries, medical and public health education had taught them that human rights could be legitimately limited in light of public health imperatives, especially during epidemics of contagious diseases. 'Leper colonies', where hundreds of men and women suffering from leprosy were forcibly confined for their lifetimes, exemplified the time-honoured appeal of this approach. Even the medical fraternity's 'Hippocratic Oath'—a key element of which requires doctors to keep their patients' ailments secret—had to be put aside in the face of these larger imperatives of public good. (The fact that Mann had broken free of this mindset and was pushing the frontiers of thinking on the issue, testified to his visionary qualities.)

So, it was no wonder that many of the students did not respond with ready comprehension during Mann's class sessions on human rights. This earned us his ire. Any poor student who dared question him was frowned at as if she or he were a nitwit, unable to grasp the most obvious of truths.

I bore the brunt of Mann's irritation too one day, when I argued that Cuba had managed to stem the spread of HIV, unlike neighbouring Haiti, where infection rates were reaching Africa-level highs, and any criticism of the Castro regime's use of harsh measures needed to be balanced by this notable public health achievement. (Cuba's doctors were allowed to test anybody they chose, including partners of infected individuals. Those found to be HIV-positive were forcibly isolated and held, presumably for the length of their remaining life, in sanatoriums.) Mann looked at me with a mix of anger and pity, cut me off mid-sentence, and then moved over to the far end of the room to speak to another student.

Despite the odds, Mann's powers of persuasion were such that, within a year of joining WHO, he had succeeded in getting the world's governments to disavow their reliance on the old coercive approaches—at least formally and at the level of policymaking—and commit to a more humane strategy based on promoting knowledge about AIDS, responsible behaviour and human rights. Every year thereafter, he strategically pushed governments to make ever-more explicit commitments on protecting human rights at the World Health Assembly, the UN General Assembly, and other UN bodies of the kind. The speed of change was astonishing.

The first global resolutions approved on AIDS, in 1987, did not explicitly mention human rights. But by the following year, the world's health ministers had declared, at a London summit dedicated to AIDS: 'We emphasize the need in AIDS prevention programmes to protect human rights and human dignity. Discrimination against, and stigmatization of, HIV-infected people and people with AIDS, and population groups undermine public health and must be avoided.'

And by 1991, a year after Mann's resignation, a UN General Assembly resolution committed governments and inter-governmental organizations to 'protect the human rights and dignity of HIV-infected persons, persons with AIDS and members of particular population groups' as well as to 'avoid discriminatory action against and stigmatization of them in the provision of services, and in employment and travel.'

All of this was an incredible achievement by Mann and his team, marking one of WHO's finest moments of global leadership. The importance of what Mann had set in motion became ever clearer to me over the years as I learnt more and more about the epidemic and its disastrous toll on human rights.

Mann had succeeded in ensuring that a virus spread by sex and drugs, popularly associated with undesirable people, be accepted as a legitimate global priority. He had also convinced the world's governments to make written global commitments that, in their efforts to control this pandemic, they would respect the basic human rights of every individual—whether it concerned people newly stigmatized for being infected with AIDS or those of us who were so reviled that they would not even mention us in these declarations.

The fate of us outlaws—whether gay men, prostitutes, or drug users—hung tenuously on those coded, formalistic mentions of 'particular population groups', of 'discrimination' and 'stigmatization', of 'human rights' and 'human dignity'. These elliptical words were the key to our protection.

Would the world's governments take them seriously? Would the UN—that imperfect, embattled mediator between hostile nations—emerge as an honest advocate on our behalf, fighting for the fulfilment of our basic human rights?

If those commitments were honoured, governments would move to provide prostitutes, gay men and drug users with effective HIV prevention services, besides legal and constitutional instruments to tackle the terrible disadvantages we faced. But, if they ignored these human rights commitments, then we were likely to be subjected to even more harm and persecution than ever before.

So, this once unimaginable development of being in the global policy spotlight augured all kinds of uncertainties for us. But whatever the outcome, we would probably not even have had these opportunities if Mann hadn't insisted that governments recognize that AIDS was a serious human rights issue just as much as it was a deadly disease.

10

The Persecuted

That summer, upon completing my public health degree at Harvard, and after a joyous reunion with Tandavan in Paris, I spent two months back in India, researching and writing several articles on AIDS, including an extensive feature for *Sunday*, a prominent Indian news magazine.

I thought often of Jonathan Mann because everything he had taught me about AIDS was visible here—the speed with which India's epidemic was growing, the challenges to action posed by the disease's long asymptomatic period, and, most graphically, the human rights abuses that were ballooning as the epidemic advanced. Yet, despite all that I had learnt in his class, I was often overwhelmed by what I was seeing, this being my first attempt to investigate the ground realities of the disease.

Though it had been just five years since the first domestic cases of HIV were detected in India—among Selvi and the five other sex workers at the Madras reformatory—more than half a million adults were infected in the country, WHO estimated. And yet, less than a hundred cases of AIDS and under six thousand known cases of

HIV had been reported to the government, mainly from hospitals as well as clinics treating sexually transmitted diseases. Such was the conundrum posed by HIV because of the years it took from the initial infection to the first signs of illness.

I began my research in the handful of hospitals, almost all government run, that were willing to care for people with AIDS. J.J. Hospital in Bombay, housed in a grim, no-frills building, was one of these rare places, under the supervision of Dr Smita Gupta, head of the department of medicine. Brusque and no-nonsense, her one comment to me before leading me to her patients was that 'even when the senior doctors look through the microscope at the HIV virus, they keep making funny remarks'. Her frustration at their idiocy, at the fact that they would care that this disease was spread mainly by sex and drug use, was visible. But their prejudice as well as their fears—of contracting HIV from patients—had far-reaching costs. They insisted that Dr Gupta treat patients with HIV in a separate ward, even though this reinforced paranoia about the disease and made it likely that the patients' identity would become known publicly.

When Dr Gupta took me to the ward, I noticed with relief that at least there was no sign identifying it as the 'AIDS Ward'—like the one I had seen just days earlier at the All India Institute of Medical Sciences (AIIMS) in Delhi, the country's leading public hospital. In every other way too, the ward was the complete opposite of the one at AIIMS. That had been empty, without a single patient, because doctors and nurses refused to care for patients with HIV, despite the public money spent on the dedicated ward. Here, each one of the seven beds was occupied. While the ward at AIIMS was spanking new and pristine, this was a general ward with metal frame beds and worn sheets. In Delhi, with no patients to tend to, the staff had stood around chatting. Here, they were so busy caring for the patients that they paid neither Dr Gupta nor me any attention.

The patients! My ability to observe came to a standstill. On every bed, there were sights of heart-rending suffering. The only thing I had ever seen that could even be compared to this horror was the sight of beggars with leprosy-gnawed limbs on Calcutta's streets.

My attention fixed on one of them because his physical suffering looked even more unbearable than that of the others. Across his long, emaciated body—only a thin sheet covered his groin—were suppurating dark boils, each the size of a clenched fist. What were they?

Whatever I had learnt at Harvard about the myriad HIV-related opportunistic infections—candidiasis, Kaposi's sarcoma, Pneumocystis carinii pneumonia, tuberculosis, ulcerative herpes and so on, the limitless A to Z of torture spawned by HIV—deserted me when faced with this living proof. He was skeleton thin. This I recognized as the condition called 'slim' disease in Africa because of the wasting caused by uncontrollable diarrhoeal infections.

There were bandages tied on so many parts of his body—one of his legs had been raised and tied to a pulley-like contraption—that it seemed as if the doctors were attempting to hold his limbs together as his flesh wasted away. Just looking at him was torture.

Those images from J.J. Hospital haunted the rest of my journey. I realized that each and every HIV-positive person I was meeting would inevitably suffer this kind of horror before the virus killed them off.

If the physical suffering from AIDS was harrowing, so too were the abuses spawned in reaction to it. Mann had described these human rights abuses as the AIDS epidemic's 'third wave', the first wave being the invisible epidemic of infection with HIV and the second the epidemic of illness that emerged some years later. However, from what I saw that summer, I began to feel that the abuses were in some ways spreading faster than the virus itself, fuelled by misinformed panic as well as by the opprobrium attached to it for being spread sexually.

Across the country, men and women whose HIV status became publicly known—typically from being leaked by their doctors—were being thrown out of their homes by their families and out of their jobs by employers. Ever so often, newspapers reported uncritically on how patients found to have HIV had been forced out of hospitals, often left to die uncared for on the streets. Prostitutes and drug users were being forcibly tested for HIV by medical authorities and the police, often at the behest of the courts. And a draconian AIDS-control law, introduced in parliament by the Rajiv Gandhi government two years earlier, would institute forced HIV testing, coercive contact tracing of past sexual partners, and even indefinite isolation of those found to be HIV-positive.

I found that no group in India had been as badly hit by these human rights violations as female prostitutes. From the outset, they had been associated with AIDS—because the first domestic cases had been discovered among Selvi and the other prostitutes at the Madras reformatory—much as America's epidemic had been associated with gay men. The association had intensified over the years as concern about the runaway epidemic in developing countries fixed the spotlight on them.

Thus, in an article that very summer of 1991, the *Economist* had asked: 'Since sex is universal, why is AIDS primarily a disease of the poor countries?' The reasons, said the magazine, were because 'prostitution and promiscuity are more common, and the traditional sexual diseases are less likely to be treated'. The most vital part of what needed to be done, said the *Economist*, was to check the spread of HIV from prostitutes to their clients, a view widely espoused by public health experts.

'Prostitutes in poor countries are often infected,' the magazine wrote. 'They and their clients played a significant role in the spread of AIDS in Africa ... [and] prostitution seems to be at the heart of the disease's spread in Thailand, a country whose troubles are less well known but may prove cataclysmic.' These dynamics were expected to be no different in India and elsewhere in Asia.

And so, the AIDS pandemic forced female prostitutes everywhere squarely into the public eye and onto the agendas of health ministries. (The attention was almost everywhere exclusively on female prostitutes, with no mention made of male or transgender prostitutes—the denial about alternative sexual behaviours and genders was so absolute that policymakers pretended away any knowledge that such reviled, criminal individuals existed in their nations.)

The attention would have been a blessing had it led to actually protecting prostitutes against AIDS. They desperately needed help—and for too many it was too late already. Extrapolations from studies suggested that 40–60 per cent of the prostitutes in several sub-Saharan African cities, and 10–30 per cent of prostitutes in such major Asian cities as Bangkok and Bombay, were already infected. Prostitutes were being wiped out at a pace that dwarfed even the devastation visited on Western gay men.

Success in stemming the epidemic amongst prostitutes as well as their clients pivoted on ensuring that their clients used condoms. This would keep prostitutes from getting infected in the first place and, in turn, keep other clients from getting infected. These goals could be directly achieved in places where prostitutes were able to demand that their clients use condoms. In fact, from the onset of the AIDS epidemic, prostitutes in Western industrialized nations began to insist that clients use condoms or forgo having sex—their clients usually agreed as they were already familiar with condoms and aware of the risk of AIDS.

Consequently, Western prostitutes who contracted HIV did so overwhelmingly from injecting drug use, common among low-income prostitutes and their partners, not through sexual transmission. Among low-income street prostitutes in the US, among whom injecting drug use—or addiction to crack cocaine—was widespread, HIV infection rates eventually crossed to more than 50 per cent.

In contrast, it remained close to zero amongst women working in legal brothels in Nevada or those employed by upscale escort services, where condom use was routine and injecting drug use virtually non-existent. Thus, it was proved that prostitutes did not really contract HIV as an inevitable consequence of their work.

But to get clients of prostitutes in developing countries to use condoms was another matter altogether. In most such nations, men were unused to condoms even as a means of birth control, and disliked using them because they 'reduced sexual pleasure'. Condoms were anyway in short supply—few developing countries even manufactured condoms—and seemed a luxury for the average man, equal to the price of a meal.

Many prostitutes, particularly in impoverished sub-Saharan Africa and South Asia, were illiterate or barely educated. This made it difficult for them to grasp the threat posed by AIDS until years later, when they saw large numbers of other women falling sick and dying. But, even when aware of the disease and convinced that condoms could prevent HIV transmission, they typically had little power to overcome the customers' opposition to using condoms. They were exceptionally disadvantaged women—impoverished, criminalized by law in almost every country, vulnerable to all kinds of abuse, and so stigmatized that virtually no one would come to their aid.

In contrast, the client was a man with money to spend. If a prostitute refused to have sex without a condom, the client would go elsewhere. The threat of losing income was a blow not just to the prostitute, but also to the pimps and brothel-keepers who brokered their business; they were often the ones who pressured prostitutes to not insist on condoms. Consequently, every factor conspired to push prostitutes into dismissing the remote threat of AIDS, its toll as yet largely invisible, and to acceding to the client's demands.

Yet, in a parallel to the pattern in the West, HIV rates remained low amongst better-off prostitutes, such as those working in nightclubs or hotels, because they had more control over their working conditions, particularly condom use. Every study showed that the poorer the prostitute was, the higher the rates of HIV infection.

This was true not just in sub-Saharan Africa, but also in Asia. Amongst the poorest groups of prostitutes in Kenya as well as India and Thailand, studies showed that an astronomical 80 per cent were infected by 1991 or so. Poorer women had to sell more sex to survive, and their dire poverty meant that they had little power in any aspect of their lives.

However, governments could not plead ignorance about what strategies would bear the best results in stemming the spread of HIV among prostitutes and their clients because WHO, under Mann's leadership of the Global Programme on AIDS, had provided detailed guidance on this issue. WHO was initially ill-prepared for the task as even its past efforts to tackle the classic sexually-transmitted diseases had focused on massive national identification and treatment programmes—a blanket approach that resulted in the organization not designing programmes specifically for prostitutes, and hence, knowing little about the health needs of women, men and transgender prostitutes as well as the complex web of difficulties they faced.

So Mann, in his characteristically iconoclastic but effective manner, had hired an American feminist activist, Priscilla Alexander, with extensive experience in working with American prostitutes. (Alexander had helped create COYOTE, a pioneering US-based prostitutes' rights organization—the acronym stands for the memorable 'Cast Off Your Old Tired Ethics'.) This was the only way of ensuring that WHO's advice was made responsive to the realities of prostitution.

On Alexander's joining the Global Programme in early 1989, she and Mann convened an unorthodox meeting on AIDS and prostitution. The participants included not just the usual public health officials but also the tiny handful of prostitutes' rights advocates—including current and former prostitutes—working in both industrialized and developing countries, ranging from the US and Switzerland to India, Nigeria and Thailand.

From the perspective of the prostitutes themselves, it was an epochal development: For the first time ever, they had a say in global discussions concerning themselves. Building on the meeting, Alexander reviewed the experiences of a handful of projects—mostly run by local non-governmental groups—that had recently come up in developing countries to work with prostitutes on HIV prevention.

The guidelines that eventually emerged from this process emphasized that narrow HIV-specific efforts—such as merely providing condoms to prostitutes and their clients—would fail because the factors that disempowered prostitutes remained unchanged. Instead, governments were urged to view prostitution, when done by consenting adults—whether women, men or transgenders—as legitimate work, and in this context, take steps to improve their overall working conditions. This could be done by establishing occupational safety standards, providing health insurance and broad health care, and ensuring them remunerative returns on their labour, all part of the panoply of rights and benefits granted to other workers. United action by prostitutes was vital to tackle the myriad factors that left them helpless, and the guidelines emphasized the need for conscious efforts to build solidarity.

To confront the intense stigma associated with the term 'prostitute' and place emphasis on the professionalism of their work, WHO introduced the new term 'sex worker' in the guidelines. This marked the first appearance of this term—coined by an American activist—in global health documents. (From this point on, I switch to using 'sex worker' instead of 'prostitute', in recognition that this positive term is now widely preferred by those in the profession.)

The importance of these developments could not be overstated: The health of sex workers was now an explicit part of WHO's responsibilities and policy agenda. And Mann had committed WHO, and through it arguably the entire UN system, to an approach focused on promoting the basic human rights of sex workers.

But Indian officials paid no heed to WHO's advice on sex work or, for that matter, the broader commitments about respecting human rights vis-à-vis AIDS that their government had made at the World Health Assembly as well as other international venues. This was so even though India arguably had the most to gain by putting in place effective HIV prevention programmes for sex workers—the Ministry of Health had recently estimated that the country had about 1 million women sex workers, far outstripping any other nation. (It was also obvious that many Indian men—of all classes—sought out sex workers, given the strictures against women having sex before or outside marriage.) Even Thailand, with its famed sex industry, had estimated that it had just a fraction of the Indian figure, at a hundred and fifty thousand sex workers.

Instead, like most other governments, India continued to take the opposite course of singling out women sex workers for mandatory HIV testing, imprisoning them if found infected, and making every effort to suppress sex work itself. Its disregard for WHO's advice on sex work was not surprising. The government's overall policy approach on HIV, embodied in the proposed AIDS Prevention Bill, was diametrically opposed to the numerous WHO recommendations it had agreed to.

This hostile policy environment fueled large scale abuse of sex workers by health officials, the police and even by the courts. The upshot was that sex workers suffered far worse discrimination and persecution than in the pre-AIDS era; their conditions became ever more desperate, and as effective HIV prevention services were not expanded, more and more fell prey to HIV.

The worst abuses were witnessed in Bombay and Madras. Thought to be the epicenters of the epidemic, the AIDS scare was most intense here. The abuses faced by Selvi and the five sex workers imprisoned in the Madras reformatory were emblematic of the persecution of sex workers across India. The six had remained under imprisonment ever since that fateful day in April 1986 when they were found to have HIV.

Every year, the number of women in state custody rose as the government continued to arrest sex workers, forcibly test them for HIV, and imprison those found to be HIV-positive. By 1989, that reformatory alone held over two dozen HIV-positive sex workers.

The number of such inmates in Tamil Nadu swelled substantially in the summer of 1990. This, oddly enough, was the fallout of mass raids on Bombay's red-light areas. Following a sensationalistic newspaper article in January 1990, claiming that 65 per cent of the city's sex workers were infected with HIV, the Bombay High Court directed the police to clear the city of HIV-infected prostitutes. That, and subsequent raids over the next months, led to the arrest of several thousands of sex workers.

The court ordered that they be tested for HIV without their consent. Whether adults or minors, HIV-positive or negative, all of them continued to be held forcibly in Bombay's reformatories. When criticism from human rights activists about the abysmal jail-like conditions at these institutions mounted, the state government decided to deport the women to their home states, as well as Bangladesh and Nepal if they were from these countries.

And so it happened that nearly nine hundred women from Tamil Nadu and other southern states, along with eighty-five of their children, were transported to Madras by a chartered train. The organizers dubbed it the Mukthi Express—Freedom Express—implying that these women had found freedom from prostitution. It was Orwellian doublespeak at its worst, because these women, like all the others arrested in the Bombay raids, had had no freedom at all from the moment the raids began. Instead, they had been subjected to astounding human rights violations, made all the more inexcusable because the abuses had taken place at the express direction of a High Court judge.

Despite not being charged with any crime, they were imprisoned for months. They were even denied a court hearing, a basic right guaranteed to every Indian. They were denied legal aid. The judge summarily rejected the plea made by several human rights groups that the overwhelming majority of the women who had been arrested were adults, and not having been convicted of any crime, had a right to liberty and to making independent decisions about their lives. The judge, instead, accused these groups of allying with the city's pimps and brothel-keepers.

By the time the Mukthi Express reached Madras Central Station, the state government had passed an order to confine the women found to be HIV-positive until 'a cure was found for AIDS'. Tests forcibly carried out on the women showed that more than two out of every three were HIV-positive.

While the few uninfected women were released, the nearly six hundred HIV-positive women were imprisoned in the state's reformatories—including the one in Madras where Selvi had been held for all these years—as well as in jails and makeshift camps.

The over-crowding of these places worsened the already appalling conditions. The hastily built camps were open to the elements despite the scorching heat of the summer. Protests by the women over not being fed led to their being thrashed by the police. Several women tried to flee the camps at night.

By every indication, Selvi as well as the many hundreds of HIV-positive sex workers newly incarcerated across the state would have remained imprisoned indefinitely. But a few months earlier, in November 1989, a young maverick journalist named Shyamala Nataraj had filed a public interest case in the Madras High Court, challenging the prolonged imprisonment of Selvi and the five women who had been held since April 1986. Nataraj, formerly a correspondent for the *Indian Express*, had gained entry to the reformatory by pretending to be a social worker. Her goal, however, was to write an article about the HIV-positive sex workers being held there.

She had been devastated by her first visit. 'Women who had tested positive since 1986 were kept in remand,' Nataraj recalled. 'Each of them had been picked up along the way over those years, and then they were cordoned off. At that time, they were living in this large dilapidated building, which was so run down that even the windows had caved in. All these women were summoned before me. This official from the remand home went out of the main building and shouted, "Hey AIDS, come here!" Just like that!

'For me to stand in the verandah and watch them approach from the building they were housed in was the most troubling moment of my life.

'They all filed in one by one. About two dozen women, all of them HIV-positive. They all stood against this wall, and the superintendent said, "Listen, she has come to help you. She is a social worker. You talk to her."

'And then this woman called Vijaya came up to me and screamed, "Who do you think we are? Are we cattle that you come and look at us, you social workers? You just make money off us."

'She looked hard at me and said, "Look at you! You are carrying a child. I have a one-year-old child outside that I never get to meet."' And then she spat on my face and screamed, "If another one of you comes along, I will commit suicide" and ran out of the room.

'And then, one by one, they all followed Vijaya, sobbing. You can imagine how I felt!

'Selvi was the one who didn't say a word. She just cried silently. And she was this sort of a child-woman, very young and innocent-looking, with this plump, round, child-like face. I noticed Selvi because there was so much anguish on her face. That's what struck me, this anguish.'

Nataraj's subsequent visits to the reformatory made her realize that the women were being held against their will, despite the official line that they were staying there voluntarily. 'Most women, when they talked to me, they simply said, "There is something wrong with our blood." And that seemed to be the extent to which they were aware of AIDS. The remand home officials had told them that they would be looked after till they were cured, and the women had been made to sign statements stating that they were willing to stay in the remand home! That's what I found out when I began to question the women.'

This revelation of the authorities' wrongdoings convinced Nataraj that she could not stop at just writing an article about the women, as she had originally planned, but had to do whatever it took to ensure they were freed. This amounted to filing a legal case challenging their imprisonment. Remarkably, in all the years since Selvi and the others had been imprisoned, no one else had been moved enough to do this.

I was struck that this epidemic was pushing people who did not have formal training in human rights law—from a public health expert like Mann to a journalist like Nataraj—into becoming invested with its principles. I was undergoing a similar process since Mann's Harvard class, realizing that human rights principles held an intoxicating potential for challenging the wrongs done to me as well as all other marginalized people.

Not only did these fundamental rights apply equally to every individual, but the pivotal ones—like the rights to life, to not be tortured or enslaved, to not be discriminated against—were 'non-derogable', and could not legitimately be taken away under any circumstance. All of us wronged, oppressed, outlawed people across the world—the women, the disabled, the Dalits, the indigenous people, the African-Americans, the sex workers, the gays and the transgenders—could use these principles to win equality with the mainstream. The irony was that so many people trained in law, such as the Bombay High Court judge who had ordered the imprisonment of hundreds of sex workers, were patently unconcerned about the fundamental rights of the people already battered by this epidemic.

Both prejudice against sex workers and irrational fears about AIDS explained why no one had sought to have the women in the Madras reformatory released until then, said Nataraj. She had seen this on vivid display when she sought help from non-governmental organizations in filing a legal case to challenge the women's imprisonment. 'They all said, "We don't work with prostitutes. Even if we help as much as we can, they will go back to prostitution. So we don't work with them."

'Astonished, I told them, "But this is not about prostitution. This is about HIV. Tomorrow, your wife might be picked up and locked away for having HIV."

'But they all retorted, "It is better that they are kept inside, otherwise they will spread HIV."'

Frustrated by the lack of support, Nataraj filed a public interest case independently. It resulted in the Madras High Court appointing an independent commissioner who asked Selvi and the other women if they had voluntarily agreed to remain at the reformatory.

The truth came out when the women told the commissioner that they didn't know what they had signed. It became clear that the government officials had abused the women's illiteracy and powerlessness to keep them in confinement.

Based on this evidence, the court—in July 1990—ordered that the women be freed. All the women being held were released, including the hundreds who had been deported from Bombay on the Mukthi Express and then imprisoned. The Madras court's decision marked a welcome, if long overdue, improvement in the judiciary's attitude towards civil liberties and AIDS, as opposed to the actions of the Bombay High Court.

Though the women were released, the government did not compensate them for the months or years of imprisonment and

Provided by author

Shyamala Nataraj

suffering they had been subjected to. Selvi and the five women who were imprisoned in 1986 had been held for over four years. The government let them out almost indifferently—as if it bore no responsibility for the hardships placed on the women.

Nataraj tried to track what happened to them after their release. She found that some were taken in by an organization called Zonta International, which had set up a house where the women could stay if they wished to. Many went back to Bombay. Though some may have tried going back to their families, it's unlikely that they were accepted, given the stigma attached to sex workers. Nataraj despaired to think of the daunting odds arrayed against them.

I felt a strong commonality with sex workers, intellectual as well as personal. Sex workers and gays seemed to share the fate of being demonized because of commonplace prejudices about sex. People thought of us as immoral, driven to sin by greed or lust. While sex workers sold their private parts for money, gays defiled theirs out of unnatural lust. I also saw myself as a kindred soul, having been portrayed as a whore by some of my hypocritical schoolmates and, as a gay man, having spent much of my lifetime being scorned and cast out.

And now, just like gay men but to an even more frightening degree, they were literally being wiped out by AIDS. But, instead of showing sympathy, people were blaming them for the pandemic (just like they blamed us for it), accusing them of being irresponsible women who were endangering naïve customers as well as their innocent wives and babies, and persecuting them brutally.

Consequently, I sought out sex workers on that first research trip in the summer of 1991. I didn't go to Madras to follow up on what had happened to Selvi and the other women released from the reformatory; the epidemic had spread so far that it didn't make sense to focus on them. Instead, as Bombay's sex workers were known to be the hardest hit by the epidemic, I concentrated on them.

A day after my visit to the AIDS ward at J.J. Hospital, I visited a health clinic for sex workers in the city's famed red-light area of Kamathipura. I had first heard of these brothels from friends at Doon and St. Stephen's. They had come here to lose their virginity in the era before AIDS became known. It was telling that the area was just a few blocks away from my friends' homes in posh Marine Drive and Altamount Road, as if the facilities were set up close enough to service the desires of wealthy men.

It was my first visit to a red-light area anywhere in the world. At least during the day, there were no signs that this neighbourhood of grimy three- and four-storeyed colonial houses, with the rainwater-logged streets choked with traffic, housed countless brothels and sex workers. It was indistinguishable from any other low-income part of Bombay. Times Square in New York City, with its innumerable sex stores and peep shows, and hookers and hustlers of every shade of gender, was far closer to my notion of a red-light zone.

The clinic was a shallow room, accessible from the street by half a dozen steps. But even so, it was dark because of the monsoon gloom. It seemed airless too, though the main door had been left wide open. On rough wooden benches running along the wall, there were about a dozen young women sitting quietly. None of them looked at me as I entered; they seemed lost in their own thoughts or worries.

The doctor at the clinic was no older than me. She ushered me into the small antechamber where she did physical examinations, saying that she had time to answer only a few questions. She spoke in a low voice, almost a whisper, presumably concerned that the women sitting outside would realize that we were discussing them. Her consideration was touching, though I doubted if any of the women could understand English. 'Almost all the women waiting in the outside room are HIV-positive,' she said. 'And yes, they are prostitutes.'

I asked her how old they were. 'None of them is older than twenty,' she said. 'And the youngest is just fourteen.' Some were already sick with HIV-related tuberculosis and other diseases, but they could not stop working until they were visibly ill. The doctor explained that they were often in debt to their pimps and madams, and as they lacked any other employable skill, they had nowhere else to go. Neither their families nor charitable organizations would offer them succor.

She asked if I wanted to speak to the women, but I said 'No!' with such intensity that it must have struck her as odd. I didn't have the presence of mind to explain my reaction. When I had planned my research, I had thought of interviewing sex workers. But after coming here, it seemed utterly pointless.

Here were these young women, some still adolescents, who were infected with HIV and certain to die in a few years. They would suffer horribly like the patients I had seen in the AIDS ward, but probably without any medical care. How would anything I ask help the articles I was writing? What would be the purpose of asking for their names, their ages, where they were from, or how they got here to Kamathipura? What could they conceivably explain that wasn't obvious already, or had shrunk into irrelevance in the face of the fact that they were soon going to die?

I couldn't bear to ask any of these questions, however relevant or logical, because it had suddenly struck me that no matter what I wrote, it would not dent the scorn and hatred that had kept people—particularly the ones in power—from helping them. Rather than feeling concern for the countless sex workers contracting this terrible disease, people blamed them for the epidemic. I was left feeling so hopeless that I could not summon the conviction to go through with documenting these women's circumstances.

Soon, on that research trip, I saw even more troubling sights. At a prison in Imphal, the dreary capital of Manipur in India's north-east, several dozens of HIV-positive drug users had been segregated in one corner of the open central compound. These young men and women sat with heads bowed, barely moving. I had never seen such palpable collective hopelessness, made all the more acute by the fact that they were largely dressed in blue jeans and jackets, the emblematic uniform of youthful liberation.

The jail warden told me that a majority of the prisoners—several hundreds in all—were drug users addicted to injecting heroin. He seemed unconcerned by what shocked me most—that they were being kept imprisoned indefinitely without trial. The state government had presumably decided that this was the best way of solving both its epidemic of heroin addiction, a spillover from the drug-trafficking Golden Triangle in south-east Asia, as well as the soaring rate of HIV infection among injecting drug users.

The only difference to the fate of Selvi and the sex workers in Madras was that most of the captives here were from middle-class backgrounds. The warden claimed that their parents felt their children were deadbeats, and had pleaded with him to keep them imprisoned. It was clear that in India, the government could violate with impunity the most fundamental human rights of social outcasts, as scarcely did anyone bother to defend them.

Yet, despite the massive scale of human rights violations I had witnessed at the Imphal jail, the brief, distant interaction with the handful of HIV-positive sex workers at the Kamathipura clinic somehow proved to have the most lasting impact on me. Over the years, I often remembered the gloomy clinic and the strangely silent women. They seemed so maligned and wronged, circumstances I had so much empathy for from my own hardships that I instinctively felt for their cause. The disparity between how scornfully the outside world saw them and how absolutely vulnerable they appeared as they sat there seemed cruelly unjust, and was a deeply familiar feeling to me.

I was not the first gay man to feel such empathetic connections between all those of us who were despised and outlawed for our sexual behaviours or desires. In a poem that I had loved ever since my undergraduate years, 'Ode to Walt Whitman', Garcia Lorca—who, like me, had struggled with corrosive shame both about his homosexuality and femininity—expressed my feelings when he wrote:

That's why I don't raise my voice, old Walt Whitman,
against the little boy who writes the name of a girl on his pillow,
nor against the little boy who dresses as a bride
in the darkness of the wardrobe,
nor against the solitary men in casinos
who drink prostitution's water with revulsion,
nor against the men with that green look in their eyes
who love other men and burn their lips in silence.

11

The Invisible

On that research trip in 1991, I didn't seek out gay men for my analysis of India's unfolding epidemic in the same way as I did sex workers. This was a conscious decision on my part.

In the half decade since HIV had emerged in India, it had not been thought of here as the 'gay plague'—it was, instead, indelibly associated with women sex workers—and we had been spared blame and persecution. And so, to avoid drawing hostile attention, I deliberately chose to keep silent about what I knew for a fact: that a large proportion of Indian men had unprotected sex with other men, and this meant that they stood an increasingly high risk of contracting HIV.

I knew this from my own sexual encounters as well as what I witnessed of others in public places. Of the countless men having sex with other men (or with transwomen) across the country, virtually none took the safe route of using condoms and water-based lubricants.

While I did my part to educate my sexual partners—or others that I talked to—most of the men appeared bewildered. As they had heard that AIDS was a disease spread by women sex workers, they ended up concluding that it was spread only through vaginal sex.

Their reasoning didn't surprise me because this was indeed what the amateurish AIDS-education campaigns of that time seemed to imply. In frightening imagery, they depicted men frantically cursing their fate after contracting AIDS from 'fallen' women—the latter portrayed as nubile but malevolent figures who were lurking on the sidelines to waylay men.

Many of the men I spoke to would confidently assert that anal sex was, in fact, known to be safe. Some even added that knowing this had led them to have sex with transwomen and stop going to female sex workers, a fact corroborated by the transwomen, many of whom sold sex.

At that point, the only Indian gay men knowledgeable about the risks of HIV infection through gay sex were the tiny English-speaking minority concentrated in the main cities. The few of us confident enough to subscribe to *Trikone*, a newsletter for South Asian gay men and women published in California, or *Bombay Dost*, India's pioneering gay magazine, published since 1990, had access to more detailed data about the epidemic as well as information about safer sex methods.

An even smaller number of us knew, through our personal networks, of gay Indian men who were HIV-positive—Dominic D'Souza in Goa; my brilliant fashion-designer friend Rohit Khosla, who had been three years my senior at Doon; Rippan Kapur, the founder of the popular charity CRY (Child Rights and You); the sexy foreign-service officer we knew who was posted in Paris.

Every year saw one or two more added to the roll call of those sick and dying. All of them were tragically young, in their thirties or early forties, when they died. With HIV beginning to take a visible toll on us privileged Indian gay men, we were largely careful to have nothing but safe sex. But we were an infinitesimally tiny minority within the vast number of gay and bisexual men in India.

I also knew that a significant (though unknown) percentage of the men who had already contracted HIV were infected through unprotected sexual intercourse with other men. But when doctors or health officials asked how they were infected, they had simply said that they were heterosexual—a pretence they habitually made anyhow—and had been with prostitutes. As most officials had little or no experience in dealing with homosexuality, they took what they were told at face value and classified them as heterosexually acquired infections.

Thus, by end-1990, just six of the several thousand cases of HIV reported to health authorities were listed as homosexually acquired. (Even that tiny number surprised me—why had these half-dozen men admitted to being homosexual, given that homosexuality was intensely stigmatized and widely known to be criminalized? I reasoned that perhaps it was a panicked admission made at the time they learnt they were infected, or possibly they were transwomen and officials automatically classed their infections as being homosexually acquired.)

It was distressing to be faced with all this evidence that AIDS was spreading rapidly amongst gay and bisexual men as well as transwomen in India. Given the vast extent of unsafe sex, I feared that the devastation could eventually be as terrible as that suffered by Western gay men. And since almost all these men were married or were going to get married, as was the social norm, their wives and babies were likely to get infected too. It was only if the government launched a frank nationwide effort to convince men to use condoms during anal sex that this tragedy could be forestalled.

Yet, in the articles I wrote in 1991, I held back, both from drawing any attention to this worrying aspect of the epidemic and advocating for gay-specific HIV prevention efforts. I had decided that the wiser course in these dangerous times was to maintain our invisibility. So I wrote strategically—saying not a word about the rising rates of HIV amongst India's gay and bisexual men and transwomen—that globally the overwhelming bulk of HIV infections had taken place through heterosexual intercourse, and this would be the primary mode of transmission in India too.

This decision also led me to decide against going to Goa to meet Dominic D'Souza, the HIV-positive gay man who had been arrested and imprisoned in 1989. Siddhartha had urged me to meet him, saying that Dominic had emerged as India's first HIV-positive activist, despite the dangers of an era when AIDS evoked hysterical fears of contagion, even among many well-educated people. I did not know then that he would not live much longer, and that I had lost my last chance to meet him.

Far from going into hiding after being released from the sanatorium where he had been imprisoned, Dominic had become a resolute activist. Isabel de Santa Rita Vaz, the professor and theatre director who had been key to securing his release, recalled, 'Dominic was naughty, child-like, and very sensitive. But he was also very strong. He didn't have a choice about what happened to him, but after that, he didn't crawl into a hole and hide either.'

Dominic's changed spirit came through in a letter, written a few months after his release. Writing to a sympathetic Bombay doctor about three impoverished, HIV-positive people—a young woman and two men—who had since been imprisoned at the very sanatorium where he had been held, Dominic wrote in frustration, 'Believe me, not one word of counseling has been imparted to the isolated HIV carriers. I am proof to this unbelievable but true attitude of our health services and Goa medical authorities ... How could the health services be so irresponsible? We have told them so many times to start educating people on how the AIDS virus is transmitted, but nothing has been done at all.'

Dominic's newfound spirit of activism reflected a unique quality about AIDS that was witnessed everywhere the epidemic spread. In a strange alchemy, it turned many of its victims—as well as relatives and friends closest to them—into do-or-die activists.

This was evident among gay men, themselves HIV-positive or mourning lost lovers and best friends, who formed the Gay Men's Health Crisis (GMHC) group in New York in 1981, publishing the first guides to safe sex as well as caring for the dying through 'buddy' programmes. It was equally evident among those who banded together in 1987, in the AIDS Coalition to Unleash Power—better known by its acronym, ACT-UP. This pioneered a confrontational, political form of AIDS activism in the US, using non-violent civil disobedience to challenge conservative groups opposing safe-sex education, and forcing the Reagan administration as well as the drug industry to accelerate the search for effective treatments. This was also true in Uganda where HIV-positive patients at the Mulago Hospital, their spouses, relatives and friends came together in 1987 to form TASO—The AIDS Support Organization—to provide counselling as well as home-care services, and to fight for medical care and humane government policies at a time of terrible stigma and discrimination.

I could perfectly understand why their activism had been triggered. It was a logical, almost inevitable reaction to the situation that infected men and women found themselves in. They knew they faced harsh discrimination of every kind that would last right until the disease killed them years later. And with death a looming certainty in the not so distant future, there was—ultimately—little at risk.

All this transformed their personal calculus. They had every reason to fight the abuses they faced, as well as challenge the failure of their governments to do more to help them or to stop the spread of HIV through sensible prevention programmes. Dominic had undergone this transformation, and so had his mother, Lucy D'Souza, and his friend Isabel Vaz.

Shortly after Dominic's release, the Goa Legislative Assembly agreed to substantially dilute the Act that had instituted draconian anti-AIDS measures, such as isolation of anyone found to be infected. Under the new amendments, the government still had the power to isolate HIV-positive persons, but this was an option to be used at the government's discretion, rather than being a mandated course of action. In practice, even this weaker set of clauses was never again used in the state.

But, oddly, Dominic and Lucy D'Souza found that the courts were less responsive to human rights principles than the Goa legislature. The Goa bench of the Bombay High Court refused to release the HIV-positive woman and men who were imprisoned at the TB sanatorium. Social class was the operative factor here—all three were from impoverished backgrounds, and so the court opined that unlike Dominic, there was no guarantee that they would behave responsibly if freed. (Eventually, the woman escaped, never to be found again, while one of the men died in captivity, cared for only by a local Catholic nun as government doctors refused to tend to him.)

Dominic himself continued to face devastating human rights abuses. On being incarcerated, he had been granted a year's leave without pay by the Goa office of the World Wildlife Fund (India). However, when Dominic reported back for work, the local head of the Fund's committee, Dr Sharad Vaidya, barred him from the office, saying that other staff-members were refusing to work with an HIV-infected person.

'Dr Vaidya didn't allow me to enter the office,' Dominic wrote later. 'I said I had every right to enter as the court has said I could go back to work. But he just refused to let me enter. If doctors behave in such a fashion, the common man is going to be even more terrified about AIDS.' After months of fighting to regain his job, Dominic ultimately accepted voluntary retirement and a cash settlement, resigning himself to this outcome because he was 'so fed up with all the discrimination'.

Yet, at the same time, there were decent-minded people rallying to challenge the discrimination being faced by Dominic and others affected by AIDS. A young human rights lawyer from Bombay—Anand Grover—had come forward to represent Dominic pro bono, upon realizing that this disease raised myriad human rights concerns. Grover's involvement in fighting for Dominic became a lasting commitment to taking on HIV-related cases, eventually advancing not just the cause of people with HIV but also of sex workers and gays in ways that could not even be imagined at that point.

Claude and Norma Alvares, Grover's friends and founding members of the Goa Foundation, an environmental group, hired Dominic on learning that he had been pushed out from his earlier job. They soon became admirers of his. 'He was never bitter or sad,' Norma Alvares recalled. 'He never wanted to go home early [from work] or anything like that. He hated being mollycoddled. In fact, we took strength from him whenever we had a problem. He was the best ambassador HIV-positive people could have.'

Dominic's activism did not flag even when he began suffering from recurrent bouts of tuberculosis and oral thrush, an agonizing infection of the mouth and throat. Since his release, he had found that people in Goa who feared that they were infected—or knew this for a fact—were turning to him for advice, given the risks of approaching a doctor or health official. After meeting other people living with HIV at an international conference in London in September 1991, he started a self-help group akin to New York City's GMHC and Uganda's TASO.

This group, known simply as Positive People, began operating out of Dominic's home, with funding from the Dutch organization Hivos. It was India's first association of 'positive people', providing confidential counseling and a support system for people 'to share their grief, experiences and anxieties,' as well as undertaking public awareness about AIDS.

But, by then, Dominic's illnesses had become life-threatening, in large part because Goa's hospitals refused to admit him for in-patient care. Finally, Isabel Vaz and his other friends admitted him to Bombay's Breach Candy Hospital, one of the few private institutions in the country willing to care for people with AIDS.

On 27 May 1992, Dominic died, two months short of his thirty-third birthday. He had lived for just three years from the time he realized he was HIV-positive, the day that he was imprisoned at the sanatorium. With better care, he would certainly have lived much longer.

It was testimony to Dominic's exceptional traits that, in this brief span of time, he had succeeded in improving public attitudes towards

AIDS in Goa and beyond. In an obituary, mainstream daily *Gomantak Times* expressed evident pride in their native son, instead of the prejudice the press displayed just a few years earlier. It said: 'This brave Goan did not quail under the burden of AIDS ... For every person who shrank from his very touch, Dominic taught ten people that there is nothing to fear ... in interacting with HIV-positive people. He showed this country that except for a little virus in the bloodstream, they are exactly like any other normal human being.'

While later piecing together Dominic's life, from all the vivid proof of his courage, I found that I was most moved by the bravery he maintained even while on the verge of death.

In his will, written in the hospital just a few days before his death, he asked that a newspaper announcement be published to 'boldly say that I died of AIDS and that I am not ashamed to say it.' It took both incredible personal courage and dedication to combating the stigma against AIDS to insist on this because, at that time, very few people anywhere in the world—even in the West—admitted to dying of AIDS. The *New York Times* obituaries, for instance, often referred euphemistically to one young man or another dying after a 'long illness,' a code phrase widely known to be AIDS.

I also ached with empathy at uncovering Dominic's struggles to come to terms with his orientation in matters of love and desire, which had intensified as his health failed. Those struggles were made even more tortured by the feeling that his orientation had led to his contracting the disease that was killing him.

In a booklet published by the Positive People group shortly before his death, Dominic wrote, 'I knew what AIDS was. But I never really educated myself. I knew how it was transmitted, but I never practiced safe sex. I had this feeling that it is not going to touch me ... I am a Roman Catholic. I kept thinking—is this His way of asking me to pay for what I have done? I felt that it was promiscuity that led me to getting this virus. I felt this was God's punishment.'

It was painful to read those last anguished sentences suggesting that Dominic had not yet come to terms with these matters. There was no way of knowing whether he had found that acceptance in the months that remained to him, but I prayed that he had, overcoming the self-loathing about being gay that all of us developed because of the condemnation we faced from every quarter of life. I prayed that he had also succeeded in overcoming the dreadful self-reproach that he himself was somehow to blame for the tragedy that had befallen him, when after all, he had done nothing beyond following his human longings for love and sex.

This statement was the closest Dominic came to publicly disclosing his orientation. It is possible that he would have become increasingly candid about this matter had he lived longer. Already, in just the space of these few years, he had gone from maintaining that he had contracted HIV while donating blood to saying that he, like most others, had been infected sexually.

Hence, in a few more years, he would have probably cast off concerns about having to bear this terrible double stigma—of being known to be HIV-positive as well as gay—motivated by knowing that while speaking the truth would not save him, it would at least set him free. This pattern was evident among gay men in the West—the imminence of death would push many young men dying from AIDS to speak with a burning, enraged candour. They would refuse to lie any more, or to remain hidden in the darkness of the closet any longer.

The writer Paul Monette, dying of AIDS in the US and having lost two lovers to the disease, was to publish the final volume of his memoir—*Becoming a Man*—just a month after Dominic's death. He wrote: 'I will never understand how the straights could have let us die like this—year after year after year, collaborating by indifference ... Why do they hate us? Why do they fear us? Why do they want us invisible?'

This candour was firing up the fighting spirit among us surviving gay people to confront the world's homophobia. And, however harsh and unsettling our honesty must have been, it was forcing many more people to begin to understand us, to understand the injustice and torments we faced, to understand our essential humanity.

So it was possible that Dominic would have eventually done what I shirked from doing at that point, what I thought wise not to do: to make us gay people visible in India by speaking honestly about the epidemic that was beginning to devastate us.

But, at the very time that Dominic was dying, another young gay man facing death took it upon himself to break the silence and end our invisibility.

12

A First Glimpse of Freedom

My maverick friend, Siddhartha Gautam, was simply not one to let things stay quiet. Though Siddhartha had given me an inkling of his intentions the last time we met, I must admit to being caught off guard by the astounding scope of what he eventually set into motion.

I had last met Siddhartha in the summer of 1991. On arriving in Delhi from Boston, I had rushed straight from the airport to his Defence Colony barsati. My longing to see Siddhartha was not only because it had been a year since we had last seen each other (when I left Delhi for Harvard), but also because his cancer had re-emerged after years of remission. He had already undergone treatment at AIIMS in Delhi, but because that had not been successful, he was leaving in a few days for New York's Sloan-Kettering Cancer Memorial Institute, where he had been treated in the past.

Siddhartha was painfully thin, and his hair was only just growing back from his last stint of radiation. But when I stood face-to-face with him, in the full wattage of his personality, my worries didn't even have a chance to be voiced.

All I could prise out of Siddhartha about his health was that he was delighted to have lost his hair because he now resembled the gorgeous Persis Khambatta in the recent Star Trek movie, and had effortlessly seduced the male doctors at the hospital (and even the fitter of the patients!). With that, all discussions about his cancer were sidelined forever.

What lovely unending hours those were. Siddhartha and I talked through the day and evening, hugging each other tight as we lay in bed, full of love for each other. As always, our conversations careened from frivolity to seriousness.

He was full of questions about what I had learned at Harvard from Jonathan Mann, whom he respected greatly, and about the articles on AIDS that I had come to India to research. But I was even more impatient to know more about his efforts on AIDS, which he had begun a few months before I left for the US, and his experiences working as a human rights lawyer at the Delhi High Court.

As Siddhartha detailed the work he had been doing on AIDS, I realized just how much it paralleled Mann's view that the AIDS epidemic had as much to do with human rights as it had to do with a disease. Siddhartha and several other activists had banded together to defend the sex workers in Delhi's G.B. Road area, who were being forcibly tested for HIV by the Indian Council of Medical Research as well as AIIMS. Their vociferous protests outside these institutions had ended this abuse, at least in Delhi. (These elite organizations had a disgraceful record through the epidemic's first decade. AIIMS was the hospital with the glossy AIDS ward standing empty when I visited it, even as legions of mortally sick people went untreated across the country. The council's top official had stoked public hysteria with his bigoted comments, which included accusing Indian women of being 'a lousy lot ... If women had taken steps two years ago and stopped cohabiting with foreigners then the situation would not have become so dangerous.') From this effort was born the activist collective AIDS Bhedbhav Virodhi Andolan (ABVA)—the 'AIDS Anti-Discrimination Movement' that fought AIDS-related abuses. It was an unusual organization, with an eclectic collection of members.

I knew several among them, having met them with Siddhartha while living in Delhi. The force behind the group was a Sikh doctor, Dr P.S. Sahni, who lived a life of frugality in common cause with the destitute. Other key figures included an activist Catholic nun, a grassroots feminist, a 'professional blood donor' (who sold blood to blood banks for a living), a prominent orthopedic doctor, several lawyers, and Siddhartha.

Despite operating on a shoestring budget raised through community donations—it refused funding from institutions on principle—ABVA not only operated a free health clinic for sex workers, but also tackled some of the worst human rights abuses raised by the AIDS epidemic. The group's most remarkable achievement had been to keep the draconian AIDS Prevention Bill from being passed into law. They did this by organizing public rallies outside Parliament and actively petitioning its members. They had drawn an astonishing range of people to the rallies, including sex workers, transwomen, gay men and lesbians, women from Delhi's slums, and leprosy patients (who, more than anyone else, knew what it was like to suffer from cruel, unjust policies mandated in the name of public health).

The AIDS Prevention Bill was now mired in controversy, and a Joint Parliamentary Committee had been constituted to review it. It was thrilling to see that even a mighty government could sometimes be forced to heed the views of the downtrodden. And this had happened only because of the efforts of a group of unpaid grassroot-level activists.

To influence public opinion, ABVA had also published two path-breaking citizen reports over the previous year, one focusing on how women—including sex workers—were being blamed for the spread of AIDS, and the other on how to make the blood-supply system safe without banning 'professional blood donors' from selling blood. Reports on other human rights issues raised by AIDS were also in the pipeline, said Siddhartha, adding excitedly that his ABVA colleagues and he were actually planning to write one on the situation of gay men and women. He said it would lay bare all the injustices faced by us.

When leaving Siddhartha late that evening, I was inexplicably filled with the dread of losing him. But I was young, and the feeling was momentary. I brushed it aside, putting it down to the usual sadness of having to say goodbye.

And then, sure enough, some six months later, I received a copy of the report on gay issues that Siddhartha had spoken so excitedly about. But it arrived in my hands under devastating circumstances.

I was back in the US, in New York City. It was late on the night of 13 January 1992. Tandavan and I had returned to our Manhattan apartment. (We had moved there together after I completed my graduate degree at Harvard, working as a consultant for UN agencies while Tandavan taught Bharatanatyam.) The flashing red numeral on the answering machine showed that I had received a message. It was from my close friend, Nilita, in Delhi, and her voice was alarmingly anxious and strained. Somehow, through tearful hesitation about leaving such news, she explained that Siddhartha had died a few hours ago. My premonition of loss when I last met Siddhartha just months earlier had been horribly true.

I called my friends in Delhi. Siddhartha had died after battling high fever for two whole days. He had been at home in his Defence Colony barsati, with his sister Anuja and friends caring for him. On the night of his death, when Siddhartha's fever spiked ever higher, Anuja had begged a neighbourhood doctor to check on him. The doctor had refused, saying that he couldn't attend to everyone suffering from a mere fever. But for that act of callous indifference, the antithesis of Siddhartha's own generous spirit, he might possibly have lived.

None of us had expected this. Siddhartha's most recent treatment for cancer at Sloan-Kettering in New York, just a few months earlier, had, by all indications, been successful. The doctors had expected him to do well for a long, if indeterminate, time. But it seemed that his immune system had been ruined by too much chemotherapy and radiation over the past decade. He was two weeks short of his twenty-eighth birthday.

It was several days before I could bear to leave our apartment and deal with the world. Tandavan stayed with me constantly, caring for me like I was his fragile child. On the way out of our apartment building, I checked our mailbox. There was a letter from Siddhartha—the envelope bore his unmistakable looping handwriting, and there in the corner was his name and Delhi address.

It was a second walloping blow. I wished that I had never found the letter, that it had been lost en route. I went back upstairs, forcing Tandavan to take a break from caring for me because I needed to be alone, even though I dreaded opening the envelope.

Siddhartha had written the letter on 9 January, three days before his death. On every inch of the plain letter paper, front and back of both sheets, crowding every margin and corner, was the handwriting I had come to love from letters that I had received in one place or another, each one of them filling me with joy from his irrepressible spirit.

'My dearest, lovely, silly boy,' Siddhartha wrote. 'Your style of stringing adjectives is infectious. I note with envy your missives to Saleem and Nilita, but I'm sure you will write to me after this one.'

I wept with remorse for not having written to him, and for knowing that it was too late to remedy my error. And I wept even more at knowing that however much I wished otherwise, I would never get to see Siddhartha's beloved face again, never hold him close like I used to, never be infected by his madcap giggling, never have him nearby to love and worry about and protect.

At the very end of the letter, Siddhartha wrote, 'I miss you immensely, especially on these beautiful, misty winter days when all the Lodhi Garden trees miss you from their barks as I do too.' It broke my heart to know that I would be the one missing him for the rest of my life.

But, characteristically of Siddhartha, the bulk of the letter was not about personal matters but about his causes. A full page focused on the efforts of the ABVA activist collective. Their energies were now focused on the World Bank, which was in discussions with the government over providing a $100-million soft loan to India for expanding its AIDS-control efforts. Siddhartha and his colleagues had been pressing the Bank to approve the loan only if the government explicitly agreed to human rights safeguards that would put an end to its current punitive policies.

If the Bank could be forced to insist on human rights protections, Siddhartha wrote, the government would, in turn, have to fall in line at this time when India was in the throes of one of its worst foreign exchange crises, and was beholden to the Bank for its support. For once, the Bank's use of 'conditionalities' as preconditions could be a positive thing.

'Please see if you can get some further information on the specifics of what the World Bank is planning,' Siddhartha wrote. 'Also, see if you can write about it—possibly interview people in charge in Washington D.C. If you do, please try and include questions from the point of view expressed in our memo. The World Bank team will be visiting India again in February to wrap up the contract. If you speak to them, ask them what their response is to our memo, and what concretely they plan to do to ensure their money doesn't finance AIDS-related human rights violations here.'

Despite my grief, I couldn't help but chuckle at Siddhartha's incredible determination. He was doing his utmost to leave the Bank no wiggle room.

Sure enough, just a few months later, the Bank approved India's AIDS-control loan after the government gave it private guarantees that it would end the harsh policies it had pursued ever since AIDS first surfaced in the country. Prime Minister Narasimha Rao withdrew the draconian AIDS Prevention Bill from Parliament, and with this, the government began to adhere to internationally agreed strategies on AIDS, at least in policy.

And then, with such evident passion Siddhartha wrote: 'I wanted you to have a copy of our latest report on homosexuality. It's a real labour of love. I've never worked so hard in my life—while pulling it together, I worked eighteen hours a day on the computer continuously for two weeks. Nor have I felt such utter isolation, of the kind that engulfed me almost wave after wave while working on it.'

He continued: 'The AIDS group was fabulous about it all. Right from gathering material, reading and discussing books, confronting their own sexuality, to debating threadbare every single argument in the document. People in the group were even selling blood to sustain our efforts financially. And we feel proud that the whole thing was done without "funding".'

'It's strange, I have for many years wanted to write something like this. Now when the chance came, my deepest impulse was to run away, postpone the whole thing. To actually sit and articulate what I wanted to say in the Indian context, to bring together years of insights, readings, mullings, wanderings, along with journalistic material, and to do it through a group of die-hard activists which includes Naxalites, Gandhians and a nun, seemed an impossible feat. But you have the product with you now, and I await your critical comments.'

The report was a 95-page pink-jacketed booklet with the smudgy type-print of that time, titled *Less than Gay: Citizens' Report on the Status of Homosexuality in India*. What a revelation it was. Even though being gay was a personal reality for me, and I had read widely about gay issues for a decade, there was so much in it for me to still learn. It even fundamentally changed my thoughts on a crucial aspect of this matter.

It was in the pages of *Less than Gay* that I saw, for the first time in systematic fashion, the historical evidence showing that homophobia was a British colonial legacy, harshly epitomized in the 1860 law criminalizing sodomy, and that Indian traditions had been markedly more tolerant of same-sex desires, of sexuality in general, and also of diverse expressions of gender identity.

'Indigenous texts, concepts and traditions revered and even celebrated sexual ambiguity,' Siddhartha and his co-authors wrote.

The Kamasutra, they noted, contained an entire chapter on the pleasures and techniques of oral sex between people of the same sex. Auparishtaka or 'oral congress', they wrote, was practised by 'male citizens, who know each other well; women, when they are amorous, do the acts of the mouth on the yonis of one another; some men do the same with women; male servants of some men carry on the mouth congress with their masters; eunuchs with males.' Vatsyana, the sage who compiled the Kamasutra in the 4th century, emphasized that these practices were allowed by the Dharam Shastras, the holy writ.

Lesbian sexuality was treated non-judgmentally in these ancient accounts. In Valmiki's Ramayana, Hanuman saw women in Lanka's palaces in a passionate embrace, 'as if they were making love to their male lovers', said Siddhartha and his colleagues. And erotic temple sculptures, such as the famed early-mediaeval ones in Khajuraho and Konark, routinely portrayed same-sex acts among the other forms of sex.

Strikingly, Indian traditions in metaphysics and religion did not make rigid male/female and masculine/feminine distinctions, in contrast to Christianity and other Abrahamic traditions, they noted, writing, 'What modern psychologists in the 20th century now acknowledge as sexual dualism in each individual was a principle enunciated in ancient traditions in India.' The worship of Shiva as Ardha-narishwara—half-woman, half-man—typifying the gender dualism present in each being, was an idea as old as India itself.

Ancient Indian accounts, including the Mahabharata, included matter-of-fact references to heroic figures who underwent transformation into transgendered individuals. As embodiments of Ardha-narishwara, 'the hermaphrodite, the homosexual and the transvestite have a symbolic value and are considered privileged beings', they noted, quoting eminent Indologist Alain Danielou. Indian mystics and spiritual seekers typically saw themselves in androgynous terms, as beings that combined male and female energies. In the past, ordinary Hindus had accepted all these ideas without surprise or discomfort.

Siddhartha and his co-authors maintained that this tolerance—and sometimes, even outright celebration—of diverse expressions of desire and gender identity was not destroyed by the spread of the Muslim rule in the late-mediaeval era, as many people assumed. Same-sex desire was a celebrated feature of court life, with the 16th century Emperor Babur writing about his famed love affair with an adolescent boy, Baburi.

Writing more broadly of Muslim cultures, they said, 'Although the Koran and early religious writings of Islam display mildly negative attitudes towards homosexuality, Muslim cultures treated homosexuality with indifference, if not admiration. The classic works of Arabic poetry and prose, from Abu Nu to *One Thousand and One Nights*, treat gay people and their sexuality with respect or casual acceptance. The Arabic language contains a huge vocabulary of gay erotic terminology, with dozens of words just to describe types of male prostitutes.' In Sufism, in India as well as elsewhere, 'homosexual eroticism was a major metaphorical expression of the spiritual relationship between god and man.'

The rupture came only with British colonial rule, said Siddhartha and his co-authors. The chasm between Victorian British and traditional Indian views on same-sex relations, and more generally on both men's and women's sexuality, could not have been wider. Victorian views were harshly intolerant, even by the standards then prevalent in Western Europe, with punitive laws used to enforce moralistic codes of sexual behaviour. The colonial elite considered its Indian subjects not just inferior but also animalistically debauched, with dusky women going about barebreasted and men just in scanty loincloths, glistening *lingams* and *yonis* being openly worshipped (instead of a Virgin Mother), temple friezes celebrating anything-goes orgies, and ancient texts promoting wanton sexual positions. (Even Hindu gods were 'absolute monsters of lust', one reformer had thundered in Parliament in 1813.) Determined to civilize and Christianize its subjects, the colonial government applied contemporary English laws to rid India of all manner of 'oriental vices'.

In the Indian Penal Code of 1860, a codification of existing English criminal law, Section 377 criminalized male homosexuality as being 'carnal intercourse against the order of nature'. Out of Victorian prudishness, Section 377 did not explicitly mention the 'abominable sin, amongst Christians not to be named' of sodomy or buggery, unlike medieval English and European laws that were written in raw language. But for all its ambiguity in phrasing, the intent of Section 377 was clear to the police, courts and administrators—to harshly punish sex between males, irrespective of whether it was between consenting adults, or involved rape or paedophilia.

Arrests under Section 377 did not require a warrant, and were also non-bailable offences. Convictions were punishable with up to life imprisonment. Only murder, rape and kidnapping earned harsher sentences, *Less than Gay* noted. With this, for the first time in India's recorded history, same-sex relations were criminalized and subject to harsh action.

These arguments helped me make sense of what I had gradually come to feel over my years of adulthood in India, as I grew more knowledgeable about the country. Indian men steeped in Victorian British culture and ways—'Macaulay's Children', as my father and most people of my background were—were almost invariably hostile to same-sex desire. In contrast, as Siddhartha and his colleagues wrote, 'notions of same-sex friendship, romance and love still suffuse the lives of ordinary men and women' whose thinking was not as heavily shaped by Raj-era cultural influences. Both Siddhartha and I had often sensed this in our encounters with non-elite Indian men, as surprisingly large numbers of them treated their desires with astonishing naturalness.

But, from the personal testimonies featured in *Less than Gay*, it was clear that Indian society's traditional tolerance had shrunk dangerously over the 130 years since Section 377 came into force.

Siddhartha and his co-authors began the report with nearly two dozen real-life stories, as if to help uninitiated readers put a human face on us gay men and women, to understand that we were human too. Most of the testimonies were just a few paragraphs long, but each of them—like a powerful short story—illuminated what it meant to be gay in India at that time. I could see myself in so many of them over the years, even though my family's affluence had shielded me from the worst of the oppression and suffering.

There were stories of guilt, of repressing the human urge for sexual and romantic connection, just like I had for years on end. A gay man from Mizoram wrote, 'I can see that I am living a big lie, but I can't really come out because of various factors. So I am going to ignore my love, sex areas and I will put all my energies into my work ... I have my yoga, exercises and work to keep me busy.'

There were stories about the fear of social disgrace. A thirty-two-year-old industrial worker from Bombay wrote, 'They think we are enemies of prukruti (nature) and sanskruti (culture).'

There were stories of love, but not one ended happily. Most ended with one or both lovers being forced into heterosexual marriages, often when their families discovered that they were in a same-sex relationship. There were numerous accounts of lesbians in loving relationships who chose death over being separated or married off by their parents.

Those who resisted marriage faced unbearably lonely lives. A woman wrote, 'Many of us enter into relationships with women in hostels during our student days. Once these break up, and most do for the obvious reason of marriage, then how are we to sustain ourselves? In fact, nearing the forties, I no longer feel anything is worth the loneliness and isolation I have faced in the last twenty years.'

There were many stories of anonymous sex, given the prohibition on legitimate gay relationships. A man from Calcutta wrote, 'Because we must seek our orgasms in darkness, too often our sexual life never extends beyond our zippers.' Others wrote that they had restricted themselves to casual sex because they knew their families and society would never permit them to have an open, loving relationship with someone of the same gender.

Even more wrenching were testimonies in a later section that focused exclusively on the persecution, blackmail, violence and rape routinely faced by gays. From every corner of India, gay men wrote to say that policemen were among the main culprits in their victimization.

A man being blackmailed by local thugs who had discovered that he was gay wrote: 'I don't know who to turn to. The police are of no help here in Cochin, and it will only cause me trouble.'

A man accosted by a gang of four strangers on Calcutta's Maidan wrote, 'They raped me brutally. I was badly injured and even needed to have stitches around my anus.'

Despite this pervasive violence and the other kinds of human rights abuses suffered by gay men and women, their problems were rarely reported and almost never addressed, Siddhartha and his co-authors noted. They explained that these abuses 'often result in intense feelings of shame, as if somehow they had brought the assault upon themselves ... In addition, there is the fear of being identified as gay in describing assaults. These feelings generally deter gay persons from going to the police, even to civil rights organizations, and even close friends and family members for redressal and support'.

They wrote, 'Whether it is blackmail or physical violence, verbal abuse or police harassment, forced heterosexual marriage or denial of homosexual marriage, gay people ... live like second class citizens, unable to obtain fair treatment because of their "wrong" sexuality.'

The root cause of all this persecution, they stressed, was Section 377 of the Indian Penal Code. 'It is true that the government has a consistently poor record for the enforcement of the sodomy law,' they wrote. 'However, because of its existence, gay men are subjected to systematic harassment, blackmail and extortion at the hands of enforcement agencies and the public. It is clear that the law exists solely to criminalize and terrorize a section of society.'

They found that Section 377 was one among several egregious laws that were direct legacies of the colonial times 'used solely to criminalize already marginalized people'. The confused anti-trafficking law—its original version dating back to 1923, now known as ITPA (Immoral Traffic Prevention Act)—which criminalized even consensual sex work by adults, had been 'used by the police to harass these already stigmatized women'. The Anti-Begging Act had been used 'to round up poor people to whom the State fails to provide jobs or social security in the first place'.

I was elated that they had placed Section 377 in this broader context. In my years working as a journalist in India, I had come to see that many of the worst colonial-era laws had got a new lease of life in the hands of the elite Indians who replaced the British as the country's rulers.

While the anti-sedition law—Section 124A of the Indian Penal Code—was used by the Raj to suppress freedom fighters, it was now utilized to squelch legitimate dissent with the threat of summary life imprisonment. The land acquisition and forest laws enabled the government to dispossess impoverished people of assets vital to their survival. The Habitual Offenders Act perpetuated the view of the Criminal Tribes Act of 1871—that both India's traditional 'third gender' communities and several hundred specified tribes and castes had a hereditary propensity to criminality and had to be harshly policed. Then there was the barbaric 'two-finger test' inflicted on any woman who filed a complaint of being raped—to judge whether her vagina was tight or loose. Any presumed looseness would be taken as proof that the woman was 'habituated to sex' and hence lost the right to refuse consent and deserve protection by the law. If India's old wrongs were not being righted, it was because our new rulers had themselves elevated these bad laws to the status of sacred cows, treating them as time-honoured Indian values rather than deplorable foreign imports.

But it was the report's opening and closing pages that were the most thrilling to read, and that had the most profound impact on me.

On the third page of *Less than Gay* was this paragraph: 'ABVA views homosexuality (and heterosexuality) as a political issue. We will strive to get consensual, adult homosexual acts decriminalized and fight for the right of gay men, lesbians and other "sexual minorities", like hijras, to enjoy equal benefits of the laws on marriage, inheritance, adoption, and privacy, among others. We feel that a clear and unambiguous stand should be taken by political parties and civil rights organizations on the human rights of gay men and lesbians. How much longer will the British-framed law on sodomy be tolerated by us? When will the Indian State recognize the equal rights of "sexual minorities"?'

There it was, unambiguous and powerfully worded: The demand that same-sex relations be decriminalized in India.

And then, at the report's very end, was an astonishing charter of demands, prefaced by this firm declaration: 'ABVA urges the Government of India to take cognizance of the following demands and take urgent steps towards their realization.' What a collection of sixteen emancipatory demands they were—if realized, we gay Indians would no longer be criminals, but equal and proud citizens!

The first, of course, was the repeal of Section 377. But then there was the demand for the Constitution to be amended to include equality before the law on the basis of 'sex' and 'sexual orientation'. There was the demand that police policies be reformed to end the abuse of gay people and gender minorities, and that a human rights commission be available to monitor the myriad rights violations they suffer.

There were demands for 'judgement-free health education related to sexuality, homosexuality, sexually transmitted diseases ... and AIDS'. For tackling homophobia, they demanded 'positive images and role models of gay men and lesbians, and of homosexuality as a viable, healthy alternative lifestyle' from school itself.

Ending the charter were demands for full equality in those vital matters of love, relationships and families—'Amend the Special Marriages Act to allow for marriages between people of the same sex (or between people who may be inter-sexed) ... All consequential legal benefits of marriage should extend to gay marriages as well, including the right to adopt children, to execute a partner's will, to inherit, etc.'

I read this charter with astonishment, almost in shock, followed by mounting excitement. I had never even dared to imagine such freedom in India—of not being criminalized, of not being perpetually fearful, of having a Constitutional guarantee that I would be treated equally in every aspect of life, of having the right to marry and have a family—let alone imagine that I should begin to expect and fight for this in my lifetime.

These were audacious, almost outlandish, demands to make in those first years of the 1990s. Homosexual conduct was a criminal offence not only in India but also in an overwhelming majority of the world's nations, besides half the states in the USA. The UN's human rights bodies were still years away from making the pioneering rulings establishing that 'sodomy' laws violated international human rights agreements. Just one country—Denmark—recognized same-sex civil unions, and only Sweden had laws protecting gays and lesbians in matters pertaining to social services, taxes, and inheritance.

No country, so far, provided constitutional guarantees of equality or anti-discrimination for gays or gender minorities. It was to be another four years, in 1996, when post-apartheid South Africa—under President Nelson Mandela—earned this great distinction, with its Constitution explicitly prohibiting discrimination based on sexual orientation or gender identity.

And yet, Siddhartha and his colleagues in the ABVA group asked for complete equality, even though there was no proof as yet that any society, let alone India, was capable of providing such justice. Perhaps it required a person on the verge of death to be able to see so clearly into the future, to know that within a quarter century dozens of countries would have begun to set right their age-old injustices against gays and gender minorities.

Let alone the practicality of such ambitious changes, Siddhartha and I had often heatedly argued about the possibility of even throwing out Section 377. His view was that we needed to build a mass movement in India seeking this goal, akin to the one for African-American civil rights. My reaction had always been that something like this was simply not possible in the India of our time. It was too dangerous. There were too few of us who were openly gay, and even fewer with a determined sense of activism.

And we had almost no allies—just a handful of supportive friends and families, and an even smaller number of forward-thinking lawyers, journalists and activists. None of the domestic civil rights groups considered matters of sexuality to be of any relevance to their work—even abroad, Amnesty International had only just begun to fight for people imprisoned because of their sexual orientation.

I argued that we would face a terrible backlash. I pointed out that in Thatcher's right-wing Britain, homophobia had intensified—the police were harassing and entrapping gay men in unprecedented numbers—while in the USA, the Supreme Court had upheld sodomy laws as recently as 1986. I was sometimes even dismissive while arguing with Siddhartha, my irritation at his impractical idealism rising to a head.

In a practical sense, I was correct. For a start, very few of even the relatively open gay men and women in India were activists to any great degree. Given the real risks of facing discrimination and persecution, it made sense to remain largely guarded, which was not possible as an activist. Tellingly, Siddhartha wrote in his letter to me, 'None of my gay friends bothered to come for the press conference or to collect a copy until a month later! Somehow I felt shocked by what seemed to be a betrayal ... it seemed that all our parties and bonhomie and friendships had come to nought ... what explains the apathy and indifference?'

And it was clear that the matter of decriminalization of same-sex relations, let alone equal human rights for us, was taboo in almost every realm of India. Thus, on releasing *Less than Gay*, Siddhartha and his ABVA colleagues presented a formal list of demands to the Petitions Committee of the Lok Sabha—but not a single Member of Parliament even acknowledged the petition, let alone championed it. Of the dozens of prominent people and organizations they wrote to (including legislators, bureaucrats, senior police officials, health experts, feminists and human rights leaders) while researching the report, only nineteen wrote back, despite several reminders. The bulk of these replies were short and evasive.

In *Less than Gay*, Siddhartha and his colleagues wrote in frustration, 'We would like to raise the following questions for all the above groups and individuals: Is there any excuse for not yet having taken a stand on homosexuality and human rights? ... The hesitation to even discuss the issue reveals what a deep-rooted stigma homosexuality still remains, within the establishment and among the anti-establishment intelligentsia.'

But on reading those brave, fighting words that morning of 1992—'We will strive to get consensual, adult homosexual acts decriminalized and fight for the right of gay men, lesbians and other "sexual minorities", like hijras, to enjoy equal benefits of the law'—for the first time I didn't care that the odds were so heavily arrayed against us.

While I realized that I had come to feel this because of the circumstances, because the ache for this freedom had literally been my beloved friend's last sentiment, it proved to be a personal turning point. I began to feel that it was only right to fight against Section 377, even if the effort lasted decades and even beyond my lifetime, instead of simply fearing it as I had and living abroad.

This report, *Less than Gay*, itself was proof that it was possible to begin this fight. Here was ABVA, a group of activist-minded individuals of whom only Siddhartha was avowedly gay, but who—through discussions and their own open-mindedness—had come to conclude that the denial of fundamental rights to gay men and women was indefensible. In fact, I didn't know what moved me more—to see Siddhartha's brave voice everywhere in *Less than Gay*, or to see that these other men and women, who admitted that they were 'ill-informed and even prejudiced to begin with', had come to see that this archaic law was an insult to justice.

And so it was that Siddhartha, in dying, forever changed my views.

In a magazine review of *Less than Gay* published a short while after his death, I wrote, 'This brief, ninety-odd page report ... written expressly to get "consensual, adult homosexual acts decriminalized", is potentially a powerful weapon with which gay Indians and activists can fight the government ... This report contains every detail necessary to challenge the Indian sodomy law as unconstitutional.' For that empowering realization I was filled with gratitude to Siddhartha, a gratitude that worsened my grief over losing him.

The power of what Siddhartha had set in motion through *Less than Gay* soon became potently evident. In early 1994, two years after Siddhartha's death, ABVA filed a public interest case in the Delhi High Court asking that Section 377 be declared unconstitutional and void on the grounds that it violates the Constitutional fundamental rights to life, liberty and non-discrimination, and obstructs AIDS prevention efforts. The immediate cause for ABVA's action was the refusal by officials at Delhi's Tihar Jail to supply condoms to prisoners—despite evidence of male homosexual conduct as well as several HIV-positive cases—on the grounds that homosexuality was a criminal offence.

The fight against Section 377 had now moved from words to reality. India's establishment was being forced to address, as a matter of Constitutional principle, something it had long refused to even acknowledge as existing in India.

And Siddhartha, aesthete and satyr, madcap and visionary, revolutionary and intellectual, had been the driving force for all this in the span of his short life.

13

More Rights—to Correct the Wrongs

In early 1993, I joined the World Bank in Washington, D.C. It was an unlikely choice for me, given my strong socialist-democratic views and the Bank's farcical advocacy of trickle-down economics. But I reasoned that I was joining the part of the Bank— the health policy division—that was encouraging genuine progress by promoting public health and even defending human rights, as demonstrated by its role in convincing the Indian government to disavow its punitive AIDS-control policies. And at my young age—I was thirty-one—I needed work experience that was as broad as possible, I told myself.

But, more than anything else, there was a pressing personal reason. I desperately needed to escape from New York. My relationship with Tandavan had disintegrated.

We still loved each other deeply, but also knew that we were no longer the happy couple that we had been five years earlier. There seemed no chance of resolving our problems, though we had long tried. These problems were the garden-variety ones that so commonly wreck relationships, especially between the young. In our case, it ranged from not being able to strike a balance between his messiness and my neurotic tidiness, to Tandavan being even more dangerously impractical about finances than I was anyway. Perhaps if we had been married or had children, we might have stuck together indefinitely, but this kind of supportive social sanction was barred to us.

Tandavan was going to stay on in New York, rather than return to France. But I lacked US work papers, and the Bank was one of very few employment options open to me outside of the UN in New York.

And so, I bolted from New York to D.C. in anguish at knowing that a momentous, happy epoch of my life—in which I had gone from being a virginal, lonely young man to experiencing great love and becoming a real adult—had come to an unhappy end. My grief was enormous; it took me a year before I even went out on a date. It would have been greater still if I could have looked into the future and seen that there were to be no comparably meaningful relationships in my life again. I was going to have a very fulfilling life in terms of following my passions vis-à-vis social justice issues, but a largely unfulfilled romantic one.

I had joined the Bank at a fascinating point. It was in the throes of adapting to a world that, because of the end of colonialism and the emergence of the 'Third World' from this multitude of newly independent countries, had changed drastically since the time the organization as well as the International Monetary Fund were established in 1944 as the linchpins of a US-designed global economic order. (The fact that the post of Bank president was an American sinecure, that the White House was just a short stroll away from the Bank and IMF, and the world's finance ministers dutifully headed to Washington each year for these institutions' joint annual meetings, spoke volumes in this regard.) The Bank and IMF were now confronting unceasing demands from legions of critics—ranging from grassroots activists and non-governmental groups to scholars of development as well as independent-thinking 'Third World' leaders—

that they stop being a stooge for the rich world and be held accountable for the outsized clout they had over the destiny of poorer nations.

The critics had ample evidence that many of the world's people were worse off because of these institutions' policies, realized through the billions of dollars that they gave in condition-tied loans to the governments of developing countries. 'Structural adjustment', the shock therapy of free-market capitalism prescribed by them since the 1980s, had left almost every country in Latin America and sub-Saharan Africa hopelessly indebted to Western creditors, bankrupted their budgets, and eviscerated whatever basic social services that had existed. Their characteristic disregard for the well-being of the downtrodden was evident in the Bank's support to the Indian government's Narmada Valley hydel scheme, which would uproot hundreds of thousands of adivasis, as well as countless other mammoth projects across the developing world that paid scant heed to whether they would worsen destitution.

In essence, by the early 1990s, the demand facing the Bank and IMF was that their performance now be evaluated, not simply by the aggregate measure of economic growth rates, but by the extent to which the burden of deprivation had been reduced in the countries they lent to. This was a far more exacting test of whether they were bringing about widely shared progress or merely enriching the already wealthy elites. The Bank soon admitted that this was indeed a legitimate measure, adopting the mission statement—'Our dream is a world free of poverty'—and attempting to reposition itself as the world's main anti-poverty organization.

However, it was a difficult challenge for a lofty, remote institution to accomplish—akin to asking the bejeweled prelates of the Vatican or other rich religious orders to genuinely minister to the destitute and the outcast. Consequently, both the Bank's considerable strengths and its deep flaws came into the spotlight.

There was no doubt that when the Bank set its mind to do something, it did so with admirable vigour and efficiency. Thus, over the past half-decade, it had already ratcheted up its financing of national programmes on education, public health and other social sectors, so as to complement its traditional investments in promoting macro-economic growth by promoting 'human capital'—a society's overall capability to generate economic development.

By sheer weight of the finances available to it, it had soon become the largest international funder of social sector efforts in low and middle-income countries. Hundreds of technocrats now worked on these issues. They were reputedly the best and the brightest, sporting specialized degrees from the Ivy League or Oxbridge. The policy and operational analysis they developed were more empirically grounded and rigorously argued than anything I had ever seen at the various UN agencies I had consulted at.

There was also a highly honed efficiency about the Bank that I had not seen elsewhere. The expensive information technology alone put it in a league of its own, providing worlds of strategic analysis and confidential data that were closed to other organizations. While the other UN agencies had been disgracefully bureaucratic, hamstrung by deadwood officials, petty infighting and Byzantine procedures, the Bank had a dynamic corporate culture. Staff worked hard, they collaborated rather than obstructed each other, and performance evaluations kept everyone on their toes. There was a welcoming of debate and constructive peer review, and an emphasis on evidence-backed thinking.

The efficiency was true too of the Bank's day-to-day handling of its vast multi-billion dollar loan portfolio, which now financed the working of virtually every aspect of the borrowing countries, from macro-economic stability to governance-improving reforms, from massive industrial projects to agricultural breakthroughs, from family planning to AIDS prevention.

The performance of these projects was meticulously audited and evaluated. Rigorous procedures governed the disbursement of these billions. Corruption and delays were rarer here than with other funders. And when the Bank realized that it had no option but to give in to the groundswell of demands that it publicly share information about its lending operations as well as its policy positions, it did this difficult task with remarkable efficiency.

These were the Bank's strengths, and they were admirable. But, on the other hand, I noted many massive structural flaws in the Bank's functioning, and consequently, in its impact on the world.

The root of these weaknesses was the fact that the Bank's technocrats were not only dangerously ignorant of the realities of poverty but also patently arrogant, convinced that they knew best what the masses needed. Inevitably, they chronically misdiagnosed the solutions to problems faced by poor countries and impoverished, marginalized people, too often worsening already precarious situations.

Indeed, there lay much truth in the branding of Bank staff as the 'Lords of Poverty', the self-serving aristocrats of the development business. Our large tax-free salaries and generous pensions put us many notches of affluence above even UN staff. At the Bank's cafeterias, we wolfed down sumptuous multi-course meals at a fraction of what we would have paid anywhere else in D.C. Rarely did any of us note the hypocrisy of the Bank in subsidizing meals for us prosperous people while slashing public subsidies on even the most basic grains and foodstuff in the debt-burdened countries then undergoing 'structural adjustment'.

The Bank's opulent new headquarters—with its walls of glass, towering atriums and expensive art—was completed a few months after I joined. It cost over $300 million, nearly double the authorized budget. The cost-effectiveness it ruthlessly demanded of client governments didn't seem to be a virtue that the Bank held itself to.

Some of our perks were so outrageous that we shared in the lifestyles of the global super-rich. The most egregious was the entitlement to first-class overseas travel for all professional staff. At the UN, in contrast, even top officials had to fly economy for flights under nine hours. Bank staffers were stripped of this indefensible perk in my first year there, following years of bitter criticism by the media and activists. However, the Bank's considerate travel agency figured a workaround, negotiating free upgrades from business to first class or the Concorde.

Inevitably, in small ways and big, the Bank's entitlements and overweening power limited its ability to promote broad-based well-being in the countries it worked in. This became clear to me on a first-hand basis from public health projects in India, Kenya and Uganda.

While on 'mission' to design or monitor these projects, a majority of my colleagues flew first class from D.C. to the capital cities of these countries. A few of us stuck to business class. ('Mission' is the bizarre term used in the international development industry to describe, typically, a quick visit by foreign experts to dispense advice to an impoverished government. It remains a mystery whether this term came into use because we were supposedly doing charitable work like missionaries, or because we imagined we belonged to the heady world of military espionage.) We stayed at the grandest hotels. We were allowed to spend without limit on meals, drinks, taxis and other facilities, rather than being constrained by the generous but capped daily allowances of the UN staff. On our return leg, we would drop by attractive European capitals for 'rest stops'. Taxpayers' money gathered from the world over paid for all this.

In Africa in particular, our work mainly consisted of meeting top bureaucrats and politicians. Though they were of the rank of health secretaries and health ministers, they would be visibly deferential to the Bank's team leader—even though he or she was no more than a mid-ranking staffer.

All we saw of the poverty in Kenya or Uganda was when we were whisked off in air-conditioned SUVs to visit some carefully selected hospital or non-governmental organization. There we were treated with the reverence accorded to visiting heads of state. We shook hands, asked a few questions, murmured comments that demonstrated both our genuine concern and exceptional professional expertise, and were then chauffeured back to our hotels.

Our reports were written at luxury hotels in country capitals, or in even more salubrious settings. On one memorable occasion, the whole team was jetted off to the plushest boutique hotel in Kenya's Masai Mara wildlife park, on the grounds that we needed peace and quiet to concentrate on our work. I was left with fleeting distant impressions of these countries, feeling rather like a rich First World tourist looking at Third World sights from a cocoon of luxury. After a year of such episodes at the Bank, I was convinced that many of my co-workers would not be able to recognize an impoverished or marginalized person if they saw one, so divorced were they from the masses they were supposed to be tending to.

In India, where I was part of a team in mid-1994 to monitor the Bank's loan for the national AIDS programme, I could be a better judge of the Bank's work because of my own prior knowledge. Disbursement of funds had begun two years earlier, and there was much to show that the Bank's money and related technical support was being used well for advancing implementation of the national AIDS programme through the National AIDS Control Organization, known as NACO.

NACO was led by a senior government official with a strong track record. His staff members were energetic and committed, and quite a few of them had technical expertise. They were working with almost every state government to raise awareness, build HIV prevention programmes, and improve medical care. The actual performance varied from state to state, depending on political commitment and overall quality of the state administration. NACO was backing the Bank's demand that poorly-performing states be pulled up, particularly on the issue of utilizing the funds made available to them. It was a relief to see that in India, by virtue of the professionalism of its senior bureaucrats, there was a largely productive working relationship between Bank staff and the government, rather than the harmfully lopsided relationships I had witnessed in Kenya and Uganda.

But even in India, and that too with a wholly beneficial project that had no complex issues of equity or harm in the manner of the Bank's support for the controversial Narmada River hydel project, the weaknesses of the Bank's work were glaringly evident. The foremost problem in India too was the fact that Bank staff remained utterly cut off from reality.

One indelible memory of that mission is of our days in Goa. Why were we ensconced at the über-luxury Taj Fort Aguada in charming Goa, I wondered to myself. (I repeated that query when our next stop happened to be an equally plush hotel in the beach resort of Kovalam, Kerala.) On our second day in Goa, with a senior state government official fussing over us, we were ferried two hours south to Baina, which was, at that point, home to one of the major sex work sites in western India. We alighted from our luxury mini-bus.

From a great distance, we watched the colourful, sari-clad women standing along the seafront or sitting on the low wall, and the scores of men propositioning them. We noted the unending, expanse of the jhuggi-jhopri shanties where the women lived and sold sex. We took in the windswept beauty of the site, with the monsoon waves rising dramatically in the background. We asked our guide—the solicitous government official—a few questions. Then we drove away.

The whole episode was surreal. I was left with scarcely any understanding of what I had just seen, beyond the few facts that our government colleague seemed to know himself. (The gist was that the sex workers were mainly from the impoverished regions of Karnataka, and that they came to Baina to sell sex during the lean agricultural months. Their clients were both locals and tourists; the day of our visit, several bus-loads of Gujarati school teachers had been their main customers.) Even a foreign tourist visiting the Taj Mahal would have learnt more than what we did in the time spent on our official visit to Baina. And, of course, I would have plumbed far more by working as a journalist in a single day, pen and notepad in hand and my feet on the ground, than on that entire ten-day trip with its countless flights across India, and the innumerable meetings and guided visits.

Nonetheless, for all the buffoonery and contradictions, the Bank was clearly attempting to refashion itself into a poverty-focused institution, rather than remaining a global bank funding mega-projects and macro-economic stability along with the IMF. The most important upshot of this repositioning was that the Bank's leaders realized they now needed to know the impoverished, the disenfranchised and the excluded—to understand them, speak their language, build bridges to them, be attuned to their needs, and win them over. This process had begun by the time I joined the Bank—indeed, the Bank's responsiveness to ABVA's demands that it should not lend to India for AIDS prevention until the government agreed to end its draconian policies was an early sign of this new responsiveness that was now gathering momentum.

The Bank began to hire staff from non-governmental and activist organizations, so as to improve communication and relationships with groups and communities at the grassroot level. It began to invest in operational research that solicited the views of the poor. It also began to ask all its staffers to spend a week or so every second year in impoverished urban or rural settings, de facto admitting that its technocrats knew far too little about the realities they were supposed to be improving. (The Bank's Intranet was soon full of slack-jawed commentary by staff members who seemingly, for the first time, realized that people in slums and impoverished villages did not have toilets or running water, lived in hovels, and often went hungry.) It moved large numbers of staff from Washington D.C. to country offices, to stay closer to their areas of responsibility and keep their ears to the ground.

In addition to this new interest in the impoverished, the Bank began to take an unexpected interest in the lives of gay men and sex workers. This was an outgrowth of the Bank's work on AIDS—the economic devastation caused by the pandemic had led the Bank to rapidly become the largest funder of AIDS prevention efforts in developing countries.

With gay men, the Bank's management already had some first-hand understanding on the subject from the considerable number of staffers who were open about their orientation. Within days of joining the Bank, I had found, to my astonishment, advertisements on hallway notice boards and the Intranet announcing meetings of a gay group for Bank and IMF staff—the World Bank/IMF Gay Lesbian and Other Bisexual Employees Association. I had gone for the first meeting I could, gratified to find it attended by several dozen staffers. Held openly on the Bank premises, the atmosphere was cheery and unafraid. The group consisted largely of American and European men, but there was a sprinkling of people like me from developing countries. It was reassuring to see several senior staff members at the meeting.

In my two years at the Bank, I found that the management was fairly responsive to our demands for equal treatment. There were eventually small but important gains—such as health insurance for same-sex partners, and prohibition of discrimination on the basis of sexual orientation. Some managers did all they could to secure visas for partners of staff wherever they were posted. Just these halting steps put the Bank far ahead of the UN system, where gay and lesbian staff continued to work in fear and secrecy because these organizations did nothing to treat them fairly. Indeed, at that point, the Bank was also ahead of the US government—this was the era of the homophobic Defense of Marriage Act (which denied recognition to same-sex partners for all federal benefits and rights), and the 'Don't ask, don't tell' policy that barred openly gay or lesbian individuals from serving in the military. Many factors contributed to this–including the value placed by top management on job performance rather than personal attributes, the Bank's operational autonomy from member countries, and the singular outspokenness of prominent Bank economist Hans Binswanger about being both gay and HIV-positive.

However, the Bank had none of this convivial familiarity with the other set of sexual outlaws—sex workers. As I witnessed in Goa, we still looked at them from a great distance, as if they were part of a tableau that we could not hope to understand. Or we read about these women, men and transgenders in the burgeoning literature on AIDS and sex work, which still left them as uni-dimensional, faceless ciphers that were of interest only in terms of slowing the pandemic.

But then, in August 1994, I was part of a small team of Bank staffers at the 10th International AIDS Conference in Yokohama. I had been to international conferences on other issues—from fighting hunger and malaria to reversing ozone depletion—but this one felt very different right from the start.

Of the more than ten thousand participants, only a tiny minority—like those of us from the Bank—were talking heads, attired in suits or other formal wear. The rest were dressed casually, often bohemian-like, and they exuded passion, anger and desperation. They included many women and men who distinctly looked ill, sometimes desperately ill. This was unmistakably a conference on AIDS—and the strong numbers of people living with AIDS, or those who had lost dear ones to this pandemic, were the reason that the conference coursed with anger at the failure to find a cure, to slow the epidemic, to care for the millions ill and dying, to stop the persecution they faced.

At one of the plenary sessions, I heard a former sex worker and activist for sex workers' rights, Ms K, speak about the epidemic's impact on sex workers. She spoke with outrage on how AIDS had been decimating sex workers since the pandemic's earliest days, even as those with the power and resources to help them did not act because of the overpowering bigotry against sex workers. I recall that everyone in that massive hall kept exceptionally quiet through the speech, as if ashamed by the truth of her words.

Somewhere in the course of her speech, I heard Ms K call for reforming the laws that criminalized sex work in country after country. While the exact words didn't register, the gist was that adult, consensual sex work needed to be decriminalized.

Decriminalize sex work! It immediately made sense, even though I had never yet heard this idea being mentioned vis-à-vis sex work.

I knew from my personal experience as a gay individual that there was no more damning circumstance than to be criminalized. Being a criminal in law and in the eyes of others was the source of all our problems. It left you corrosively ashamed because others reviled you—and that sense of shame was the most disempowering force. It kept us outlaws from protesting against even the most inhuman abuses we faced, while the police and courts, those all-powerful enforcers, thought us unfit to deserve any of the most basic citizenship rights, let alone real justice.

Decriminalization was always the most pivotal step in an outlawed community's journey towards emancipation—when no longer a criminal, you can begin to fight for all your other rights, even eventually for equality. So I could immediately understand that just as decriminalizing homosexuality was the first step that we gay men and women needed to emancipate ourselves, so too was decriminalizing sex work in order for sex workers to begin tackling the myriad hardships they faced, of which HIV was just the latest.

Coming from Ms K—someone with as personal an experience of sex work as I had of being gay—the call to decriminalize sex work had an unquestionable authenticity. And her words made such an impression on me because they came soon after I read the demands made by Siddhartha and his ABVA colleagues in *Less than Gay*, suddenly opening up new options that hadn't previously seemed possible.

I was so impressed that I sought out Ms K, a self-assured woman with the charismatic style of a nightclub singer, to ask if she would contribute an article to the health policy newsletter that I edited at the Bank. Would she write about what sex workers thought the World Bank should do to turn around the pandemic's onslaught on sex workers and their clients?

As she seemed taken aback by my suggestion, I assured her that she would have an attentive and influential audience, considering that the Bank was by then the world's largest funder of HIV prevention programmes in developing countries. Ms K eventually agreed, on the condition that she would ask a colleague to author the article, given the short deadline.

A week later, the article arrived by email. It turned out to be written by Priscilla Alexander, the activist and researcher on sex work whom Jonathan Mann had recruited to WHO's Global Programme on AIDS in 1989. Alexander had left WHO in 1993 to coordinate the efforts of the National Task Force on Prostitution, a coalition of US and Canadian organizations for sex workers' rights.

Alexander's article was fascinating. By now, I had read reams on HIV and sex workers, but almost all of it took the narrow perspective of understanding them only in the context of HIV prevention, with no wider, genuine interest taken in their thoughts or realities. (With few exceptions, this was indeed true of all HIV prevention research. Little effort was made to understand people in the context of their lives—whether the complex drives of sexuality, the compulsions of financial survival, the human needs for intimacy and support, or the power of social and cultural factors.) Alexander's article was very different.

She began by discussing the terrible stigma and persecution that have been visited on women sex workers for eons in most societies. 'Prostitution has often been called the oldest profession,' Alexander wrote, 'However, it has rarely, if ever, been respected as a profession. Thus, for centuries, it has been governed by punitive and discriminatory rules, regulations and laws, but virtually no efforts have been made to promote the welfare or health of the prostitute ... The laws, and regulations and rules about prostitution have been, for the last several thousand years, aimed at keeping prostitutes out of sight—forced to live on certain streets, confined to "closed" brothels, or subject to banishment from the city.'

According to Alexander, the animus against prostitutes was so overpowering that 'the occasional regulations related to health, without exception, never had the health of prostitutes in mind'. The emergence of AIDS and 'epidemiologic characterizations of female prostitutes as vectors who will speed up transmission of HIV to men, to men's wives, and to babies', had worsened the vilification of sex workers as well as legitimized a spate of brutal health regulations, such as the mandatory HIV testing of sex workers and the incarceration of those found positive.

'Papers in prestigious medical journals have described female prostitutes as "reservoirs of infection", "pools of contagion", "vectors", and—my favourite—"core groups of high-frequency transmitters"', Alexander wrote acerbically. (For all her frankness, Alexander was being diplomatic—she could have noted that the Bank was also a leading offender in using exactly these alarmist, blame-the-victim terms in its works on HIV.)

She showed up the wrong-headedness of these characterizations, writing: 'These views are considered legitimate despite the fact that every study shows that it is the prostitutes, not their clients, who are most vulnerable to HIV infection; and it is the clients, not the prostitutes, who, in every country, resist the use of condoms.'

The punitive laws criminalizing sex workers were the root cause of most of the problems affecting them, including their vulnerability to HIV, Alexander argued. She said they forced sex workers to operate in an illegal market with all its inevitable dangers. Sex work was illegal in all but twenty-odd countries, with countries varying only on the extent of criminalization and the specific aspects of sex work that were prohibited.

While many countries specifically criminalized the selling of sex, others also criminalized buying it (as is the case in the USA). Others, including Britain and India, criminalized sex work indirectly by prohibiting every aspect of selling sex rather than the sale of sex itself—such as soliciting, advertising or being found in a brothel.

This made it impossible for sex workers to engage in their profession without breaking the law. In practice, most countries used every possible law to prosecute sex workers, typically combining specific anti-prostitution laws with discriminatory use of broad laws targeting vagrancy, public nuisance, adultery or sodomy (in the case of male or transgender sex workers).

Revealingly, whatever the precise shape of the laws, the brunt of punishment always fell on the sex workers themselves—mostly in terms of monetary fines, jail terms of varying severity, and being listed in public records as a 'common prostitute' or 'sexual offender'. In a handful of countries, women convicted of prostitution were put to death.

'The need to avoid being arrested sharply restricts the ability of the sex worker to negotiate with clients, or to get a sense of whether a client is likely to be abusive,' Alexander emphasized. In contrast, in areas where laws are markedly less repressive, such as the Netherlands and some states of Australia and New Zealand, 'it has been easier for sex workers to collaborate on efforts to establish common practices, such as routine condom use to prevent HIV and other STDs.'

And then Alexander asked: 'What would be the most effective reforms to protect women sex workers from HIV and other health problems? From severe economic exploitation? From rape, physical assault and murder? From being forced to do sex work? What reforms could help to prevent the recruitment—including through debt bondage—of children into sex work?'

She wrote, 'At the present time, as we near the end of the 20th century, there are essentially three dominant paradigms for how society should approach the subject of prostitution. The oldest one is "control the prostitute", which has, as its corollaries, "protect the client", "protect the neighbourhood" or "protect society" from the prostitute. The second is "rescue the prostitute", from herself, from the clients, from the pimps.' These two traditional paradigms were the ones that had 'left sex workers so vulnerable to violence and disease'.

In contrast, Alexander wrote, 'A new voice has begun to make itself heard, the voice of sex workers powerfully enunciating a new paradigm. This paradigm is "control working conditions", in the context of sex work as a legitimate occupation.'

Building on this last paradigm, Alexander's article ended with a brief section laying out what sex workers' organizations wanted in terms of action from the World Bank and governments. They were just a half-dozen bullet-points, stripped of any flourishes, as if to tell even a prejudiced reader: 'Look, how can you disagree with the evident truth of what I'm saying, what I'm asking for?'

Alexander asked for decriminalization of sex work—specifically, the repeal of all laws that criminalized adult consensual sex work and related activities. Alongside this, she pushed for a tight crackdown on forced prostitution and child prostitution (often called sex trafficking), advising against prostitution-specific laws—that were not just misused but also fueled the stigma against sex workers—in favour of improving and enforcing of general laws against rape, sexual assault, kidnapping and child abuse.

She also laid out ways to ensure better work conditions for sex workers through paid sick leave, health and disability insurance, retirement pensions and broad healthcare. She emphasized that sex workers needed the right to engage in collective bargaining and various kinds of advocacy, just like workers in other industries.

From everything that I had seen, read and understood of sex work so far, these demands seemed legitimate and reasonable. By their comprehensiveness, they also seemed vastly more likely to be effective in stemming the spread of HIV in sex work settings than the narrow prescriptions of the Bank and other major organizations, which focused almost entirely on promoting condom use and treatment for sexually-transmitted infections, without sparing any thought for the power dynamics that stood in the way or the grave risk of worsening the persecution of sex workers. I thought that my Bank colleagues' notions about sex work and HIV would be effectively challenged by Alexander's article.

But Alexander now wrote, her frustration evident: 'With any other occupation, such basic demands would not be controversial, but with sex work, few policymakers are even willing to participate in an open discussion.' Those closing words of hers—about the unwillingness of policymakers to even discuss these matters—were prophetic.

My immediate boss for the past few months, on reading Alexander's article, curtly told me that he would not allow it to be published in the Bank's health policy newsletter. I was appalled. When I had checked with him at the Yokohama AIDS conference before asking Ms K to contribute to the newsletter, he had been wholeheartedly enthusiastic. But he now maintained that it was inappropriate for sex workers to tell the Bank and its partner governments what they wanted, and that too in such forceful terms.

I argued that we had made a commitment to both Ms K and Alexander, that too on a sensitive matter, and we could not renege on it. He retorted that if I didn't like his decision, I was free to resign. From his expression, it was clear that he hoped I would.

But I resolved to fight, and referred our dispute to the director of the division. A few weeks later, the director told me that he and other senior staffers had decided that Alexander's article should be published in its entirety.

I was overjoyed. It renewed my admiration for the Bank's organizational procedures as well as its markedly open intellectual culture. I knew that almost no other international organization would have run such an article. Whatever my criticisms of the Bank's functioning and impact, there was no doubt that there was greater freedom for debate here than at other comparable institutions.

Eventually, Alexander's article appeared as the lead front page item in the fall 1994 issue of the Bank's health policy newsletter, which was distributed among Bank staff as well as to the public. It covered three full pages. I noted candidly in the introduction that the Bank had solicited this article 'because of the continuing disregard by decision-makers of the views of sex workers' rights organizations'.

If I could have spoken from my heart, I would have said more. I would have admitted that my own personal investment in promoting the views of sex workers was fed not just by the hope that the Bank would address the many injustices faced by them, but also the larger hope that this new dialogue would ultimately lead to rational, hypocrisy-free societies where censure and persecution for any kind of consensual, adult sexual behaviour would be ended. I ached for dignity to be restored to every kind of sexual outlaw, whether sex workers, gay people or transgender individuals.

As I expected, Alexander's article attracted more attention than any other in the newsletter's history. One major reason was that it marked the first time a community so severely affected by AIDS had the chance to convey to Bank staff, indelibly in print, their view of what the Bank and its partner governments needed to do to make real headway against the epidemic. Several years later, when the Bank first fully enunciated its thinking on HIV prevention among sex workers and their clients, I was gratified to see that it was informed by Alexander's perspective—particularly her insistence that criminalization harmed the well-being of sex workers as well as the goal of tackling the spread of HIV.

But though I felt glad that I had played a role in opening a dialogue, I was never confident that it would deepen into genuine understanding and acceptance, akin to that being shown by the Bank's management towards gay men and women. We gay people were no longer outcasts at the Bank, welcomed on staff and even in leadership positions. But sex workers remained outcasts and distant, and I wondered whether that great distance could ever be bridged.

14

Rising from the Ruins

I had left my work on AIDS at the World Bank at the end of 1994 to write a book on the lives of the many millions of Indians marginalized by poverty and caste. It was research that immersed me for a long time in the realities of village life, giving me a genuine understanding of India—particularly of the aspiration for emancipation that was gripping every downtrodden group as democracy became more of a reality—for which I was forever grateful. Several years later, I returned to researching the impact of the AIDS epidemic on sex workers and gay men, this time for a book focused on India's escalating problems in this regard.

By this point, at the end of the 1990s, AIDS had devastated the lives of India's sex workers like no force ever before. In the decade and a half since Selvi and the five other sex workers in the Madras reformatory were found to have HIV, thousands upon thousands upon thousands had died, were dying, or were falling mortally sick. In Bombay, for instance, estimates suggested that every second woman sex worker in the downtown red-light areas had contracted HIV—as high as the worst rates recorded among gay men in New York City or San Francisco.

'I cannot even begin to tell you the amount of deaths we have seen,' said Shilpa Merchant, a public health specialist who, in 1991, began HIV prevention efforts in Bombay's traditional red-light areas of Falkland Road and Kamathipura for Population Services International, a global non-profit organization. 'From 1993 to 1996, this whole lot of sex workers died. We used to offer voluntary counselling and testing, and from that we had a positive rate of 70 per cent!'

'The death toll in Falkland Road was much greater than even Kamathipura, because Falkland Road is a poorer area, where women come much cheaper. In the 1990s, Kamathipura women charged Rs 50 per client. Falkland Road women charged less than half of that. The lower price made your power of negotiation even less.'

'The madams would keep them as long as they were somewhat healthy and useful. Most of them, even if they could not be sex workers anymore, became the ayahs there—cooking, cleaning and doing odd jobs for the others. So, till they were useful, they were kept. But they were usually turned out on to the street when they were sick and dying. So, while only a few died in brothels, a great many died on the streets.'

The epidemic had outstripped even the worst-case scenarios expected for India, and sex workers were among the worst-hit. By 1999, less than fifteen years into India's epidemic, more people were infected with HIV than in any other country (with the possible exception of South Africa), the UN estimated, somewhere between 3.5 to 5 million adults. While half a million more were contracting HIV every year, over three hundred thousand were dying of AIDS in the same period. It was a mind-boggling toll but, almost certainly, far worse lay ahead.

The consensus amongst close observers was that the government's prevention efforts—despite massive funding from the World Bank, UN and bilateral donors—were so patchy on the ground that they could not hope to check the epidemic, given how far it had advanced. 'Outside of Africa, India likely has the world's most worrisome AIDS crisis,' a *New York Times* editorial commented. 'India suffers the same virulent strain of AIDS that is killing Africans, its general health conditions are poor, and heterosexual transmission is common, putting the whole population at risk.' The US government's National Intelligence Council, an expert research arm of the CIA, warned that India would have 20–25 million HIV-infected people by 2010.

The change in scale was shockingly evident. On my first research trip in 1991, there had been so few people hit by the epidemic that I could remember virtually every such encounter, from the wrenching scene at the AIDS hospital ward in Bombay to the hopeless group of HIV-positive drug users jailed in Imphal. But now I met countless people with HIV, desperately searching for care at hospitals as well as support from the 'positive-people' groups and HIV-focused NGOs that had recently sprung up.

I also came to realize that for all the havoc it was wreaking in the lives of India's sex workers, the epidemic had also catalysed a few positive changes for them—and, astonishingly, some of these changes were so promising that they could even bring about a sea change in the lives of those who survived the epidemic.

One source of these changes had emerged from the HIV prevention projects begun for sex workers by NGOs. Most of them never went beyond trying to control the spread of HIV, and usually had a limited impact on even this goal. Some would even do the sex workers outright harm by aiding in forcible testing, or by duplicitiously using them as guinea pigs for experimental drugs. But a small handful took a very different path.

Though they also started off with the narrow goal of HIV prevention, they were rapidly transformed into broad efforts run by sex workers themselves, fired up by the larger vision of transforming every aspect of their lives. (I was immediately struck by how similar their hopes and demands were to what I had recently witnessed among impoverished Dalit families in rural India, and how, like the Dalits too, they remained unbroken despite all the oppression they had suffered, beginning to fight fiercely for their emancipation once they had even a little cause for hope or a few reliable allies.) These unusual organizations began to catalyse once-unimaginable changes—from forcing the government and the women's movement in India to pay attention to the welfare and basic rights of sex workers to profoundly influencing global thinking about sex work.

I sought out three of the most remarkable of these groups, which were coincidentally founded in the very same year, 1992, in far-flung reaches of the country—Calcutta, Madras, and the small agricultural town of Sangli in Maharashtra. Though they had been established and developed independently, the common thread linking them was that their founders acted on the evidence that if sex workers saw that their overall welfare was genuinely at the heart of these efforts—that their most hated burdens were being tackled—they themselves rose up to fight determinedly for their overall well-being, of which protection from HIV was an important part.

My extensive visits to these groups, as well as others over the years, began to give me a real understanding of the topsy-turvy realities of sex work in India. They punctured the stereotypical images of big-city brothels and helpless women, the impressions I had got from superficial earlier research and reading. Instead, I came to realize that the world of sex work was not only infinitely complex but also astoundingly counter factual.

Thus, I was to find that in India a vast majority of sex workers didn't operate out of brothels, and that sex work was common in many rural areas. I found that many women who sold sex did so as a temporary measure—often to tide over a period of dire need for their families—rather than as a lifelong occupation, with this being the most lucrative trade available. From the many women I interviewed, I came to learn of the myriad abuses inflicted on them by the police, courts and other branches of the state, persecution that often dwarfed what they suffered at the hands of clients, pimps or madams, commonly thought of as their worst oppressors and exploiters. I was also left with an unforgettable understanding of the capacity of many of these women to challenge their all but insurmountable odds—to somehow fend for themselves, their children and families—particularly if given some support.

The Madras organization had been set up by Shyamala Nataraj, the journalist who, in 1989, had filed the legal challenge that won Selvi and the hundreds of other HIV-positive sex workers imprisoned in Tamil Nadu their freedom. She had quit her successful career in journalism soon afterwards. Her experiences at the reformatory had left her determined to do practical things to help sex workers confront this killing epidemic as well as the worsening abuses they were facing. It was an unconventional undertaking for a well-off young Indian woman of that era, but with her characteristic independence of mind, Nataraj set up the South India AIDS Action Programme (SIAAP).

The impressive name belied the fact that the fledgling organization had no budget, no staff beyond a part-time assistant and Nataraj herself, and operated from a tiny rented room. It didn't even have a blueprint for action—Nataraj had no prior training in grassroots work, and there was as yet no bank of knowledge in India or elsewhere on the most effective ways to support sex workers, given the fact that these women had been shunned by civil society groups as well as governmental services the world over.

Even so, the organization rapidly took on an effective shape. A key reason for this, said Nataraj, was that Selvi and several of the other women from the Madras reformatory had found their way to the fledgling organization. They were to change it in ways that Nataraj said she could never have foreseen.

'From what I understand, Selvi had first gone back to Ulundurpettai to live with her husband, to try and make things work with him,' Nataraj recalled. 'But she found once again that she could not get along with her husband and her in-laws. She came back to Madras, but decided she was not going to sell sex anymore. She heard through the grapevine that I had set up a place to work on AIDS. So, one day, she walked into my office and just said: "I want to work with you".'

'Realizing that I clearly did not recognize her, she said, "Don't you remember me? You met me in jail, in the remand home. I am one of the women you freed".

'I asked her, "What work will you do?" There was no money available at that time to hire anyone to work on AIDS. She gave that question some thought, and then answered, "I will tell other people what I went through. Whether you pay me or not, I will come and work".

'And then for the next many years, until her death in 1998, Selvi was really a tireless crusader. She would go to other sex workers and literally say, "Hey, I had sex without a condom. Look at me now. Don't let this happen to you. This doesn't need to happen".'

This is how peer education on HIV prevention began for SIAAP, said Nataraj. It was to expand rapidly because the sex workers whom Selvi met trusted her, as she had also been a sex worker until recently. Soon, overcoming their fear of informers, they began to attend educational meetings at the organization and, from there, were drawn to joining as part-time peer educators themselves.

Similarly, from all that Selvi had suffered in her life—her abusive marriage, her years of selling sex to support herself and her young son, her HIV diagnosis and long years of imprisonment—she knew better than any outsider about the realities faced by these women, and what exactly would help them the most. This enabled the group to tailor itself to the characteristics and hardships of sex work in Madras, said Nataraj.

In Madras, and generally across Tamil Nadu, brothels were a rarity and sex workers picked up clients from the street, typically in crowded areas like bus stops and railway stations, cinema halls, and highway rest sites. Particular spots were associated with sex work, known to both clients and to sex workers, rather like the gay cruising areas known to men seeking men. The women would then service clients in cheap hotels—popularly known as 'lodges'—or deserted areas like parks and railways lines.

So Selvi and the other sex workers who had joined SIAAP began to identify convenient spots to leave supplies of condoms that the women could access. They would be placed in public toilets, inside broken lamp posts, or left with helpful vegetable vendors or tea stall owners. They even negotiated with lodge owners about placing condoms in the rooms.

The group began to address the labyrinthine burdens the women had been suffering for long. From the discussions at the group meetings, Nataraj realized that a critical first step would be to help the women 'build their self-respect and stop viewing themselves as "doing wrong". She was struck that they castigated themselves so bitterly for selling sex, despite the dire pressures and compulsions that had propelled them into this work.

'Many of these women entered sex work because they had been abused or deserted by husbands, lovers or family members,' said Nataraj. 'Others wanted to supplement their husbands' earnings because the money they made was too little for their families to survive on. In any case, entry into sex work also displayed the autonomy of these women, rather than solely their victimhood.

'So we encouraged them to share their life experiences—not only about the desertion, abuse and violence, but also about survival as well as hopes and aspirations for their children, and their own relationships with husbands, lovers and other family members. These helped reveal to the women their own values, strengths, and motivations. They gradually began to see themselves as strong women, women who would not be easily cowed.'

The women also desperately needed practical support, and so SIAAP began building broad alliances with healthcare institutions, lawyers, and the government's national commissions for women as well as human rights. Healthcare personnel were invited to SIAAP to brief the women on sexual infections and HIV. Women activists and progressive lawyers introduced the women to issues related to their rights as citizens, and to debates about gender and patriarchy. And they, in turn, were sensitised to the particularly harsh difficulties faced by sex workers, marking the beginnings of an engagement between feminist activists and sex workers.

The group, almost immediately, turned to tackling the violence the women suffered at the hands of the police. Nataraj recalled, 'I soon realized from the regular group meetings with sex workers that their one common desire was to get the police off their backs.'

SIAAP first used persuasion. 'Selvi, some sex workers from the locality and I would go together to the local police station and discuss the issue,' said Nataraj. 'The key was to touch the humanity of the cop in a completely non-judgemental way.'

'We pointed out that sex work had existed through the ages and often was a product of sexual desire of the client on the one hand, and the poverty of the woman on the other. We would tell them that there was no right or wrong involved, and the risk of HIV made it urgent for them to help both parties protect themselves—rather than take a moralistic stand.'

'I think the cops bought the logic because many of them were also clients of sex workers. They appreciated our approach as well as the condoms and education material we left behind.'

'For their part, the women became more circumspect in their behaviour at the pick-up sites, making sure that they did not show up tipsy or dishevelled. They also made a pact amongst themselves to stop pimps from exploiting underage girls, threatening to report them to the police with SIAAP's help. In any case, over time, the police in Madras began to treat the women better. The abuse and arrests reduced considerably, even more so when we began to send letters of appreciation to police stations.'

Even so, confrontation was unavoidable, said Nataraj, because a core of policemen continued to exploit and abuse sex workers. With the guidance of human rights lawyers who had begun to support SIAAP's work, the group decided to challenge the police whenever any of the sex workers known to the organization were arrested.

On closely analysing the laws under which sex workers were mostly arrested, Nataraj and the human rights lawyers had realized that they did not criminalize the act of selling sex itself, but penalized every activity related to this—such as soliciting, pimping or operating a brothel. The confusion reflected an unresolved contradiction in the laws, which followed British colonial jurisprudence and had inherited the tensions existing in this between the government's goal of eradicating prostitution and a reluctance to be seen as punishing the 'victimized' women in prostitution too harshly. They saw an opportunity in this confusion.

'Everybody—the women themselves as well as the police and lawyers—thought that sex work was clearly illegal in India, rather than a grey area,' Nataraj recalled. It was because of this assumption that sex workers had helplessly and unquestioningly pleaded guilty to whatever charges the police filed against them when produced in court, even if they were false.

Nataraj and the lawyers knew that it would be difficult for the police to provide hard proof that sex workers were soliciting—unless they had been entrapped by the police—and decided to focus on this weakness in challenging future arrests. 'We knew that the women would win if only they found the confidence to plead not guilty,' said Nataraj.

'But, given the risks,' said Nataraj, 'it took a few years before one brave woman—Saroja—agreed. But she won! And then more women began to challenge their arrests. And they won too! We had soon overturned dozens of arrests in the state.' The sex workers were soon confident enough to challenge arrests on their own, without turning to Nataraj or Madras-based lawyers.

By the time I first visited SIAAP in the winter of 1998, the group's proven utility was such that two thousand sex workers had joined local collectives launched by it in cities and towns across Tamil Nadu. These collectives were run by the sex workers themselves, with office-bearers chosen through regular elections. In the collective's formative years, SIAAP provided seed funding and matching grants but, in time, their expenses were met entirely by membership fees.

Being part of the collective provided huge benefits, ranging from the material to the psychological. The women had the confidence that comes from numbers and solidarity, as well as the legitimacy that comes from being part of an institution. This helped them negotiate with local politicians, government officials and the police, rather than keeping as far from them as possible out of fears of abuse. The collective's members got free condoms, small loans and support for child-care as well as schooling. SIAAP pressured the state and local administrations into giving voter identity cards and ration cards to the women even when they didn't have formal proof of their residential address.

Each gain produced further gains that once seemed impossible. Thus, having their names on the voters' list brought the women the power to negotiate for support from local politicians, using this backing to convince local schools to admit children on the basis of the mother's guardianship alone, rather than requiring a father's presence.

I also saw that one of SIAAP's distinctive strengths was that it catalysed and supported spin-off efforts by the women. One person in SIAAP would inspire another to begin something that the women critically needed. Then SIAAP would support the initiative, with seed funding and technical advice. A thousand unexpected things bloomed because of this.

One such person was Mary Thomas, a sex worker from Kerala. 'I joined SIAAP in the early-1990s. I didn't join because of the salary—it was just a hundred and eighty rupees a month! I joined because I was impressed that the women in SIAAP would help me and other sex workers in case we ever got into trouble with the police. Because of my son, whom I was raising alone, I was always paranoid about this. I used to be scared even to stand at a bus stop.'

When Mary was hired at SIAAP, Selvi was already working there. The two struck up a close friendship. She said that Selvi was 'very

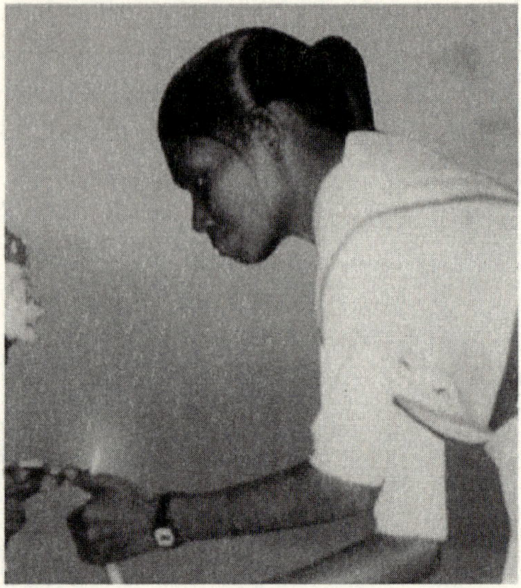

Selvi

bold and passionate' when talking to other people about AIDS, but also very patient when it came to dealing with other sex workers. 'You know what comes to mind first when I think of Selvi?' said Mary. 'The fact that she taught me how to write reports! I was almost illiterate till then.' (The more I learnt from Mary and Nataraj about Selvi's transformation—from the silent, traumatized young woman jailed in the Madras reformatory, to this trailblazing activist who had left such a legacy of progress for Tamil Nadu's sex workers—the more intensely I regretted that I did not get a chance to meet her. She had died just months before I began my research.)

But it was Selvi's final years as an AIDS patient that had the most impact on Mary. 'She really suffered,' Mary said. 'She became like a child, having loose motions all the time. You couldn't even wash those clothes because they were so dirty. We bought them in bulk, the way we buy clothes for babies. We wore gloves while looking after her.'

Selvi was moved from hospital to hospital, but in a strange twist of fate she came to be tended in her final stretch by Dr Suniti Solomon, the professor of microbiology who had unwittingly brought about Selvi's long years of imprisonment at the Madras reformatory. Solomon had left the government's health services to establish a non-profit hospital in Madras, which soon came to set the benchmark for providing subsidized medical care to people with HIV. It was impossible not to interpret this as some kind of atonement on Solomon's part.

'When Selvi was terminally ill, at least I was there for her,' said Mary Thomas. 'But there were so many people worse off than Selvi. I saw a lot of people who could do with some help. I saw people lying everywhere in the hospital premises, especially in the TB sanatorium at Tambaram. Many patients could never leave the hospital even if they got better, because they had been thrown out by their families for having AIDS. They even brought their children with them because they had no place to leave them. When I would take food for Selvi, she'd share it with everyone who didn't have enough to eat.'

'I was provoked by seeing all this. Who was there to care for them or their little children? They were in a pathetic state, especially the patients who had no caregivers but were still worried about how their kids would survive once they were gone. I decided to do something for them. It was truly Selvi's case that provoked me.'

The day after Selvi's death, Mary told Shyamala Nataraj and others at SIAAP of her ambition to start a short-stay home near the Tambaram TB hospital to help the most disadvantaged of the patients with AIDS. These would be the people, as she put it, for 'whom no one cares, the kind of people left to die on railway platforms or pavements'.

Though Nataraj warned Mary that it would not be an easy project to sustain, she provided her with all the support she needed. The shelter was registered as a charitable trust named after Selvi—the Selvi Memorial Illam Society. (Illam means shelter or house in Tamil.) The demand proved to be so great that the shelter was always full to capacity, and the trust had to gradually expand its efforts into providing home-based care for people living with AIDS, organizing support groups, arranging for admissions to hospitals, and caring for the victims' children. I'm not sure what moved me more—to see how deeply Selvi had inspired others even in such a short, truncated life (she was just in her mid-thirties when she died), or to see the extraordinary things that Mary had achieved in memory of her beloved friend.

I was also to find that the impact of the combined efforts of Selvi, Mary and Shyamala Nataraj went far beyond the grassroots, however vitally important this was. They had also collectively succeeded in pushing the issue of sex workers' rights and well-being onto the agendas of the government as well as broader civil society movements. This made me appreciate that, though India's democracy was generally hostile to the well-being of the poor and marginalized, it also offered potential for remarkable breakthroughs—in this case because an egalitarian-minded activist had come together in common cause with sex workers determined to change their circumstances.

Thus, in great part because of Nataraj's urging, the new chairperson of the National Commission for Women—prominent social activist Mohini Giri—committed herself to preparing an in-depth report on sex work in 1995. She also agreed to Nataraj's insistence that the Commission's members pay heed to the sex workers' views and demands, rather than decide matters without their participation. Eventually, Giri herself met more than two thousand sex workers, and a near-final draft of the report was opened up for discussion and comments with forty select sex workers, including Selvi and Mary Thomas.

Sex work was an unlikely choice of issues for this governmental body because the women's movement had paid little heed to the working conditions of women in sex work, focusing its energies on more mainstream matters such as domestic violence, 'dowry' killings and inheritance rights. The broader non-governmental sector, with its concentration on rural poverty, had ignored sex workers as well, at the most intervening with moralistic rehabilitation efforts.

Only rank prejudice against women who sold sex could explain this prolonged neglect by these otherwise forward-thinking sections of society. Even in a country where many, if not, most women are brutally treated through the entire course of their lives, sex workers were arguably the worst treated and most critically in need of support from feminists and human rights activists. It spoke volumes that it was activist-minded journalists and public health professionals who had ended up defending the rights of these women and instituting progressive feminist models of empowerment.

The Commission's report—*Societal Violence on Women and Children in Prostitution*—was published in early 1996. I read it with astonishment.

The opening page began by saying, 'Women in prostitution are first and foremost equal citizens of India ... The fundamental rights towards basic amenities, comfort, freedom and dignity should be available to these women as much as they are to all the citizens of India.' I had never imagined that a report bearing the imprimatur of the Indian government would ever take this position, given how disgracefully it had treated them so far.

Indeed, the report—in essence—was a catalogue of the grievous wrongs done to sex workers by varied branches of the state. Clearly, Nataraj's urging that the Commission's members hear the views of sex workers had led them to understand how shamefully they were treated by governmental institutions.

'The state's key institutions, such as the police, schools and hospitals, are dismal in their attitudes and responses to these women', said the report. 'In fact, most of them have served as the opposite of their designated functions; they double their exploitation and extortion, along with exerting violence of varying degrees upon these women and their children.' Even basic social services such as government clinics and hospitals 'are virtually beyond their access due to discriminatory attitudes and behaviour of both the medical and the para-medical and the administrative personnel'.

The Commission's most scathing criticism was of the police, and the impunity with which it brutalized and terrorized sex workers. 'The one constant refrain from women at all meetings held by the National Commission for Women was to "do something about the police,"' the report noted bluntly.'

'The women are arrested under charges of "possession of condoms", or even on false charges of "possession of narcotics" ... The women are rounded up at the end of the month when the target for petty/minor offences are not met by the particular police station ... Some police officers are known by name to be self-avowed crusaders against "prostitutes". Instead of protecting these women from the goondas and criminal elements, the police adds its own violence and abuse to that of other criminals. Eviction and demolition of shelters and homes of these women by the police and other administrative authorities are common.'

Adding insult to injury, the police routinely raked in a large fortune from the hard work of these impoverished women through the 'haftas' and 'mamool' they extorted, the Commission noted.

The Commission also lambasted India's laws and judiciary. The laws and their prejudiced application—whether it was the ITPA or the myriad state and local laws employed against sex workers—'victimizes the women rather than deter and punish perpetrators of prostitution', the Commission noted. For instance, anti-vagrancy laws that regulate the uses of public spaces, including footpaths and parks, were routinely used to arrest sex workers. The Commission wrote sharply: 'No other citizen is usually charged for the offence of vagrancy, which is the law most often operating against the women in sex work.'

One egregious section of ITPA gave magistrates unchecked power to have a sex worker evicted from her home or premises in the 'interests of the general public' or 'if there is a complaint against her'. The Commission asked, with palpable outrage, 'How will such a procedure stand the test of "reasonable restriction"?'

After surveying the innumerable ways that state and society had sinned against sex workers, the Commission made reams of recommendations, seeking sweeping reform of the laws, an end to police abuse, and guaranteed affordable housing, ration cards, and electoral cards for sex workers to exercise their basic citizenship right to vote. The recommendations made for heartbreaking reading, despite being in dry, terse language, because they showed that sex workers had so far been denied absolutely everything—even the most basic of human rights—because of the impunity with which everyone abused and shamed them. (Though the Commission's recommendations were not legally enforceable, they carried influence in the government and also affected public opinion.) Thus, the Commission even had to urge that condoms should be considered 'life saving equipment', not used as a pretext for the police to arrest them!

I was particularly happy to see the Commission push for the removal of any clauses that permitted 'imprisonment of adult women in prostitution', and for prostitution cases to be tried in civil rather than in the criminal courts—steps that would loosen the police's oppressive power over the women as well as roll back the stigma that sex workers were criminals.

Quite beyond its sympathetic stance, the report set a precedent in India by establishing that sex workers—like all other citizens—had a right to be heard in matters concerning them, even at the rarefied level of national policymaking, rather than summarily ignored. I was filled with admiration for Mohini Giri upon noting that she had left intact the views of sex workers, prominently highlighted in boxed sections, even when they strongly disagreed with the Commission.

This disagreement was nakedly evident on the crucial issue of legal reforms. The sex workers clearly felt that the Commission had not gone far enough, even though it had recommended wholesale reform of the laws affecting sex workers. They wanted real freedom once and for all—the law and the police had to be entirely removed from their lives, through a complete repeal of all prostitution-related laws. They stressed that as long as the law and the police intruded on their lives, they would not be safe. And they had no patience for reforms that implicitly disapproved of sex work and sought its ending, when this was the most lucrative of the work options available to them as impoverished, largely illiterate women.

Thus, they stated categorically: 'There should not be any laws against prostitution; ITPA must be removed; there should be no fines; there should not be "demand reduction" in our services or else we will starve'. (I was struck that these sex workers had arrived at many of the conclusions of Priscilla Alexander and other Western advocates for sex worker rights, despite hailing from a completely different setting.)

There was so much about the Commission's report that impressed and moved me. However, the most moving revelation was to be found in the report's very last pages—the text of a recent petition by Selvi and six other sex workers, addressed to the government's National Commission for Human Rights. Their petition focused on the arrest of several hundred sex workers in Bombay in February 1996—on the orders of the High Court—who were then forcibly tested for HIV and deported to their home states. Many months later, they were still being held captive.

Selvi and her co-signatories urged the Human Rights Commission to press for the release of these sex workers. They submitted the petition as members of the Representative Inter-State Committee of Sex Workers in India. 'The members of this committee,' they wrote, 'have discussed this situation and the violations, and wish to record their anger and deep sorrow at the gross injustice that is being done. We submit that the below mentioned parties be held responsible, and urged to remedy the inhuman and illegal situation thus created.' Their petition was directed against Bombay's Commissioner of Police, the National AIDS Control Organization and state health officials.

I was so deeply moved, because the petition came almost exactly a decade from the time Selvi had been imprisoned in the Madras reformatory. And here she was, a decade later, fighting for the hundreds of women who were in exactly the same unjust predicament.

The reasons for despair as well as hope were embodied in this. The terrible abuse of sex workers by the police, judiciary, health officials and other oppressors hadn't diminished even one iota. But what had changed radically was the fact that sex workers were not only overcoming the shame that had crippled them, but also insisting that it was not enough that they be tolerated, pitied or even treated sympathetically as victims: they insisted on being treated as equals. They insisted on speaking without secrecy or shame. They insisted that their basic human rights be honoured. They were organizing to fight for all this. And not only had they won allies to their cause in civil society as well as influential policy positions, they were also—astonishingly—often leading these battles themselves.

These developments were so extraordinary that they ameliorated some of the anger I had been left with after researching poverty in rural northern India, on realizing that there had been so little material progress for hundreds of millions of impoverished people there. I began to appreciate that India's democracy had—at least by now, a half-century since Independence—started offering real opportunities vis-à-vis grassroots and civil society activism. This activism offered even the most deeply downtrodden groups some chance to improve their social position, if not usually their material circumstances. Whether the mobilization of sex workers could be translated into meaningful legal and policy changes to benefit them was still unclear.

Another path-breaking sex workers' collective I visited was the Durbar Mahila Samanwaya Committee—Bengali for the 'Indomitable Women's Collaborative' Committee—in the Sonagachi red-light area in my hometown of Calcutta. It had already won fame far beyond the limits of the public health fraternity. the *New York Times*, the *Economist*, the BBC and innumerable other media organizations had showcased how the collective had rapidly succeeded in checking HIV as well as securing across-the-board progress for Sonagachi's sex workers.

Sonagachi, the largest and oldest of Calcutta's twenty-plus red-light areas, was in the congested, older part of the city that I barely knew, a world apart from the airy southern side built by the British where I had grown up. It abutted the Marble Palace and other opulent mansions of the Bengali merchant-princes and zamindars who had prospered hand-in-glove with the British.

This proximity reflected Sonagachi's history, from the early 19th century, as being the residence of rich men's mistresses as well as talented courtesans. But after Independence, the comprador fortunes had been lost, the mansions had crumbled, and Sonagachi had gone from being the venue of courtly pleasure for elite Bengali men to a place where primarily blue-collar workers and migrant labourers bought cheap sex.

By now, it had lost its distinctive architecture. The three- and four-storey buildings that lined the narrow lanes and even narrower by-lanes were dilapidated and of no clear vintage. But what struck me was that there was neither the intense sexuality nor the overwhelming filth of Bombay's major red-light areas, such as Kamathipura and Falkland Road.

Though there were women lining the pavements as well as every doorway and verandah, more often than not they were engrossed in conversations with each other. Only a few flirted with prospective clients. Most looked like middle-aged Bengali housewives—dressed in traditional sarees, hair pulled back in simple buns or thick plaits, foreheads often adorned with large red bindis, wearing conventional jewellery. Very few wore the gaudy sarees, tight pants and revealing halters favoured in the Bombay areas.

The men didn't seem to be driven by urgency either, casually eating or chatting in groups at the area's countless hole-in-the-wall food stalls. I spotted just one liquor store, a large place that functioned as a cheap, informal bar, in contrast to the innumerable places selling alcohol in Kamathipura and Falkland Road.

Calcutta's chaotic everyday life continued all around—scooters and hand-pulled rickshaws fighting for space while small shops and pavement-hawkers sold everything from vegetables to cheap clothes.

There were barefoot children in rags working at eateries, and street cats and dogs scrounging through the refuse. Bengali pop music blared from a music shop, and Bollywood songs and television chatter emerged from many a building. Though narrow open drains ran along the sides of every lane, the area was no dirtier than any other low-income residential area in Calcutta.

The sex work here was very different from that of both Madras and Bombay. In Sonagachi, an estimated ten thousand sex workers operated from small rooms and brothels, while Madras had no comparably large population of brothel-based sex workers. And while a large proportion of Bombay's brothel-based sex workers came from outside Maharashtra—from as near as Karnataka to as far as Nepal—the overwhelming majority of Sonagachi's sex workers were Bengalis from the same state or across the border, from Bangladesh. A small proportion were 'Agrawalis'—women from Agra or other parts of northern India, who had lived in Bengal for generations, commanding higher rates by tradition and now owning or working at high-end brothels on two adjacent streets, their large, well-furnished rooms even boasting of air-conditioners.

The exact terms on which women worked in Sonagachi varied, with their operations ranging from one-woman businesses to brothels that housed two to three dozen women. A large number of women gave their landlord or brothel-keeper half their daily earnings, in exchange for a place to live as well as do business—the dank cell-like rooms, all of two hundred square feet, that almost every old or new building in Sonagachi had been divided into.

A substantial number of women were self-employed, renting their rooms. Their numbers included several thousand 'flying' sex workers, the local term for low or middle-income housewives who commuted to Sonagachi during the day, supplementing their household incomes by servicing clients at high-end brothels or in rented rooms.

The worst-off among Sonagachi's residents were those who had been trafficked as girls or young women, and remained bonded sexual labourers to their madams—forced to work under brutal conditions, with no rest or choice over clients and sexual practices. This would continue until they escaped or paid off the amount they had been 'bought' for, a process that typically took years.

The changes that transformed the condition of Sonagachi's sex workers had begun innocuously. In 1992, the government's All India Institute of Hygiene and Public Health, located in Calcutta, started an HIV prevention project in the area. The project, like other mainstream efforts of that time, intended to treat sexually transmitted infections as well as promote condom use through peer educators drawn from sex workers themselves. But Dr Smarajit Jana, a young Bengali epidemiologist, who had been assigned to run the project, quickly realized that the effort would make little headway if it retained its narrow focus on AIDS.

He saw that it was only when he began to ask the sex workers about their lives and problems, rather than their sexual infections, that they began confiding in him. 'It touched my heart to know that they were not only supporting their children but also their extended families, which often included parents, brothers and sisters,' said Jana, a slight, bespectacled man a decade older than me. One result was that instead of treating just syphilis and gonorrhoea, the health clinic that opened in Sonagachi wound up providing primary care to women and children. For the first time, Sonagachi's sex workers had an alternative to quack doctors.

Without conscious direction on anyone's part, the project began to knit together the sex workers, beginning with those who had been hired as peer educators. The peer educators surmised that only when all the sex workers in each and every brothel in Sonagachi banded together, could they ensure that some women did not break ranks and operate without condoms. Together, they could also challenge pimps or madams if they tried to force women to accept customers opposed to using condoms.

Though these women had often been in desperate competition

with each other, they were now beginning to unite. One telling sign of this new sense of solidarity was the fact that the literate women in the project had started teaching the others to read in makeshift daily classes, a practice that has since continued.

This deepening sense of solidarity led the women to begin demanding things that went far beyond the project's HIV-focused mandate and instead, addressed head-on the oppression they had chronically suffered. They wanted the terrifying police raids, with their risk of arbitrary imprisonment and abuse, to stop. They wanted the police to protect them from abusive hoodlums and madams. They wanted a place to borrow money at fair rates, rather than end up indebted for life to local moneylenders, who would flagrantly cheat the largely illiterate women by charging interest rates extending even to a thousand per cent a year.

This resolve was less surprising in Bengal than probably anywhere else in India. Several centuries of progressive movements had emancipated Bengal's women in many ways. While poor and low-income women were far more assertive and autonomous than the norm for India, middle and upper-income women were often highly educated and held professional jobs as doctors, teachers and academics. Tellingly, few younger women in Bengal ever kept their heads covered with their saree pallus, or looked down when interacting with men, the unrelenting norms of subservience for ordinary women in much of India.

The upshot was that, in 1995, with Jana's backing, Sonagachi's sex workers formed a collective to fight for their rights, with its assertive name of Durbar Mahila, or Indomitable Women. The Durbar, as it is popularly known, is essentially a labour union, rather than merely a collective, and by 1999, when I first paid it a visit, the group had about thirty thousand members, all of them sex workers. The state rules governing co-operative societies required the workers to be euphemistically passed off as housewives, but Sonagachi's sex workers pushed Bengal's Left government to amend them to officially allow sex workers to form a financial co-operative. That was the first breakthrough in getting the government to consider sex work as legitimate work.

The co-operative began to break the vicious cycle of debt caused by the moneylenders' exorbitant rates and cheating by providing loans to its members at nominal rates. Later, it also began a micro-credit fund and alternative employment scheme for retired or out-of-work sex workers, who were otherwise reduced to begging.

Another immediate target of the Durbar was to quell the violence they suffered at the hands of local criminals, abusive brothel-keepers, and the police themselves. Thuggish local men, a common feature in Calcutta's slums and lower-middle-income neighbourhoods, were an especially strong force in Sonagachi and other red-light areas, running gambling, liquor or drug dens, or acting as pimps and procurers. They extorted money and free sex from sex workers, especially the newer ones.

They could act with impunity because many—despite their criminal activities—were also leaders of neighbourhood association 'clubs' and even branch offices of political parties. The local police did not act against them as they were deeply corrupt themselves, profiting from weekly or monthly bribes from brothel-keepers. In any case, the keepers of the law behaved just as criminally towards sex workers, extorting money or sex under the threat of fines or arrest, or summarily beating and imprisoning them.

These old patterns of abuse were challenged as hundreds of the Durbar's members held noisy protests at police stations whenever any woman faced abuse. Their collective strength and militant show of resolve tipped the balance in their favour. The local police grudgingly began to reform themselves, thinking twice before abusing or exploiting the sex workers. They also overcame their reluctance to act against the thugs and brothel-keepers, and this source of violence fell dramatically. The Durbar had turned into a force to be reckoned with in Sonagachi—a place where only madams, pimps, hoodlums and moneylenders used to reign, and the only governmental presence was that of the corrupt, exploitative police force.

In the year I first visited Sonagachi, the Durbar also formalized its efforts to combat the trafficking of girls or women who were sold or forced into the trade. The women abhorred the brutality inflicted on trafficked persons, some of them having suffered this cruelty first-hand too. It was also in their self-interest to check trafficking, considering that the availability of girls took lucrative business away from them in a market that prizes youth.

The Durbar began 'Self-Regulatory Boards' in each and every red-light area that they worked in. Every new entrant to the red-light areas had to appear before the board, where she had to prove that she was over eighteen and was willingly joining the profession. To ensure rigour and honesty, each of the boards had broad community and governmental representation, including members of the Durbar; a reputed local lawyer and doctor; local staff from the government's social welfare, health and labour departments; and an elected official, typically a local city councillor or member of the state legislature. At the state level, the steering committee of the boards included representatives from various West Bengal state commissions, such as the women's commission.

Soon, hundreds of women were being quizzed by the board each year. As a result, according to project surveys, the percentage of trafficked girls or women in Sonagachi and other areas dropped from about one in four in 1992 to about one in thirty by the end of the decade. It was only among the 'Agrawalis'—who viewed themselves as superior and ethnically different from the poorer Bengali women of the Durbar—that trafficking persisted, with young women from their communities continuing to be forced into the occupation. With the visible decline in the trafficking of girls, the police began to cut back on raids.

Education for sex workers and their children was another priority for the Durbar. Just one in six of Sonagachi's sex workers had any level of literacy in 1992. In less than a decade, as the adult literacy effort was formalized and expanded, nearly one in two were functionally literate. For their children—who inevitably abandoned schools after being tormented by teachers or fellow students because of their Sonagachi connection—the sex workers started crèches, tuition centres, residential schools and vocational training programmes.

On the public health front, the original intention of the effort, the gains were enormous. The percentage of Sonagachi's sex workers who reported that they always insisted on condoms rose from almost nothing to 90 per cent by 1998. HIV prevalence eventually peaked at a little over 5 per cent, a fraction of the levels reached among sex workers in brothels elsewhere in India, including Mumbai or Pune, where more than half of them were HIV-positive.

These dynamics meant that by the year of my first visit to Sonagachi, a narrow HIV prevention effort had been transformed into a large sex worker-led collective that tackled the social injustice as well as health risks faced by them. The Durbar's goal was to win radical improvements for themselves, their children and other dependents. The collective now covered several red-light districts in Calcutta as well as other places in Bengal. It operated thirty-three health clinics, and its staff included 261 sex workers as educators and team leaders, besides a hundred other professionals, ranging from accountants to doctors.

In that very year, the Durbar even took over the management of the HIV prevention efforts from the All India Institute of Hygiene. Every aspect of the Durbar's work was now entirely led by sex workers themselves. Though Jana was still a pivotal presence, providing counsel and encouragement, he no longer led the effort. A sex worker explained his continuing role in the Durbar as being that of 'a father and a mother to us'.

There was no doubting the changes wrought by the Durbar. Every sex worker I met, even the quietest in demeanour, had an underlying sense of confidence about her. Many were exceptionally assertive, talking to me as an equal and displaying neither nervousness nor the sense of imbibed shame I often saw among sex workers I had interviewed. They had found self-respect through their collective power.

Equally telling of this change was that the Durbar women strove to improve public opinion and policies about sex work just as much as they tried to alter their grassroots realities. Echoing the thoughts of Selvi, Mary Thomas and the other women who had contributed to the 1996 National Commission for Women report, the paramount demand voiced by the Durbar's women was that sex work should be decriminalized.

But, strikingly, the Durbar's women had a corollary demand—that the government recognize their occupation as legitimate work, with sex workers being guaranteed the same rights as other workers.

In the 'Sex Workers' Manifesto' published in 1997, the Durbar's women wrote, 'Sex work is also an occupation, and it is probably one of the oldest professions in the world because it meets an important social demand ... [But] we are refused enfranchisement as legitimate citizens or workers, and are banished to the margins of society and history. The kind of oppression that can be meted out to a sex worker can never be perpetrated against a regular worker. The justification given is that sex work is not real work—it is morally sinful.' Here, they asked unapologetically: 'Why cannot sex workers remain in the sex industry and demand a better deal in their life and work?'

While this would have seemed an unrealizable claim almost anywhere else in India, in Bengal the demand had mainstream legitimacy. It resonated with the state's ethos of peasant and workers' movements, dating back over a century and culminating in decades of democratic Leftist administration. Even in Tamil Nadu, with its long history of social reform movements, sex workers at SIAAP and other organizations focused on decriminalization alone, rather than also demanding workers' rights. This difference was rooted in the fact that workers' movements in this state have never enjoyed the power and status they command in Bengal.

And indeed, the Durbar's assertion that sex workers deserved the rights due to all workers readily found acceptance amongst Bengal's intellectuals—a particularly influential force in shaping public

DMSC

Durbar's sex workers demonstrate against punitive laws

opinion in the state. They included littérateurs Mahasweta Devi and Sunil Gangopadhyay, playwright Badal Sarkar, film directors Goutam Ghosh and Rituparno Ghosh, and numerous activists and leftist political leaders.

There was soon vivid proof of this widening acceptance, something that amounted to a gigantic cultural shift. In late 1997, the Durbar hosted India's first national conference of sex workers, and the chief guest was none other than the country's Home Minister, the legendary Communist leader, Indrajit Gupta. In an opening speech delivered in Bengali, Gupta told the cheering audience of three thousand sex workers who had gathered from places across India, that he supported their demands for decriminalizing sex work and providing the full panoply of labour rights. He assured them that he would take this fight to Parliament.

My regret at not being at the conference intensified when I heard of Gupta's extraordinarily courageous statement. I knew of no precedent in India, or almost anywhere else in developing countries barring Brazil, of a person in such an influential government post advocating for the rights of sex workers. But, given what I knew of Gupta (my admiration had led me to interview him on rural poverty during my journalism days in Delhi), I was not surprised that he had displayed the courage to officially take this stand. Ever since his days in the freedom movement, and for forty years in the Communist Party, he had unwaveringly stuck by positions and causes he held to be right—no matter how controversial or unpopular. That resolve had clearly not waned, even though Gupta was now in his late seventies. Gupta's speech raised my hopes that he would initiate far-reaching legal and policy reforms on sex work, but this came to nought with the fall of Prime Minister I.K. Gujral's government just a few months later.

The extraordinary scale of the Durbar's achievements became even clearer to me on my next trip to Calcutta, in early 2001, for the launch of my book on AIDS. I had timed this visit so as to not miss the first-ever national mela of sex workers, organized by the Durbar.

They called it the Millennium Milan Mela. Milan means a celebratory gathering in Bengali and Hindi, and this gathering was to celebrate the dawning of a new millennium in the worldwide struggle of sex workers for their rights. By this time, the efforts of a number of national and international networks, including the informal coalition that would become the Global Network of Sex Work Projects, had brought sex workers from the global north and south together. They together declared the mela's opening day—3 March—as International Sex Workers' Rights Day.

The friends I had made at the Durbar told me that they had received thousands of visitors every day, surpassing their best hopes. So it was that I went with much anticipation to visit the mela. But what I saw far outstripped even my expectations, leaving me awestruck at what these women had managed to achieve in less than a decade.

To begin with, the mela—like the 1997 national conference—was also held at Salt Lake Stadium, the iconic site of countless political rallies, rather than some minor venue. This itself testified to the Durbar's influence in Bengal. And then, when I reached the stadium, I saw that there were huge crowds milling and queuing up for tickets outside, as if they were at a routine fair or circus. Inside, the normality was the most astonishing thing.

The crowd of thousands consisted overwhelmingly of average, everyday couples and families with children of all ages. All of them seemed to be enjoying every aspect of the mela—the food stalls, the folk dances and puppet shows, the workshops and panel discussions about the realities and hardships faced by sex workers. Nobody reacted negatively to the fact that the people manning the stalls, doing the dance performances, and speaking up with great passion during the discussions, were women sex workers and their children, with a sprinkling of hijra and kothi sex workers. There was no leering or rudeness. There was complete normality, just like a conventional mela for families.

I was elated. The Durbar's paramount goal—that they be treated with the same respect as other workers—was being achieved. They were being accepted as regular, ordinary people by Calcutta's public—as equals. I felt enormous pride in being a child of this city, with its celebration of rational thinking and its humanistic ethos.

I even began to hope that what I was witnessing at the Calcutta mela could eventually be the norm for all of India. Perhaps the marked gentleness, characteristic of many Indians, the generally live-and-let-live attitude and the lack of polarized views on most social matters—in such sharp contrast to the US, where many people seemed to be permanently inflamed with self-righteous moralizing—meant that we Indians had the potential to gradually rid ourselves of the abhorrent legacies of British colonialism. I wanted to believe this—that we Indians had a unique potential at this point in our history for acting humanely, for building a just and caring society. Otherwise, what would be the point of the egalitarian possibilities offered by our new democracy, the highs of philosophical understanding that had emerged here over the millennia, and all the evidence that many people here were singularly compassionate?

My sense that things could start improving radically for sex workers was also encouraged by changes at the global level. An increasing number of influential organizations—including the Ford Foundation and key UN bodies—were speaking up for their well-being and human rights. Some of that attention had emerged from distinct, recent global movements, ranging from efforts to tackle violence against women worldwide to greater recognition of sexual rights as an integral part of universal human rights (whether it was the right of women to freely make decisions about their sexuality and reproduction, or the right of gays to express their sexuality as well as to be treated on a par with heterosexuals in every sphere of life.) But the most powerful impetus had been the AIDS pandemic.

The UN's efforts to tackle the pandemic had fallen into disrepair after Jonathan Mann's resignation from the World Health Organization in 1990, but half a decade later it was rejuvenated by the launch of the UN Joint Programme on AIDS (UNAIDS), which synchronized the AIDS-specific efforts of several UN organizations and the World Bank through a Geneva-based Secretariat. I was filled with admiration for the fledgling effort when, within a few years, it published two landmark sets of guidelines to help policymakers protect human rights, while responding to the mammoth challenges raised by AIDS.

In both, much of the focus was inevitably on the marginalized groups hardest hit by the disease, including sex workers and gay men. The advice on sex work drew on the lessons learned from Sonagachi and other effective HIV prevention efforts, which had been closely documented in 'Best Practice' studies undertaken by UNAIDS. Consequently, because of UNAIDS's intense efforts, there was now an impressive body of knowledge about the situation of sex workers worldwide as well as judicious guidance on the most sensible policies.

The keystone of the UN's guidance was the *International Guidelines on HIV/AIDS and Human Rights*, developed jointly by UNAIDS and the UN Office of the High Commissioner for Human Rights in 1998. This compendium had been formulated by human rights experts from academia and civil society, and representatives of organizations of people living with HIV. The guidelines general position on sex work and other outlawed sexuality was clear from a comment that noted, 'Criminal law prohibiting sexual acts (including adultery, sodomy, fornication and commercial sexual encounters) between consenting adults in private should be reviewed, with the aim of repeal'.

And specifically on sex work, the guidelines emphasized, 'With regard to adult sex work that involves no victimization, criminal law should be reviewed with the aim of decriminalizing, then legally regulating occupational health and safety conditions to protect sex workers and their clients, including support for safe sex.'

It was striking to see that the international experts writing these guidelines had arrived at precisely the same conclusions urged by the sex workers of Sonagachi's Durbar as well as Priscilla Alexander in her World Bank newsletter article. This convergence of views had come about at astonishing speed, considering that it had been less than five years since Priscilla Alexander wrote despairingly, 'With any other occupation, such basic demands would not be controversial, but with sex work, few policymakers are even willing to participate in an open discussion.' A viewpoint that had nearly cost me my job at the World Bank was now accepted by several UN organizations, the Bank itself and other pillars of the international system. They had been convinced by the plain merits of the argument that the grievous wrongs suffered by sex workers could be corrected only by providing them more rights.

And then, a year later, UNAIDS and the Inter Parliamentary Union—an influential association of the world's parliamentarians—published a detailed, five-hundred-page handbook to guide governments and legislators the world over in taking action against HIV, in line with international human rights commitments.

The handbook commented, 'Most prostitution laws are founded on 19th century notions of morality and were ineffective then, as now, in suppressing the industry while there continues to be a demand-driven market. By treating sex work as a personal service industry which is neither condemned nor condoned, public health objectives are much more likely to be achieved than under the criminal law.'

Like the guidelines, the handbook also advised governments to 'decriminalize sex work where no victimization is involved, and regulate occupational health and safety conditions to protect sex workers and their clients'. And, crucially, it emphasized that criminalization itself fuelled a cycle of brutally unjust practices because sex workers were seen as 'criminals'. Some of these practices were 'automatic reductions in penalties for rape of prostitutes', their imprisonment 'in rehabilitation centres or medical programmes against their will', and the requirement that they 'use special identity cards, or have their papers, such as passports, marked with their occupation'.

This sea change in thinking had begun to impact global opinion leaders. 'The inexorable trend, in both law and public morals, is towards legalisation of what is already tolerated,' the *Economist* commented in an extensive article on sex work. 'That would free law-enforcers to concentrate on what is not tolerated, such as the sexual exploitation of children. And it would put the greater part of the sex business where it ultimately belongs—as just another branch of the global entertainment industry.'

All this made me begin to hope that governments the world over would now gradually be convinced of the need to act fairly towards sex workers. Despite my doubts of the past and the clear odds—it was one thing for the UN to recommend sensible policies, but quite another for governments to accept or act on them—I began to feel guardedly optimistic that the momentum was favourable for their emancipation, particularly in democratic India. Only then would the sacrifices made by all the sex workers who had suffered and died—and who had fought so bravely for their rights—not have gone in vain.

15

An Era of Uncertainty

The AIDS epidemic was also irretrievably altering the lives of Indian gay men and transwomen. But these changes were so rife with contradiction and paradox that I often could not decide where they were leading us, whether they spelt the start of freedom or the worsening of oppression.

I began to learn about many of these changes in the company of Sekar, a gay man in Chennai who generously volunteered to help me with research for the book on AIDS that I was working on in the late 1990s. Sekar was resolutely open not just about being gay but also about being HIV-positive. I felt afraid for him on both counts.

Barely anyone outside elite circles was open about being gay. And even now, fifteen years into India's epidemic, people discovered to be HIV-positive were being thrown out of jobs and homes, refused medical care, and driven to suicide. But here was Sekar, a slight, bedraggled figure in a colourless safari suit that hinted at his precarious finances, looking immeasurably older than his mid-thirties because of his thinning hair and the dark skin turned grey from ill-health, insisting on speaking out on both matters.

Provided by author

Sekar

Sekar had been diagnosed with HIV in the early 1990s. He had soon sought out Shyamala Nataraj at SIAAP, as she was one of the few people in the city known for non-judgemental advice and support. His activism had been catalysed at the group, watching the example of the numerous HIV-positive sex workers, including Selvi, working there as peer educators. In 1996, with seed funding and technical advice from SIAAP, Sekar branched out on his own to set up Ambu Illam—or House of Love—an organization meant to provide counselling on HIV to gay and bisexual men.

But at this point, the Tamil Nadu state government dismissed Sekar's urging that large numbers of men were contracting HIV from sex with other men or transwomen. 'The government kept insisting that the "MSM" population is very small,' Sekar explained. MSM is the acronym for 'men who have sex with men', an expansive term coined in HIV prevention in an attempt to describe the reality, particularly outside the industrialized West, that men who enjoy sex with other men or transwomen often do so without considering themselves to be gay or even bisexual.

'I told them that the population is, in fact, large and that many were getting infected,' said Sekar. 'It is only that these men are not visible—that it is a hidden population. But the government did not listen. They didn't understand that whenever a man who is gay goes to the hospital, when doctors ask him questions about how he got infected with HIV or an STD, he always says that it happened from sex with women. No man will admit that he had sex with another man or aravani! They know they will face discrimination if they tell their true story.' (Aravani is the preferred Tamil term for India's traditional 'third gender' as well as other transwomen, referring to the Mahabharata legend that Lord Krishna took on the female form of Mohini to marry the Pandava prince Aravan.)

'So the results make it seem like hardly any of the men infected are MSM, making the government say that MSM are not at risk of AIDS,' he added.

Failing to find consistent financial support, Ambu Illam folded in a matter of years.

But Sekar's dogged openness turned him into living, incontrovertible proof that the AIDS epidemic was taking its toll among our ranks and that HIV prevention services were desperately needed. He didn't seem perturbed to take on this fraught role, which even Dominic D'Souza, despite his courage about being HIV-positive, had avoided less than a decade earlier.

This was so in part because Sekar was among the second generation of HIV-positive gay men in India, and though they faced a dangerous world too, it was much less hostile than what Dominic and the others—whose infections came to light in the 1980s—had to face. Thus, by this time in the late 1990s, AIDS was no longer an unknown danger, igniting hysteria among officials and the public. Year after year, India's wildfire epidemic had been making headlines, and virtually everyone at least knew about such a disease. Countless Indians had become infected. Many who knew their status had joined 'positive-people' groups, like the pioneering one started by Dominic in 1991, finding a blessed sense of support and community.

And now, astonishingly, there was even hope that AIDS was not inevitably a death sentence. Since 1996, treatment with anti-retroviral drug combinations had given HIV-positive individuals in rich countries a potentially indefinite lease on a healthy life. The annual AIDS death toll in the US had fallen by half within just two years, from a peak of over fifty thousand deaths in 1995, immediately before the treatments became available, a decline that almost defied belief. Though only wealthy Indians could afford treatment (as the drug combinations cost $16,000 a year), everyone began to hope that by some miracle—however improbable—they would get a regular supply of this elixir of life.

For all these reasons, the new generation of activist gay men, particularly those who contracted HIV, had begun to break the tacit agreement we had maintained in the epidemic's early years to refrain from drawing attention to the fact that HIV was spreading amongst us. Instead, they had started demanding HIV prevention efforts for the country's vast numbers of gay and bisexual men, emphasizing that they were at grave risk.

Their demands were amplified by a handful of HIV-positive transwomen. The amorphous pan-sexuality of many non-elite Indian men meant that they had sex interchangeably with women, other men and transwomen, often hinging simply on what was most easily available. Consequently, they were all part of the same epidemic cycle.

The most forceful of the transwomen activists was Noori, whom I also met in Chennai. Noori was a decade or more older than me—a tall, angular figure in a saree wound awkwardly around her like wrapping paper, the traditional make-up and jewellery sitting oddly on her strong square-jawed features. She had worked with a 'positive people's' network before starting her own grassroots group, focused on aiding transwomen.

'I found out many years ago that I was infected with AIDS,' Noori told me. 'I was in Bombay then, living in a rented house with other aravanis. I earned most of my money through sex with men. But after finding out that I was infected, I never sold sex again.'

'I moved back to Chennai once I fell very sick, as I longed to be with other Tamil people. And it's cheaper here, so my savings will last longer. They also treat you better in Chennai hospitals. In Mumbai, hospitals won't treat aravanis even if they don't have AIDS! The prejudice in that city is so bad, the police won't even allow aravanis to beg!

'Anyway, most of my aravani friends in Mumbai are dead or dying. But now, so are many of the aravanis here and in other parts of Tamil Nadu. We finally got some money from the government to educate ourselves about AIDS. But it's too late for most of us!' Her voice was filled with anger.

At some point, in the course of the days I spent with her, I realized that Noori's forcefulness went far beyond even the obvious. She was the only person living with HIV who seemed dismissive about the disease and uncaring about the future. There was none of that feverish preoccupation with the impending death sentence that HIV brings or that desperate quest for a regular supply of anti-AIDS medicines, which I witnessed with virtually every other HIV-positive person in India. Even in the preternaturally calm Sekar, these anxieties broke through occasionally.

But Noori talked about AIDS as if it were just another one of the many unpleasant things life had dealt her. Perhaps the constant trials she endured had developed this exceptional toughness in her. Whatever the precise reasons for her forcefulness, it helped Noori become a formidable activist for HIV prevention for transwomen, pushing the government of Tamil Nadu to begin funding HIV prevention efforts far before any other state.

I came to appreciate just how essential it was for transwomen to develop this toughness while interviewing several younger aravanis in the city. The dangers and hardships that beset them were of an extreme that far dwarfed even that borne by gay men. The crux of the difference was that while we gay men were largely invisible, having learnt to pass ourselves off as straight men, transwomen wore their gender change publicly all the time—facing reactions that were almost always hostile the minute they left the neighbourhoods they lived in (where there was often some tolerance and even acceptance as people knew them personally).

'There are always problems when an aravani ventures outside her area,' a young transwoman, who looked more adolescent than adult, told me. 'I go twice a week to Mount Road for begging. But we can't travel in the public bus in peace! Even educated men, especially the youngsters, behave indecently. They speak such filthy words! The young men will say a thousand things, call us dirty names and sing obscene songs. No one will help us! They will just watch! But if we say one thing in response, that will become a big issue. A fight.

'As for going to see a movie, it is almost impossible! It is an ordeal to sit through a movie in a theater. The men sitting behind us pinch us or keep shoving us with their legs! And even if we manage without problems inside the movie hall, it starts once we come out after the film!'

However, this harassment was a mere irritant compared to the terrible sexual violence they suffer. It was chilling to hear that almost every one of these younger transwomen had been raped, often by policemen or by gangs of men. The most gentle of them, a slight, dark woman in her twenties, told me in a trembling voice that just a few weeks ago she had been staying overnight at her mother's hut when a gang of men broke open the door, lifted her up, and tried to carry her away. She was saved by their immediate neighbours in the shantytown.

It was clear that many men thought of the transwomen only as sexual objects for having voluntarily chosen to become female, almost as if they imagined that transwomen had changed their gender out of an unquenchable desire to be fucked. The sexual violence against them was of the same unhinged intensity as that against women sex workers—as if the association with sex had debased them so much that they had forfeited their claim to be treated as humans.

From every one of the transwomen I spoke to, including Noori, it was apparent that the police, far from providing help, were probably their worst oppressors. Though the colonial-era Criminal Tribes Act that criminalized 'eunuchs' had been scrapped in 1949, the police retained the notion that transwomen were inveterate criminals, bent on kidnapping young boys to castrate and force into prostitution, or involved in petty theft and extortion. Their reliance on sex work, begging and public dancing—conventional jobs being closed to them because of intolerance—also fed the police's animus.

The upshot of these prejudices was that transwomen were routinely persecuted by the police under the anti-sodomy Section 377 as well as India's multitude of vagrancy, public nuisance and anti-begging laws, all dating back to the colonial era. The police singled them out for any crimes that occurred locally. The police also felt emboldened to act against them en masse—for instance, fining or imprisoning dozens in anti-begging drives, irrespective of whether any of them were involved or not—treating them as a homogenous mass of criminality and perversion.

These interviews left me shaken and enraged in no small part as I could see myself in these younger aravanis, with their stories of how they felt feminine as children and wished to dance and wear women's finery. If I had been born to an impoverished or even a middle class family rather than a wealthy, anglicized one, I might have had no choice but to be one of them. This was the only traditionally available space—however dishonoured and reviled by now—for Indian males to express femininity and same-sex desire.

By the late 1990s, the open advocacy by Sekar and Noori in Chennai as well as a handful of pioneering activists in other major cities had begun to convince key government officials that a significant proportion of Indian men had sex with other men as well as transwomen, and that increasingly large numbers were contracting HIV. By now, there was also enough data to back these claims.

Studies in Goa, Mumbai and Tamil Nadu—typically conducted by the fledgling groups that had recently launched HIV prevention measures among gay and bisexual men and transwomen—reported HIV prevalence rates ranging from 2 per cent to over 50 per cent. (These huge variations reflected the small sample sizes—many people avoided HIV tests for fear of finding out that they were infected—and the use of differing methodologies.)

Research commissioned by the government's National AIDS Control Organization about sexual behaviours showed that a substantial share of men, whether in cities or smaller places, were bisexual or pansexual, variously having sex with women, other men or transwomen—a 2001 nationwide survey found that nearly one in three men who visited female sex workers also had sex with one or more male or transgender partners in the past year alone. There were wide but unexplained regional variations: in Manipur, less than one in six clients of female sex workers admitted to recent bisexual behaviour, while nearly one in two confessed to the same in Maharashtra, Goa and Gujarat. (Anyhow, these figures were likely to underestimate the true extent of same-sex relations because of the reluctance of most people to admit to outlawed sexual behaviour, even in anonymous surveys.)

An inflow of international funding now made it possible for grassroots activists and groups to begin expanding HIV prevention services for gay and bisexual men as well as transwomen. As with funding for HIV-focused sex worker groups like the Durbar and SIAAP, the lead was taken by forward-thinking donors like the Ford Foundation and Hivos, and then by the official aid organizations of Western European governments. The government did not stand in the way of this funding going directly to non-governmental groups. But barely any of the government's own, larger funding—from the World Bank-financed national programme—was directed to gay-focused HIV prevention efforts, reflecting lingering prejudices within NACO's leadership.

Even so, the net result was an enormous and rapid increase in the number of groups focused on gay and bisexual men and transwomen. Thus, even till the late 1990s, there had probably been no more than half a dozen such grassroots groups, all concentrated in major cities. But, by 2005, there were dozens spread across even provincial capitals and small towns.

The upshot was that gay and bisexual men as well as transwomen in cities and towns nationwide now began to encounter outreach workers—typically, local gay men or transwomen themselves—in their cruising areas after nightfall. They advised them about safer sex, provided condoms and illustrated safe-sex guides, urged them to join their support groups or meet their counsellors, and offered to help intervene in family conflicts or with police raids. Telephone helplines manned by these groups gave advice and support to those unwilling to risk being seen at the offices of HIV-focused organizations.

It was very far from being enough to end the epidemic's onslaught among them, but it was still a quantum leap from the utter neglect of the past. And, crucially, the spread of these groups ended up fuelling gay and transgender activism across India in pursuit of their needs and rights.

One outcome of these changing dynamics was that in December 2001 the Delhi High Court admitted a second petition challenging the constitutional validity of Section 377 of the Indian Penal Code. This came nearly eight years after ABVA, the activist group in which my friend Siddhartha had been a driving force, had filed a first challenge in the same court.

That case had petered out, becoming a victim of the deadening pace of India's appallingly under-resourced, inefficient and often corrupt judicial system where cases can drag on unresolved for decades—sometimes even when all the original litigants have long passed away. (A Chief Justice of the Delhi High Court famously noted that at its current pace of operations, it would take the court nearly five hundred years to clear just the backlog of pending criminal appeal cases.) But, there was reason enough to hope that this second challenge would make more headway than the 1994 case. The two civil society groups that had filed this challenge were better resourced than the ABVA collective, and were therefore probably better placed to deal with the judiciary's institutionalized weaknesses.

The petition against the government had been filed in the public interest by the Naz India, one of the very first groups to begin HIV prevention efforts for gay men and transwomen. The Delhi-based group was founded in 1994 by Anjali Gopalan on her return from New York City, where she had worked as a grassroots counsellor with gay men and substance users. The legal challenge was being handled by Anand Grover, the human rights lawyer who had become deeply involved with HIV-related law since representing Dominic D'Souza in 1989.

Neither Grover nor Gopalan was gay, but they had taken up the cause of gays as well as gender minorities because they could see the gross injustice inflicted on them by homophobic prejudices and laws. They both made me hopeful about India, that activism by forward-thinking individuals had flourished to the point where they were willing to take up causes long considered beyond the pale of respectability.

In the decade since he had fought for Dominic D'Souza, Grover and his colleagues at the Lawyers Collective had taken on dozens of cases of AIDS-related abuses, fighting them pro bono. They had sued employers who sacked HIV-positive employees. They had fought hospitals that refused to care for the HIV-positive or flagrantly leaked their test results. Most recently, they had challenged global intellectual property laws that priced life-saving anti-retroviral drugs far beyond the reach of all but the wealthiest of Indians.

Grover and his team—which included several openly gay lawyers—brought this vast experience to bear in framing the Naz India petition. It challenged the constitutional validity of Section 377 on several grounds.

Like the 1994 challenge by ABVA, this petition also emphasized that decriminalization of consensual, adult same-sex relations was now urgently needed as Section 377 jeopardized HIV prevention efforts among 'men who have sex with men'. They were driven away from health services and other HIV prevention efforts by realistic fears of police abuse and social discrimination spawned by Section 377. The higher risk of HIV that these individuals consequently faced was a violation of the right to life guaranteed in the Indian Constitution. 'Section 377 is therefore dangerous and irresponsible legislation which infringes upon the right to life,' the petition argued.

Additionally, the Naz petition noted that Section 377's prohibition of private, consensual relations violated the right to privacy, which is guaranteed 'within the ambit of the right to liberty' in the Constitution. As these were private, consensual relations between adults, the state could not show a sufficiently compelling interest on the grounds of 'public morality' to justify such restriction of the fundamental right to privacy. It also argued that the punishment of ten years to life imprisonment prescribed in Section 377 was 'unconscionably harsh, especially since the impugned provision encompasses private sexual activity between consenting adults absent any evidence of palpable harm'.

Throughout, the petition emphasized that Section 377 reflected the imposition of colonial English law and Victorian morality on Indian culture, as the criminalization of 'sexual acts which are "against the order of nature" ... is based upon traditional Judeo-Christian moral and ethical standards, which conceive of sex in purely functional terms, that is, for the purpose of procreation only'.

The petition noted, 'Until the enactment of Section 377, there had been no record in Indian culture of the harsh criminal punishments employed in Europe and the Americas for persons engaging in the sexual acts encompassed by Section 377. Indian ethos and culture do not share the same historical intolerance of alternative sexual behaviours. Thus, the legislative object of Section 377 enjoys no historical rationale in Indian society prior to its introduction in the IPC by the British Raj.' Section 377 was an archaic, alien law, and the time had come to end its use in independent India.

Another key theme of the Naz India petition was emphasizing the precedents in international human rights norms that had, by now, established that the criminalizing of adult, consensual same-sex sexual conduct was a violation of basic human rights. The turning point had come a few years earlier, in 1994, when the United Nations Human Rights Committee—which interprets and monitors compliance with the International Covenant on Civil and Political Rights (ICCPR)—decided, in the case of *Toonen v. Australia,* that an Australian law criminalizing sexual contact between consenting adult men was a violation of that country's obligations as a party to the ICCPR, violating the right to privacy and the right to non-discrimination.

This decision explicitly rejected the regulation of 'public morals' as justification for the criminalization of homosexual relations. It concluded that the anti-discrimination provision of the ICCPR should be understood to prohibit discriminatory treatment on the basis of sexual orientation. After this, the Human Rights Committee, other UN treaty bodies and the UN's Special Rapporteurs began to urge governments to decriminalize same-sex relations and address discrimination as well as other abuses. The Naz petition drew from these developments.

The petition also emphasized that there had been other epochal turning points over the past decade in securing essential freedoms for sexual and gender minorities, which India needed to acknowledge and follow. In virulently homophobic Africa, Mandela's South Africa had emerged as a beacon of right-mindedness by becoming the world's first nation—in 1996—to explicitly prohibit discrimination based on sexual orientation in its Constitution. Two years later, South Africa's highest court struck down an anti-sodomy law akin to India's Section 377.

The Naz India petition extensively cited this thoughtful ruling—*National Coalition for Gay and Lesbian Equality v. Minister of Justice*—which had concluded: 'The harm imposed by the criminal law is far more than symbolic. As a result of the criminal offence, gay men are at risk of arrest, prosecution and conviction of the offence of sodomy simply because they seek to engage in sexual conduct which is part of their experience of being human. Just as apartheid legislation rendered the lives of couples of different racial groups perpetually at risk, the sodomy offence builds insecurity and vulnerability into the daily lives of gay men. There can be no doubt that the existence of a law which punishes a form of sexual expression for gay men degrades and devalues gay men in our broader society. As such, it is a palpable invasion of their dignity.'

And across Europe, Central Asia, the Americas and Australasia, country after country was moving to end the outlawed, outcast status of gays by legislating vital protections and rights. This ranged from the basic steps of decriminalizing same-sex relations and prohibiting discrimination to recognizing civil unions, social benefits, and even marriage as well as adoption of children by same-sex couples. In 2001, the Netherlands became the first country to recognize same-sex marriage and adoption by same-sex couples. Two years later, the US Supreme Court explicitly overturned its own 1986 ruling that had upheld the constitutionality of sodomy, effectively apologizing by saying that its earlier ruling 'was not correct when it was decided, and is not correct today'. Between 1985 and 2005, forty-one countries decriminalized consensual adult same-sex relations, so that for the first time in the contemporary world, homosexuality was legal in a majority of nations.

A growing number of countries granted political asylum to individuals persecuted for their sexual orientation, a policy change backed by the United Nations High Commissioner for Refugees. A handful of countries began to legally recognize same-sex relationships for purposes of immigrant sponsorship.

All these governments were acknowledging that they had been profoundly wrong through the centuries, that they had criminalized us, condemned us as sick or degenerate or disgusting, denied us even the most basic of human rights. At least in these dozens of countries, we gay men and women could finally hope to begin having lives that had some of the same potential for happiness as heterosexuals—to not be thought of as criminals or sinners or perverts, to not live in fear of violence or ostracism, to have legitimate, recognized relationships, to have children, families and homes.

Coming after the persecution and hate that gay people had faced for aeons in so many parts of the world, these possibilities seemed almost unbelievable. I knew that they might not have been won so widely had it not been for AIDS, the 'gay plague' that galvanized so many of us to fight for our survival, uniting us across national boundaries.

The AIDS epidemic was the precipitating force shoving India's gay men and transwomen into the public glare. But by the end of the millennium, another force was pushing in the same direction—in the shape of the astonishing changes sweeping across urban India as the economy grew at record speed and the well-off integrated into the globalized world.

The familiar, stern India of socialist rationing, earnest Five-Year Plans and 'garibi hatao' rhetoric began to fade away. In its place rose today's schizophrenic ever-mutating nation—the cities a consumerist sprawl of malls, traffic-choked flyovers, gated communities and high rises, peopled with billionaires, multi-millionaires and every gradation of the middle class; the villages and hinterland remaining the desperate Bharat of hungry masses. These epochal shifts in India's fortunes held all kinds of opportunities as well as dangers for gay and transgender Indians.

For well off and upwardly mobile gay men and women in the major cities, these changes soon made life an approximation of contemporary gay life in the West. Instead of the utter invisibility I had known while living in Delhi in the 1980s and mid-1990s, gay people were suddenly becoming visible everywhere. The wealth-fuelled demand for the fine things in life made celebrities of fashion designers, interior decorators, beauticians, boutique hoteliers and artists, many of whom were gay and now had the financial freedom and assurance to be open about this matter.

English-language TV channels aired Hollywood films as well as documentaries and newscasts on gay issues. Local programming began to cover Indian gay men, metrosexuals, drag queens and transgenders, often as creatures of fable and frivolity, but sometimes more empathetically. Indian publishers released a slew of gay-themed books, ranging from the novels of Ranga Rao and anthologies of gay and lesbian writing to scholarly works like Ruth Vanita and Saleem Kidwai's *Same-Sex Love in India: Readings from the Literature and History*.

Gay support groups for English-speaking gay men and women, such as Gay Bombay and Bangalore's Good As You, flourished, arranging parties, discussions and parents' meets. Several city editions of *Time Out* magazine started dedicated coverage of gay events; its Mumbai edition launched a regular column on gay issues written by Alligator, the nom de plume for gay journalist Vikram Doctor. Upmarket bars began to openly offer weekly gay evenings. All these changes bred a public familiarity with gay people that had never existed in India before.

The Internet was another source of liberation, connecting gay, lesbian, bisexual and transgender people in every corner of India as well as the globe through e-mail 'list serve' groups and online sites. They could strike up friendships and relationships. They could organize and advocate in the knowledge that they had allies. They could find out everything they wanted to know about gay issues, whether it involved obtaining practical advice on how to have safe sex or investigating theories about same-sex desire and gender variance.

Two facts said everything about the astounding scale of change. In the mid-1980s, at our parties in Delhi, there were just a dozen avowedly gay men and women. However, by the close of the 1990s, massive gay parties with several hundred revellers were being held regularly at the homes of wealthy gay men and women. Even more tellingly, in the cloistered worlds of fashion and design, I began to encounter gay men—a generation or two younger than me—who were astonished to hear that homosexuality was a criminal offence in India. It was the first time they had heard of it! I both envied and celebrated their insouciant ignorance. Their reality was so different from the one I had faced while living in Delhi just fifteen years ago.

But, in this raw new India, there was an ever-widening gap between winners and losers. In this case, lower-income gay men and transgenders failed to get their share of the liberation that was transforming the lives of their well-off peers. Not only did the burdens of the past remain intact—for instance, the lack of places to meet, barring risky public spaces like parks and toilets—but a potent new danger was also added to them.

This new danger was that homophobia had become immeasurably more concerted and politicized, driven by the governing right-wing Bharatiya Janata Party and its Hindu-supremacist backers like the Rashtriya Swayamsevak Sangh, self-annointed, bullying arbiters of who qualified as a deserving Indian. Our fellow sexual outlaws, women sex workers, were another of their main targets.

The prime victims of this politicized homophobia were gay men and transwomen not affluent enough to sequester themselves in the enclaves of privilege. The groups working on the frontline to promote HIV prevention among low-income gay and bisexual men and transwomen were ready targets. A 2002 investigation by Human Rights Watch documented serious police abuse of the staff of such organizations in Lucknow, Mumbai, Chennai, Sangli, Bangalore and New Delhi. There was now far greater use of IPC Section 377 by the police, in addition to the old abuses of extorting money and sex.

In the most concerted case of persecution, four staff members of Naz Foundation International and Bharosa Trust—two accredited non-governmental groups working on HIV prevention in Uttar Pradesh's capital Lucknow (with the BJP government of Rajnath Singh in power)—were jailed after the police raided their offices in July 2001, accusing them of 'promoting homosexuality', running a gay 'sex racket', and selling pornography. (Naz Foundation International is not affiliated to Naz India, the Delhi group that filed the legal challenge to Section 377 later that year.)

Even though there was no evidence of sodomy or other sexual acts, they were charged under IPC Section 377—which has a strict, narrow requirement of actual sexual acts—along with charges of criminal conspiracy, abetment and obscenity. Although both these were NGOs recognized by the Uttar Pradesh State AIDS Control Society and were working within the guidelines laid down by NACO, Lucknow's chief judicial magistrate accused them of 'polluting the entire society by encouraging the young persons and abating [sic] them to committing the offence of sodomy'.

One of the men arrested, Naz Foundation International's Lucknow director Arif Jafar, later told Human Rights Watch researchers: 'For the first ten days, they provided nothing for us, not even clean water. We were not provided utensils for eating, and we couldn't take baths. We were cleaning drains and toilets with the same utensils that were all we had for eating. Even for going to the toilet, we had to use dirty drain water. We were harassed. The first news reports that came out about our arrest said that we ran a 'gay den' and had made seventy lakh, so the police had the impression that we had money, and that, combined with their idea that we were doing "unnatural" things, made them harass us. We were abused and beaten and threatened ... I have kidney stones, and in prison they would not allow me to have medication. I was in terrible pain. It was so painful—at that time, I wished to die.'

Jafar, a Muslim by birth, said that the police had told him that he was 'trying to destroy our country by promoting homosexuality' and that 'Hindus don't have these practices—these are all perversions of the Muslims'.

Because arrests made under IPC Section 377 are non-bailable, the four men were imprisoned for nearly two months before a higher court ruled against the police, concluding that they had falsified facts and appeared to be framing the men. Tellingly, through these weeks, the government's AIDS policy leadership did not come to the defence of the arrested men, clearly adhering to directives from the ruling BJP government.

At the same time, individual cases of persecution and sexual violence by policemen and thugs against gays and transgenders multiplied, each more horrific than the previous. Because homosexuality was already criminalized and stigmatized, they could act with brutality and impunity. The worst abuses were against kothis—feminized men—and transwomen. In June 2001, kothis who had attended a meeting at a Delhi drop-in centre were severely beaten by local hoodlums armed with sticks and metal batons. Two of them were so badly beaten that they had to be hospitalized. In 2004, Kokila—a transwoman, who was a community mobiliser with the Sangama group in Bangalore—was raped by ten men, known to be local goons. The perpetrators then dragged her to the police station, where, rather than being given protection, she was stripped and tortured by the police.

This violence and persecution was part and parcel of a larger conservative assault on what—according to Hindutva groups—was the Westernized, anti-Indian lifestyle of the urban middle and upper classes. India seemed to be at war with itself, one part of its people ambitiously bent on shaping the 21st century world, while another part was adamant about upholding every one of India's old wrongs in the name of tradition. Anything relating to sexuality, however tangentially (such as any expression of women's autonomy), became a flashpoint targeted as 'Western threats to our culture and moral order'.

Sushma Swaraj, Minister of Information and Broadcasting, banned educational programmes on sexual health from national broadcaster Doordarshan, despite the vital role this played in rural AIDS prevention efforts. The Fashion TV channel and several ads were banned for showing too much flesh. The Hindutva rank-and-file was given a free hand to operate as fanatical moral police across India. They were a Hindu Taliban, ordering women to dress in sarees and salwars instead of jeans, and beating couples for merely holding hands or embracing. Bookshops were torched just because they sold Valentine's Day cards.

Homosexuality was especially demonized. It was almost as if the Hindutva obscurantists could not stomach us gay men and women having even a paltry sum of openness and freedom, of reprieve from our centuries of stigma and persecution.

The 1998 Canadian-Indian film *Fire*, a drama depicting a lesbian relationship between two of its main characters, was running to full houses when Shiv Sena, Bajrang Dal and BJP mobs vandalized theatres in Maharashtra, Delhi and Uttar Pradesh. Maharashtra Chief Minister Manohar Joshi , of the Shiv Sena, supported the mobs, remarking, 'I congratulate them for what they have done. The film's theme is alien to our culture.'

Sena leader Bal Thackeray rhetorically asked in a magazine interview: 'Is it fair to show such things which are not part of Indian culture?' And then, without waiting for a reply, he answered: 'It can corrupt tender minds. It is a sort of a social AIDS.'

Defending the marauding mobs, BJP ideologue Swapan Dasgupta wrote, 'So widespread is the new gay evangelism that during the contrived controversy over Deepa Mehta's film *Fire*, there were loud claims of homosexuality and lesbianism being part of the Indian "heritage", a claim that angered many Hindu activists.'

Dasgupta, a 'Macaulay's Child', educated in Britain, but now intent on portraying himself as a paragon of Hindutva culture, took it upon himself to attack homosexuality in his newspaper columns. The brutal 2004 murder of two gay men in an affluent Delhi area—one of whom worked for USAID—far from encouraging any empathy, led him to write: '(The) case has brought into the open a nexus between employees of international aid agencies and the gay underworld. Of particular concern to many is the possibility of the lavishly funded anti-AIDS campaign being misused to create a gay network ... to buy cheap sex with poor slum kids ... Courtesy the steady degeneration of liberalism and the systematic assault on family values, ordinary, decent people are wary of speaking out against the perversions in the gay community lest it be construed as intolerance.'

Adding to the sense of worsening threat was evidence that Naz India's legal challenge to Section 377 in the Delhi High Court was making no progress, obstructed not only by the judiciary's slow pace but also by the reluctance of the judges to grapple with this difficult matter. Two years passed before the BJP-led Union government filed its counter-affidavit. (It argued, unsurprisingly, that 'by and large, Indian society disapproves of homosexuality ... This disapproval is strong enough to justify it being treated as a criminal offence'.)

And then, in late 2004, when the petition eventually came up for hearing before a bench headed by the Chief Justice, it was dismissed on the specious grounds that Naz India did not have the right to file this public interest challenge because the foundation's chief executive and listed appellant, Anjali Gopalan, was not gay and had not been personally harmed by Section 377. (Indian courts had long established that public interest litigation could be moved by anyone, and the involvement of an affected individual or community was not necessary.)

Years had ground by fruitlessly. It now seemed likely that this case would also die from attrition like the ABVA challenge a decade earlier.

Seeing the increasing numbers of gay men and transwomen contracting HIV, the worsening persecution by police and Hindutva zealots, and the stalling of the legal challenge to Section 377, I often feared the worst in those dark years of BJP rule. Rather than being the glorious dawning of a new millennium of freedom and acceptance for us, I wondered if this new India of virulent homophobia would become an even worse place than the past India of fearful invisibility. Would the courage of Sekar and Noori as well as other activists come to nought because the arch-conservatives in power were so vehemently opposed to our just claims?

To keep myself from despairing, I had to consciously focus on all the positive changes that had occurred in the past few years in India and abroad, and tell myself that they were proof of an inexorable momentum that would secure freedom for me as well as other gay Indian men and women.

16

A World War

The persecution of vulnerable minorities in India— whether gays and sex workers, or Muslims and Christians—that was ratcheting up under the BJP and its Hindutva backers was the only dark blot in a period where I felt an unexpected sense of optimism, on the personal front as well as on matters relating to AIDS and the outlawed. My optimism seemed appropriate to the dawning of the new millennium, the 21st century. I somehow expected that humankind would automatically progress at an exceptional pace from now on, that in this new golden age there would be no place for the primitive bigotry of the BJP and the Bush Republicans.

On the personal front, my sense of renewal had much to do with my move back to New York City from Delhi in 2000, after completing the two books—on rural poverty and on AIDS—that had consumed much of my time since the mid-1990s. I was close to turning forty and was relieved at the prospect of having a relatively settled life again, rather than the whirlwind travel and unceasing changes of the past decade.

Though I was a misfit in New York City's gay world, with its obsession for fashion, muscles and parties, I hoped to find romantic love again after so many years of being single. I had innumerable close friends, and half a dozen god-children. I got myself a puppy, a singularly sweet-tempered Portuguese Water Dog, whom I named Lorca after the great poet. The city began to feel like home.

Even on matters relating to AIDS, I found that there were unexpected reasons for optimism. At first glance, any optimism seemed wishful as the pandemic was inflicting worse havoc than ever before. Every year, another five million people were contracting HIV and over three million were dying, in addition to the thirty-five million already infected and the twenty-two million killed. But, even so, for the first time it seemed like real change was happening, two decades since AIDS first became known.

Most crucially, the insistence by AIDS activists and a handful of visionary individuals that it was unconscionable to let many millions die when lifesaving anti-AIDS medicines existed had led to a revolutionary breakthrough—the launching of a global effort to make these medicines affordable to the millions of impoverished HIV-positive people in developing countries who would otherwise die soon. A 2001 world summit had brought together 144 heads of state and government at the UN General Assembly to chart a course for checking the pandemic. A global superfund had been established to raise and manage the billions needed annually to make both anti-AIDS medicines as well as HIV prevention services available across the world, even for the poorest of people in the poorest of nations.

And the epidemic's depredations had mobilized some of the most marginalized people, including sex workers and gay men, to demand that their well-being and rights be taken seriously. They had won powerful allies to their cause within the UN, major donor institutions and other establishment organizations. The myriad chronic wrongs they faced were now widely recognized to be systemic human rights failures.

But just as these positive developments felt like they were gathering momentum, they became the victims of George W. Bush's ruinous involvement.

Unexpectedly, in his January 2003 State of the Union address, Bush took on the task of battling the pandemic in developing countries as his personal charitable cause, a 'work of mercy'. He committed the astonishing sum of $15 billion in US aid to tackling AIDS in fifteen hard-hit countries, mainly in sub-Saharan Africa but also including Haiti and Vietnam. But Bush's right-wing dictatorial insistence meant that some of America's most unjust social policies were to be forced on the world, including the failed public health policies that had led the US to have by far the worst AIDS epidemic of any industrialized nation. Marginalized people everywhere would suffer most grievously—AIDS prevention efforts for them would be crippled, and the larger progress that had been made in challenging their burdens of criminalization and stigma would be abruptly reversed.

The pandemic was an inexplicable choice for Bush. He had ignored the disease's domestic toll, not only in his five years as governor of Texas, but also during his 2000 presidential election campaign. In his first term, he had considered the closure of the White House Office of National AIDS Policy. None of the populations among whom America's epidemic was concentrated—gay men, injecting drug users and African-Americans—mattered to the Republican party or Bush's electoral chances. What's more, the reactionary Republicans and hardline Christians who had been key to bringing Bush to power, considered AIDS a disease of the hated homosexuals.

Reverend Billy Graham, the celebrity preacher and Bush's spiritual guide, had called homosexuality a 'sinister form of perversion'. (Bush credited Graham with transforming him from a failed businessman hooked to alcohol into a 'born-again' Christian convinced that God had chosen him to lead America.) At the very point when AIDS was taking its most bloody toll on gay Americans, Reverend Jerry Falwell welcomed it as 'God's punishment for homosexuals'.

Senator Jesse Helms, an influential ultra conservative ally of Reagan and the Bush family, had called homosexuals 'morally sick wretches' and pronounced that 'there is not one single case of AIDS in this country that cannot be traced in origin to sodomy'. He demanded that AIDS funding be slashed because homosexuals contract the disease through their 'deliberate, disgusting, revolting conduct'.

Unsurprisingly, superpower realpolitik calculations explained Bush's motivations for breaking with this record of animus. That State of the Union address justified Bush's impending invasion of Iraq as well as the launch of his worldwide 'war on terror'.

'As our nation moves troops and builds alliances to make our world safer, we must also remember our calling as a blessed country to make this world better,' Bush pronounced. America would fight evil abroad through its military might while the billions from the US President's Emergency Plan for AIDS Relief (PEPFAR) would prove to the world that America was a charitable, righteous empire.

PEPFAR marked a massive increase in money for tackling the runaway epidemics in the worst-hit developing countries. The US was now providing nearly twice as much to the global effort against AIDS as the rest of the world's richest governments combined. But the American billions brought with them a plague of problems.

'Is it churlish to criticise Bush over his spending on AIDS?' asked *The Lancet*, an influential health journal, in an editorial. It replied: 'Leading scientists, physicians, and public-health advocates ... have judged that the size of the US investment into AIDS renders President Bush immune from criticism. They are badly mistaken.'

PEPFAR was not only unabashedly unilateralist—almost all its funds had to be distributed by US governmental agencies rather than the better-qualified and international Global Fund to Fight AIDS, Tuberculosis and Malaria—but the recipients of its funds also had to abide by myriad dictatorial demands or lose funding. At precisely the point when Bush was insisting that the world accept his trumped-up evidence of 'weapons of mass destruction' in Iraq as well as America's unilateral use of military power across the world, the Bush AIDS plan was yet more proof of the administration's bullying approach to foreign affairs.

One cause of outrage was the Bush administration's insistence that pricey branded anti-AIDS drugs made by American pharmaceutical giants be used in all the countries that PEPFAR was going to concentrate on—rather than the cheap, equally effective generic copies made in India and Thailand that were being used as part of the larger UN-led global effort. Ethics demanded that as many people as possible be brought on to treatment speedily, and the use of generic drugs would give that assurance to many more people.

A year's supply of generics for an individual cost under $300, less than a dollar a day, while the branded drugs cost up to $15,000. The generics also had immense operational advantages. They were available in potent three-in-one combination pills—made possible precisely because patents were not at issue—thus allowing patients to pop just a single tablet twice a day rather than a bewildering mix of six or more pills if branded drugs were used.

Unswayed, Bush's AIDS team—led by US Global AIDS Coordinator, Ambassador Randall Tobias, a former chairman of American pharma giant Eli Lilly—insisted that countries helped by PEPFAR use only branded American drugs. This intransigence, which cast intense doubt on the genuineness of Bush's commitment to tackling AIDS, even on the plainly humanitarian matter of saving millions of lives, embittered observers the world over.

As it was, the American government's reputation on the matter of fair access to the life-saving anti-AIDS drugs was already tarnished. For years, the Clinton administration had battled on behalf of American pharma giants against the few governments that had attempted to use generic drugs to save their HIV-positive citizens, threatening to impose punitive trade sanctions on Brazil, South Africa and Thailand, for alleged violations of intellectual property laws.

American officials and the pharma giants had also spread the canard that developing countries should not undertake AIDS treatment as their health services were too shoddy to deliver these modern drugs, or to ensure that patients religiously took their medicines. They held up the apocalyptic spectre of drug-resistant strains of HIV sweeping through the world because of Third World irresponsibility. Before Bush so unexpectedly made AIDS his cause, Andrew Natsios, his appointee to the US Agency for International Development, had contemptuously proclaimed that Africans could not be expected to take the drugs in accordance with the prescribed schedule because they 'do not know what watches and clocks are. They do not use Western means for telling time. They use the sun'. To the contrary, Africans in even the most impoverished nations of the continent soon showed that they could adhere to treatment regimens better than many Americans.

So, there were ample grounds for concluding that if the American government and Western pharma giants had had their way, putting profits before saving lives, the world would never have embarked on the effort of making anti-AIDS drugs available affordably in developing countries—something that rapidly proved to be one of the greatest public health success stories, saving over half a million people every year from death and giving millions many years of healthy, productive life.

Criticisms of the Bush administration's approach to HIV prevention were soon equally intense, when it became evident that America's might and billions were being used to advance Bush's evangelical notion that Biblical 'morality' was the best solution to the epidemic. Indeed, a key reason why Bush's hardline Christian backers had overcome their aversion to dealing with this abhorrent gay-related disease was learning that a vast majority of people in Africa and elsewhere in the developing world had contracted the infection heterosexually. Thus, the epidemic could be defeated by encouraging Africans to embrace 'biblical values and sexual purity', proclaimed arch-conservative Senator Jesse Helms, who had long fought against spending on fellow Americans at risk of AIDS but now backed massive government aid for AIDS prevention abroad.

The millions of African families devastated by AIDS also offered the Christian right-wing unprecedented opportunity for spreading their brand of hardline religion. Soon, across sub-Saharan Africa, PEPFAR and other US government aid money was being used by these churches to mix preaching with AIDS-related services, even though US law forbids organizations receiving federal funds from evangelizing. Human Rights Watch noted that it was sometimes hard to tell whether the aim of these organizations was preventing AIDS or spreading their brand of Christianity.

With the response to AIDS cast as a Christian crusade, an extreme moral righteousness came to drive American foreign assistance on HIV. Poorer countries were bullied into accepting 'Biblically-inspired' interventions of utterly unproven use.

A mainstay of this approach was to promote 'abstinence-only-until-marriage' programmes. These maintained that heterosexual intercourse within marriage was the only acceptable form of sexual behavior and contraception, and the only fail-safe means of preventing the spread of HIV (rather than safer-sex options and condoms). President Bush, a fervent advocate himself, was quoted as saying, 'If you're worried about teenage pregnancy, or if you're worried about sexually transmitted disease, abstinence works every single time.'

But the truth was that 'abstinence-only' interventions didn't work. Every domestic US abstinence-only effort ever evaluated had failed to reduce rates of teen pregnancy or sexually transmitted diseases. Many young people wanted to be sexually active before marriage.

Rather, abstinence and fidelity were valuable options only when promoted within a comprehensive approach to safe sex, alongside condoms, so individuals would know all the effective ways of protecting themselves from HIV and choose those best suited to them at any point in their lives. The one billion dollars of PEPFAR's funding earmarked for abstinence-only efforts abroad was certain to be a waste of precious funds as well as a distraction from the substantive HIV prevention efforts that were so desperately needed.

The damage done by the administration's insistence on promoting the abstinence-only solution extended immeasurably further, because, astonishingly, the Bush team—as a corollary—attacked the use of condoms in preventing HIV. The US government's most respected health bodies—such as the US Centers for Disease Control—were forced to censor their public advice on condoms. In contrast to their original clear recommendation that condoms are 'highly effective' against the spread of HIV and other sexually transmitted diseases, they now said that condoms could only 'reduce the rate of STD transmission' and 'cannot guarantee absolute protection'.

Groups receiving US government funding were barred from discussing condom use with young people or mainstream adults. It was recommended only 'for those who practice high-risk behaviours', defined as 'prostitutes, sexually active discordant couples, substance abusers, and others'.('Discordant' refers to a couple in which only one partner is HIV-positive.)

These bullying tactics aimed at denying people accurate information about the safety of condoms would have been reprehensible at any time, but in the age of AIDS, it was criminal, arguably no different from culpable homicide. In much of sub-Saharan Africa, with one in ten, and in some places, nearly one in two adults already infected, every adolescent and adult person faced a frighteningly high lifetime risk of contracting HIV. They needed to know every possible thing about how best to navigate these dangers, not to be callously denied knowledge about the only effective barrier protection that existed.

I was enraged because I still remembered with acute clarity the crippling fears in my twenties about how to have sex without exposing myself to HIV, and the hopelessness I had felt from lacking clear, explicit advice I could trust and act on. It was condoms that had kept me utterly safe despite my having had sex with many men over the years. How anybody in a position of responsibility could insist that this life-saving knowledge be withheld from others was beyond my understanding.

And then, yet more concerted and damaging still, were the Bush AIDS team's strategies on HIV prevention specifically among both drug users and sex workers.

One of the first efforts of the Bush AIDS team was a global campaign to ban 'needle exchange' programmes, in which injecting drug users were given free sterile needles and syringes in exchange for used ones. This ensured they did not share injecting equipment, and therefore risk spreading or contracting HIV and hepatitis. Numerous studies had shown needle exchange to be one of the most effective strategies for preventing the spread of HIV through injecting drug use. WHO, UNAIDS and other leading health institutions recommended needle exchange programmes as a vital element of the harm reduction approach to drug use, a complement to the more difficult and longer task of treatment. Australia and numerous Western European countries had contained injecting drug use epidemics of HIV through giving out millions of free syringes and needles and providing other elements of harm reduction.

In the US, in sharp contrast, President Ronald Reagan banned the use of federal funds for needle exchange programmes in the late 1980s. He did this against the advice of the US National Institutes of Health—which had emphasized that the provision of clean needles did not encourage drug use—and all the heartbreaking evidence that AIDS was devastating drug users. (In New York City, every second drug user was already infected.) This stance reflected the characteristic US approach of waging a 'war on drugs' through criminalizing drug addiction and funding repressive anti-drug strategies, instead of treating addiction as the medical disorder and public health problem that it is.

So far, while Washington had not directly funded needle exchange programmes abroad, it continued to aid groups that did so. However, this changed dramatically with the Bush administration. Its officials summarily told the bosses of UNAIDS, the UN Office on Drugs and Crime (UNODC) and other UN organizations to stop recommending needle exchange in their policies, and remove all references to such efforts from their websites and public materials. It began to cut off funds to organizations that funded or supported needle exchange in any way.

With half a million people worldwide contracting HIV every year from contaminated injecting drug equipment—the world's fastest-growing HIV epidemics were fuelled by intravenous drug use in Asia, Eastern Europe and the former Soviet Union—the Bush campaign had deadly human costs. 'The United States should help pay for these important programs,' the *New York Times* editorialized. 'If it cannot bring itself to do so, it should at least allow the rest of the world to get on with saving millions of lives.'

Sex work was the other target. The United States Leadership Against AIDS, Tuberculosis and Malaria Act of 2003, the legislation that created PEPFAR, portrayed sex work as being indistinguishable from sex trafficking of women—and, based on this breathtakingly mala fide conflation between willing sex workers and actual victims of exploitation, explicitly sought the 'eradication of prostitution'. All recipients of US foreign assistance would, in the future, have to sign a pledge 'explicitly opposing prostitution and sex trafficking' or lose funding. This monetarily-tied demand gave the Bush administration enormous power to dictate how organizations worked with sex workers across the globe.

In one stroke, all the profoundly unjust and harmful aspects of domestic American policies on sex work—which harshly punished sex workers with jail terms of up to five years, left them defenceless against an abusive and corrupt police force, and denied them opportunities for a democratic debate over policy—were to be forced on countries the world over. This sounded the death knell for the rational discussion of sex work worldwide.

Explicitly prohibited were efforts that 'promote or advocate the legalization or practice of prostitution and sex trafficking'. This sweeping clause banned precisely the kind of support for sex workers that worldwide experience of HIV prevention had shown was essential—from helping them organize to gain self-respect and collective power, to fighting for better payment terms or against police or other abuse, or to advocating for the repeal or reform of unjust laws.

Equally damaging, a signature on the anti-prostitution pledge entitled US government officials to vet projects for compliance. Because the wording of the provisions was vague and open-ended, almost anything could be considered a violation, giving them unlimited room to deny or withdraw funding from groups that opposed or displeased them.

Even the use of the terms 'sex work' and 'sex worker' could be taken to imply support for prostitution—the Bush administration wanted 'prostitutes', or preferably 'trafficking victims'. Publications and websites of US-funded groups began to feature notes nervously explaining that their use of the term sex work did not imply support 'for the legalization or practice of prostitution or sex trafficking'.

It was an astonishing turn of events. The pioneering groups that had worked most respectfully with sex workers on the frontlines and shown that enormous improvements in their lives could be secured alongside tackling trafficking and preventing the spread of HIV, were suddenly being told by an alien government that they had to prove their bona fides and establish that they were not promoting prostitution.

And to prove this, they had to be party to a pledge that deceitfully conflated willing sex work with sex trafficking—specifically defined under international law as criminal abuses involving abduction, violence, fraud, debt bondage and coercion related to tradition—and denied adult women in sex work any right to self-determination.

Then, making matters worse, just some months after launching PEPFAR, Bush declared in an address to the UN General Assembly that besides its celebrated 'war on terror', the US would also lead the world in a global war against sex trafficking. As with the language of PEPFAR's prostitution gag-rule, sex work was intentionally confused with both child prostitution and the sex trafficking of adults. And the vast, confused problem of human trafficking, spanning extreme kinds of exploitation of men and women alike—including forced labour, domestic servitude, debt bondage, child labour, forced marriage and the harvesting of human organs—was reduced to a lurid concentration on sex trafficking alone. This was doubly tragic because the sex trafficking of women was rooted in the conditions of deprivation and powerlessness that gave rise to the broader forms of exploitation, often affecting whole communities, and could never be solved on its own.

Asserting that 'hundreds of thousands of teenage girls, and others as young as five' are trafficked into the sex trade every year, Bush—in his UN speech—called the sex 'industry' a 'special evil' amounting to 'modern-day slavery' and a violation of the 'moral law that stands above men and nations'. His fiery rhetoric was patently a bid to claw back some moral high-ground after the catastrophic damage done to America's reputation by his misdeeds abroad. (The horrific abuses at Iraq's Abu Ghraib prison were just beginning to get exposed, with their damning evidence of the US military and CIA systematically using torture, physical and sexual abuse, rape and sodomy against the men, women and even children detained there.)

The outcome was that, within the space of a few months, the eradication of sex work had become a centrepiece of US foreign aid. Bizarrely, more emphasis was placed on eradicating sex work than on eradicating HIV. And in the place of the broad, empowering policies carefully recommended by the UN to tackle the complex challenges of sex work, the Bush administration was now irresponsibly pushing this distorted cure-all—the abolition of sex work—however patently unworkable and damaging to the best interests of women.

With the billions from PEPFAR, anti-trafficking funding and other US official foreign aid, the Bush administration and the coalition of domestic groups backing this crusade wielded extraordinary power to force their will on poorer countries as well as on UN policies, crippling the poorly funded nascent movements for sex workers' well-being and rights. Even the Republican crusade in the 1980s to deny the world's women safe abortions had never been anywhere so concerted or so well funded. (A gag-rule issued by President Reagan in 1984, and reinstated by Bush on his very first day in office, banned family planning groups that received US funds from performing or even counselling about safe abortion, although unsafe abortions were killing tens of thousands of women every year and gravely injuring millions more.)

Ironically, despite the Bush and rightwing assault on women's reproductive rights both within America and abroad, an influential section of American feminists—even ostensibly progressive leaders like Gloria Steinem—now allied with them in the anti-sex work crusade. They ignored the almost exact parallels between sex workers who were being denied the right to self-determination and pregnant women who were being denied the right to safe abortion, both being cast as ignorant victims or shameless sinners who needed to be protected from themselves, by force if necessary. How feminist-minded women could support policies that would worsen the criminal penalties against sex workers and leave them even more at risk of abuse by the police was beyond my powers of comprehension.

They also turned a blind eye to the fact that both the prostitution gag-rule and the anti-trafficking law were the work of a noxious opponent of reproductive rights—Republican Congressman Chris Smith, a hardline Catholic infamous for calling abortion 'child slaughter' and fighting to deny abortion even to victims of rape. (Despite my years of living in the US, I was always freshly flabbergasted by every new instance of the power of the American right-wing to cripple social progress on a staggering number of fronts, whether it was gun control, health care, race relations or mass imprisonment, or the intensely polarized matters of sexuality and reproduction.)

Rounding off the leadership of such crusaders were individuals such as *New York Times* columnist Nicholas Kristof, hugely popular amongst well-off, do-gooder American readers for describing the developing world to them in terms of chronic dysfunction and barbarism—and consequently in abiding need of American advice and charity. Everyone in this motley but powerful coalition to end 'modern-day slavery' was fired up with moralistic and often religious fervour about rescuing hapless women in backward countries from lustful, exploitative men. Consequently, they ignored every inconvenient fact—the likelihood that the options facing sex workers in impoverished countries were often far worse than being in sex work; the evidence from the UN and leading researchers that sex worker collectives had been singularly effective in tackling trafficking and exploitation; and, the incontrovertible proof that soon began to mount of the awful harm being done to sex workers the world over by the US-led abolitionist crusade itself.

In spring 2004, just a year into Bush's taking up of AIDS as his cause, I testified against this rising tide before a US Congressional panel focused on human rights and the AIDS pandemic, chaired by a group of forward-thinking members of Congress and the Senate. I was speaking in my personal capacity, and therefore did not hold back from bluntly voicing my criticism, saying, 'Official American support has recently become—to speak frankly—misdirected, unhelpful and indeed damaging ... Millions of Indians are done a great disservice by US advocacy for abstinence-only and anti-prostitution approaches, which strengthens the most ideological forces in Indian officialdom ...

'Instead of putting its influence and money to supporting and empowering sex workers, men who have sex with men, transgender persons, young people and other vulnerable groups, the current US push delegitimizes them and their rights and needs ... These positions have marred the US government's reputation amongst Indian civil society, so much so that many leading people are loathe to be associated with official US assistance on HIV/AIDS.'

This was honest if unsparing criticism. It would have been immeasurably harsher if I could have looked into the future and seen the full extent of the harm the Bush administration's policies would eventually cause sex workers, drug users and the many others who desperately needed help in protecting themselves from HIV.

Within months of Bush being re-elected President, I left the US and my beloved New York City—depressed at this confirmation that America's citizenry would not come together to oppose him despite all the damage he was doing to the world. But there was no escaping Bush anywhere. Even in Switzerland, where I joined the UNAIDS Secretariat on 1 January 2005, as a senior advisor and speech writer to executive director Peter Piot, I found I had hopped from the proverbial frying pan into the fire.

Only the UNAIDS Secretariat, as the core of a UN-wide effort to tackle the AIDS pandemic, had the global legitimacy to halt the Bush administration's drive to destructively rewrite international HIV prevention strategies—whether relating to the efficacy of condoms or the strategies most needed for sex workers and drug users. Knowing the Secretariat well from the extended consulting assignments I had done a few years ago, I didn't doubt that it would live up to this responsibility.

Just a decade old, it was one of the rare UN bodies that had not fallen into irrelevance, like so many of the other organizations I had worked for or knew. I admired the things that the Secretariat had helped achieve against all the odds—the advocacy that had won attention and funds from the world's political leaders; the careful putting together of a knowledge base of what worked; and the guidance that balanced the imperative of tackling HIV with those of protecting human rights.

I also relished the Secretariat's committed work environment, so refreshingly different from other UN organizations. With its informal dress code and nondescript offices, it looked like a non-governmental organization operating on a shoestring budget, and—just like the best of them—the commitment of its staff members was palpable. Many had begun working on AIDS when it was still a disgraceful, stigmatized matter. Several were living with HIV or had lost loved ones to the epidemic—among them women and men who had been pioneers in their countries when it came to confronting the stigma and persecution that followed AIDS. The fact that staffers who were living with HIV or who were openly gay or lesbian held senior positions at the Secretariat, and obviously were not discriminated against, was still a rarity across the UN. (Nearly a decade after the World Bank and IMF, the UN system was now tentatively beginning to provide basic benefits to gay employees and their partners. This had earned Secretary-General Kofi Annan the ire of right-wing governments, allying the Bush administration with the Vatican and African, Middle Eastern and Eastern European despots. As the vice-president of the UN gay employees association, I had seen up close the hostile pressures that Annan had to confront.)

And though I had met the Secretariat's executive director Peter Piot only briefly over the years, I admired him for combining exceptional scientific skills—he had co-discovered the Ebola virus while still in his twenties—with vast experience in policy making on AIDS (having led the Secretariat since its founding in 1995). A tall, energetic fifty-six-year-old in 2005, Piot cut a beguilingly different figure in the dull world of international diplomacy, his geeky spectacles and finely tailored suits stamping him as a policy powerhouse while his trademark 'condom' ties made him appear iconoclastic. All in all, when I joined the Secretariat in those snowy winter days of January 2005, it was with boundless enthusiasm and goodwill—it was all that I hoped global development organizations would be, yet never had been in my experience so far.

But with astonishing speed, I was left utterly disillusioned. This was not because of my colleagues as a whole, but with Piot's abeyance of his leadership responsibilities as the Bush assault on global AIDS policies gathered strength. On every matter of ideological importance to the Bush administration—whether it was sex work, drug use, or abstinence over condoms—I saw Piot cave in rather than use diplomacy and confrontation to challenge the administration's destructive views.

My disillusionment began to take root in the run-up to the June 2005 meeting of UNAIDS's governing board, where a crucial strategy on HIV prevention was to be negotiated. In late April, I read the penultimate draft of the prevention strategy and was astounded by the document's poor quality, to the point where I first wondered whether a raw draft had been mistakenly forwarded to me.

Despite this being a strategy focused only on how to strengthen HIV prevention strategies and programmes, the steps they listed were almost retrograde when compared to the *Global Strategy Framework on HIV/AIDS* that I had helped prepare in 2000-2001, or even the weak *Declaration of Commitment* hammered out at the 2001 global summit on AIDS. (The Secretariat had been the lead actor in developing these earlier strategies.)

Bizarrely, there was far less focus on the vital role played by condoms, the need to protect the fundamental rights of sex workers and drug users, or the need for adolescents to be guaranteed access to life-saving sexual health knowledge and services. There was hardly any mention of the fact that respecting the principles of human rights was key to HIV prevention. In a nutshell, every single thing the Bush administration opposed in HIV prevention, and more broadly on the matter of human rights, had been censored out of the draft prevention strategy.

Though puzzled, I left it at that. At the back of my mind was the thought that Piot would angrily tear apart the draft when it reached him for review, and he would insist that it be reworked. (The materials sent to the board were each reviewed and signed off by Piot himself, given their importance. One of the hardest-working people I've known, Piot read every sentence of every important document, from talking points and speeches to major reports, giving detailed feedback in his precise handwriting, and woe betide the person who didn't address his every point.) Piot and I had had a working lunch a few days earlier, and when I referred to the poor quality of the draft, he had commented that the prevention strategy needed to be 'more explicit and business-like', adding that condoms were vital as they were 'the only barrier that exists'.

Consequently, I was flabbergasted to read the final version of the prevention strategy several weeks later, on the day it was sent off to board members after being approved by Piot (as always, a month in advance of the meeting itself). I had been astonished by the weakness of the April draft, but this final version left me enraged—it was even weaker than the April draft, the language carefully censored and key sections either deleted entirely or moved to where they would be less noticeable. If the April draft had reeked of self-censorship with a keen eye on the wishes of the Bush administration, this one stank of active collusion with the Bush administration's AIDS team, of their hands-on editing and direction.

There was no end to the omissions, however bizarre their absence in a document about HIV prevention. In this ten-thousand-word document, condoms were mentioned just three times in the body text—less than half the number of mentions in the far shorter April draft. Inexcusably, despite the epidemic's devastating impact on particularly vulnerable populations in most countries, such as sex workers and drug users, the final version had only two terse, woolly sentences reserved for them. This was an unmistakable rupture with the agreed direction of global, UN-led strategy ever since it had been laid out during Jonathan Mann's time at the World Health Organization in the late 1980s. Previous global strategies, such as the 2001 *Global Strategy* and the *Declaration of Commitment*, had detailed recommendations running into several pages on the priority needed to be placed on key vulnerable populations—most so in prevention efforts.

No less astonishing, this final version gave even shorter shrift to human rights than the April draft—it was nowhere to be found in the scene-setting opening pages where it had been in the end-April draft. There was no mystery about why human rights had been excised; Bush was, by then, leading a full-scale assault on human rights and international laws that he found inconvenient, even challenging the application of the Geneva Conventions' ban on torture to prisoners of war held in Abu Ghraib and Guantánamo.

Reading this draft marked the end of my smooth working relationship with Piot. Though we maintained an appearance of civility, the strain and the antagonism between us was evident enough. Only my utility kept him from doing what he did to others who questioned him, which usually involved shunting them off to a distant corner of the headquarters or to an unpleasant posting somewhere. (As for me, I stayed put for personal reasons—soon after arriving in Geneva, I had started dating a lovely man, a lawyer ten years younger than me who was relocating from his native Germany so that we could live together. I was loath to imperil this happy prospect.)

The tense three-day board meeting in June, dominated by discussions over the prevention strategy, revealed just how far Piot had taken the Secretariat from the long-established fundamentals of global policy on AIDS. Within hours of the meeting's opening, the corridor talk was that many governments—including that of Canada, the UK and quite a few major developing nations—were upset by the weakness of the draft strategy. Their representatives on the drafting committee were going to revise it together, an unprecedented occurrence in the decade-long history of UNAIDS. This amounted to a sharp rebuke of the Secretariat, an indication that its draft had fallen way short of minimum standards.

And indeed the revised draft, worked on by the board members, was enormously stronger. Human rights headed the principles of effective HIV prevention as well as the list of essential policy actions, in line with the UN-led global consensus. There was far greater focus on the nuts and bolts of prevention, including discussion of sexual behaviours, the particular prevention needs of vulnerable populations, and the efficacy of condoms in preventing the sexual transmission of HIV as well as of needle exchange and other harm reduction methods in preventing transmission through drug injecting.

Nonetheless, because of the appalling quality of the Secretariat draft, even the revised draft could not meet the standards of earlier strategy documents. To bring it to that quality would have required trashing the Secretariat draft entirely and writing a stronger one from scratch.

The events of the day on which the governing board tabled the prevention strategy gave me an insight into some of the factors that allowed Piot to become so complicit with the Bush administration's demands without being held to account by progressive governments or activist groups. I made it a point to attend this session of the governing board meeting, held in the elegant main meeting hall at the neighbouring World Health Organization's headquarters. While it could seat nearly five hundred people (I had seen it full during the yearly World Health Assembly discussions), today—to my surprise—I found that no more than a third of the seats was occupied. The heads of delegations were already seated at long tables at the centre of the hall, their supporting colleagues gathered in the ranks.

I felt an overwhelming rush of depression. Here were these life-and-death matters up for debate—how to keep AIDS from infecting and killing tens of millions more—and all we had was this quiet, almost-empty hall and a civil, emotionless debate between health bureaucrats and a sprinkling of NGO representatives.

Was this the sum total of how much the world's governments cared about a global crisis that had already killed over twenty million people? Was this what all the years of struggle and activism and sacrifice around the world had amounted to? I remembered that even the World Bank's in-house annual conference on development economics always saw far larger attendance and more animated debates.

I sat through the entire session, even though the conclusion was known to everyone by now—the US delegation would not force a vote on the prevention strategy, given the vocal opposition it had faced from so many countries. A face-saving compromise was reached on the US's vehement opposition to needle exchange programmes for injecting drug users—this was to note, in the minutes of the board meeting, that the strategy did not require donor countries to fund 'activities that are contrary to the donor's national laws or policies'.

But, all in all, even though the board process had kept the Bush administration from wreaking even more damage on HIV prevention policies, it had failed to ensure that a substantive prevention strategy existed to guide the world's governments. UNAIDS's governance system was so weak that it was failing to be responsive and accountable to the people who most needed a well-functioning UNAIDS—the tens of millions living with HIV, and the even larger millions particularly vulnerable to this virus because of being criminalized or downtrodden. Instead of living up to its responsibility of guiding the world's efforts based on science, evidence and human rights principles, the UNAIDS Secretariat was acceding to the ideological demands of its major donor, the US government.

Piot's acquiescence to the Bush administration's destructive positions on AIDS puzzled many observers. For an extensive article I was writing for Piot, to be run in the *Economist*'s Viewpoint section, I had asked a handful of people whose views I respected to suggest issues that the article should tackle. Peter Gill, a former BBC journalist who was completing his book *Body Count: How they turned AIDS into a Catastrophe*, on the leaders and institutions that were to blame for the tens of millions infected or dead, wrote back, 'I cannot see how Peter and you can write the piece without wielding an iron-bar bluntness about the Vatican and condoms, the Americans on drugs, the Americans on prostitutes, the Americans on abstinence, the Americans on pretty well anything sensible in the prevention field! I keep being told how much the Americans admire your boss, and then these people scratch their heads a bit about why that should be!'

As the Bush onslaught against sex workers gathered force, incident after incident spotlighted Piot's failure to challenge him. This gave me some insight into the personal reasons for his failure, beyond the simple fact that the US was UNAIDS's largest donor.

By mid-2005, the Bush administration had turned to targeting the path-breaking sex workers' collectives in India. These groups had shown that collective empowerment could not only stem HIV among sex workers but also radically improve their well-being and tackle sex trafficking. Consequently, they posed the most potent counter-evidence to the Bush assertion that prostitution was irredeemably synonymous with sex trafficking and sex slavery, and therefore had to be eradicated.

They were also the most powerful critics of the administration's views, preferring to return US government funds rather than sign the prostitution gag-rule. (Embarrassingly for the Bush administration, so had Brazil's government, refusing nearly fifty million dollars in US grants because the prostitution gag-rule amounted to 'interference that harms the Brazilian policy regarding diversity, ethical principles and human rights.') They had been prime movers behind a recently released open-letter signed by human rights and AIDS groups around the world that criticized the Bush administration for its cynical conflation of willing sex work with sex trafficking.

Audaciously, the Bush administration set about accusing these groups of being complicit in child prostitution and trafficking of women. The sex workers' collective VAMP (Veshya Anyay Mukti Parishad or 'the collective to free sex workers from injustice') and its parent organization Sangram became its first targets.

Late on the afternoon of 20 May 2005, Gokul Nagar, a shantytown of narrow rustic houses on the outskirts of Sangli in southern Maharashtra, was raided by a contingent of nearly a hundred Indian policemen and policewomen. Bizarrely, leading the police action was a white American man—later identified as Greg Malstead, the head of a hardline Christian organization, Restore International, bent on 'rescuing' women from prostitution.

The police kicked in doors, abused the women, and thrashed several of them. Nearly fifty women from Gokul Nagar were then locked up in Sangli's reformatory—most of them on the grounds that they were children and had been trafficked into sex work, and others accused of being brothel managers abetting trafficking—not to be released for over a month.

There was an outpouring of support for Sangram/VAMP (as the group is commonly known) from many quarters. Yet, the UNAIDS

Secretariat kept silent, not issuing a public statement of support as it often did when HIV prevention groups faced human rights abuses. Eventually, a prolonged judicial investigation concluded that not one of the women had been trafficked, and none of the brothel managers were involved in trafficking.

It said everything that the area where Sangram/VAMP had worked for fifteen years to fight sex trafficking had been targeted for the raid rather than crime-beset Mumbai, just 500 km away, where trafficking remained a significant problem. If the abolitionists had been truly interested in curbing trafficking, rather than attacking the collective's invaluable, painstaking efforts that had brought down the incidence of trafficking to a fraction of what it had been, they should have raided Mumbai's hotspots instead.

A second, equally violent and abortive raid followed that summer, this time in the adjoining town of Miraj. But the breathtaking culmination was that in end-September the Bush administration

VAMP

Sangram/VAMP members protesting raids

accused Meena Seshu—the feminist and social worker who had founded Sangram in 1992—of trafficking children and women into prostitution, and opposing their rescue from brothels.

'US accuses NGO of trafficking', blared a *Hindustan Times* headline. It quoted US Ambassador John R. Miller, the conservative former Congressman appointed by Bush to lead the Office to Monitor and Combat Trafficking In Persons, as saying: 'I want to believe this is an exception, an anomaly. But we are reviewing other programmes and if there is any specific information that an organization is trying to keep people from being rescued from any kind of trafficking, we will be looking into it ... If the US is going to play a leadership role in abolishing this modern-day slavery in the 21st century, then we need to ensure that US funds go to support that effort and not frustrate it.'

It was a surreal charge. Seshu, whom I knew well, had recently been honoured by Human Rights Watch, the international rights group, with their annual 'Human Rights Defender' award for her work alongside sex workers. She was a member of UNAIDS's Reference Group on Human Rights and HIV. Sangram/VAMP's work had long been praised as 'best practice' by UN agencies as well as USAID. She and her husband, Vasant, a prominent newspaper editor, had adopted several children of sex workers.

As it happened, the very next day after Seshu had been accused of being a 'trafficker' by the US government, I found myself seated next to Mark Dybul, the second ranking official in the Office of the US Global AIDS Coordinator, at the opening session of a strategy retreat hosted by UNAIDS. I couldn't hold myself back from telling Dybul how disappointed I was by the US government's actions against Seshu and Sangram, that this was a historic low point in America's AIDS-related efforts in India.

Dybul looked astonished—no doubt taken aback that anyone from UNAIDS would speak so critically to a senior American official—but then caustically replied that the Indian government had admitted to Sangram's involvement in child trafficking. I retorted that everyone working on AIDS knew well that governments rarely stood up for sex workers and other reviled citizens, and so its views were hardly likely to be accurate. (As it was, to the embarrassment of the Bush administration, the Indian government insisted a few days later that the US Embassy in Delhi publicly retract its charges against Seshu and Sangram.)

Soon after, Dybul was promoted to the post of US Global AIDS Coordinator, replacing Tobias, and became ever more clearly an apologist for the Bush administration's policies. Here was an openly gay man advancing the pernicious agenda of a President who had attacked gays in his own country and done nothing against even the most barbaric incidents of homophobia abroad. (Bush had packed key posts with people hostile to gay rights, and exploited conservative opposition to gay marriage to mobilize support in the 2004 presidential elections. Earlier, in his 1994 campaign to become Texas governor, he had defended the state's sodomy law as a 'symbolic gesture of traditional values'.) Dybul ought to have had some instinctive empathy for sex workers given his likely personal experience of stigma as a gay man—not so long ago, being gay was no less damning to a public career as being a sex worker. Instead, he praised the administration's dictatorial, brutalizing policies, calling them a 'compassionate response' to prostitution.

Those few minutes of taking Dybul to task were the only positive ones in that meeting, which otherwise only served to show me yet another depressing aspect of Piot's decline. This was that Piot had also developed the 'Lords of Poverty' syndrome, the chronic addiction of many in the international development set to enjoying high luxury on public expense. (*Lords of Poverty* was the title of a 1989 book by British journalist Graham Hancock that excoriated the international development industry.) The venue for the two-day meeting—touted as an 'envisioning exercise' to plan the long-term response to the pandemic—was the grand palace-hotel of Le Mirador Kempinski at the exclusive Swiss resort of Mont Pèlerin.

Why UNAIDS was hosting a meeting at this château-like building with its magnificent views of Lake Geneva, and paying for sumptuous Michelin-starred feasts at baronial dining tables, I could not understand. The hundreds of thousands of Swiss francs wasted on this pointless talk-fest would have run a small country's AIDS-treatment services for a year. I wondered if other participants, such as legendary South African AIDS activist Zackie Achmat, were also upset by this excess. Were they also trying to figure out what all this luxury had to do with the focus of our deliberations—the tens of millions of people living with AIDS who fretted constantly about how to pay for their next meal and their next dose of medicines, or the millions of impoverished young women and transgenders reduced to selling sex to pay for their daily needs?

The excess was on a par with the worst that I had seen at the World Bank or the most mismanaged UN organizations. To see it coming from the UNAIDS Secretariat was devastating. I was relieved that I had been assigned to a cheap place nearby, rather than being implicated unknowingly in this shameless waste.

It was obvious that a decade of being a top UN official—Piot was now in an unbroken third five-year term as the Secretariat's boss, thanks to a loophole in administrative rules—had corrupted his sense of right and wrong. His life as the UN Under-Secretary-General handling the era's global cause célèbre had left him dangerously divorced from reality. The endless hours of hobnobbing with politicians, billionaires, celebrities and royalty had led Piot to forget the hoi polloi whose survival he was supposed to be fighting for, the tens of millions living with HIV as well as the many millions of marginalized people at grave risk of contracting HIV.

I was to see that in his third term, Piot had become visibly disenchanted with dealing with the nitty-gritty realities of the world's efforts against AIDS, particularly now that he was being criticized by activists and observers for his complicity with the Bush administration's destructive policies. Piot should have either lived up to his responsibilities or, if he felt he no longer had the dedication to combat the Bush administration, handed the job to someone who could do it justice. Instead, he clung to office, kept the Bush administration happy, dismissed constructive criticism as malice, and frittered his formidable energy on bombastic thinking and grandiose projects.

Piot's later speeches and articles, to my frustration, became an unending bravura attempt to display his genius as a thinker—celebrating pointless complexity instead of the practical doable, and making the erroneous argument that everything from poverty to gender inequality had to be set right in the world before the pandemic could be slowed. And akin to the Mont Pèlerin meeting, he organized one vanity project after another—each of them grossly expensive, consuming a great amount of staff time, and contributing little or nothing to the fulfilment of the Secretariat's core responsibilities. Half a million or one million dollars, or even vastly more, were frittered away on reports and initiatives of little value, read and used by no one.

There was *AIDS in Africa: Three scenarios to 2025*, a coffee-table tome on the future of the continent's epidemic. Bizarrely, it was told through folksy, illustrated stories, as if to suggest that Africans cannot grasp anything more complex. There was a two-hundred-and-fifty-page public relations chronicle on the first decade of UNAIDS's work, which itself took three years to be published. There was 'AIDS 2031', touted as planning the long-term response to the pandemic, 2031 being fifty years from the initial medical reports of AIDS patients in 1981. These fed the gravy train for highly paid staff and consultants in the multi-billion-dollar AIDS industry; neither any money nor any good trickled down to the grassroots.

When the UNAIDS Secretariat moved from its homely, nondescript offices to the latest addition to the UN's gleaming modern buildings in Geneva, boasting sky-high atriums and acres of tinted glass, Piot told the assembled staff that we should be proud to have the nicest building and the best art collection of the city's international organizations. I noticed that quite a few of my colleagues seemed baffled to hear this, no doubt wondering where the once-committed scientist and hardworking leader had disappeared to. This glacial new building symbolized how much the Secretariat had changed in recent years under Piot—it had become a prosperous, self-serving bureaucracy, like the World Bank and countless UN organizations, not the lean, almost NGO-like body it had been during its early years. I wished fervently that I had worked there in the days it had been driven and committed, rather than now.

In the fall of 2006, my disagreements with Piot coming to a head, I resigned from the Secretariat. Within months of leaving, I realized that public frustration with Piot's abeyance of leadership had mounted to such an extent that—for the first time in its short decade of existence—UNAIDS was embattled rather than praised. It faced a barrage of criticism on myriad grounds from policymakers, public health experts, activists and non-governmental organizations around the world, its reputation reaching such a nadir that there were calls for the programme to be disbanded altogether.

One of the major charges against the Secretariat was that for several years it had consciously exaggerated global estimates of the number of people living with HIV, refusing to accept convincing evidence from outside experts that the epidemic had peaked even in sub-Saharan Africa and was not expanding relentlessly anywhere else, including China and India. Eventually, in its 2007 epidemiological report, the Secretariat cut its estimates of the worldwide number of people living with HIV from forty million to thirty-three million, and the number of new HIV infections from nearly five million a year in the previous year's estimate to 2.5 million.

For India alone, the estimates of people infected were more than halved, falling from 5.7 million to 2.5 million. In one sweep, this transformed India from being a country with an uncontrollable HIV epidemic to one that had only seen it grow sluggishly over the past twenty years.

The stunning scale of the revisions did irreparable harm to the Secretariat's reputation for technical excellence. To many, it was evidence that the Secretariat had been motivated by the desire to keep AIDS high on the global political agenda, or, less excusably, by the self-serving goal of ensuring that AIDS continued to command the lion's share of global donor funds.

Another storm of criticism was triggered by a 'Guidance Note on HIV and sex work' posted on the Secretariat website for consideration at the summer 2007 meeting of the UNAIDS governing board. It was the first major UNAIDS publication on sex workers in years, a pall of self-censorship having gripped the programme since the Bush administration began its global anti-prostitution crusade, with the words 'sex workers' rarely finding mention in the reams of paper, it produced.

The Guidance Note broke completely with UNAIDS's previous 'best practice' guidance on sex work and, instead, parroted the Bush administration's abolitionist views. It was met by outraged criticism by sex worker rights networks as well as other human rights groups. The protests forced the Secretariat to pull the document from the website, and the governing board eventually instructed UNAIDS to revise the guidance note in consultation with sex workers' rights groups.

On reading the guidance note, I was not surprised either by the outraged reactions or the governing board's demand that UNAIDS improve it. The eight-page document was poorly argued, and had an abysmally weak evidentiary base.

The oddest aspect was the fact that its argumentation and recommendations broke completely with UNAIDS's past understanding of sex work, which had been detailed in numerous documents, such as the 1998 guidelines on HIV and human rights that I so admired. There was no explanation given for why UNAIDS had turned its back on the closely considered guidance of the past. In a bizarre but revealing omission, the guidance note did not list any of those reports in its footnotes or bibliography.

The grubby fingerprints of the Bush administration were visible all over the guidance note. The kowtowing to the administration's duplicitous equating of sex work with sex trafficking began right from the opening section, which read: 'The increasing feminization of migration and the involvement of families, kin networks and local communities in the movement of women and girls, blurs the difference between trafficking and sex work.' Astonishingly, there was not a single footnote or reference provided to back this stunning claim. (In telling contrast, the most comprehensive review of sex work by UNAIDS had concluded just five years earlier that the 'forces that drive people into sex work ... can vary—sometimes widely ... Many people enter sex work for economic reasons; that is, it may be the only, or the best-paying, employment option. Others are coerced into sex work through violence, trafficking or debt bondage. Some, particularly adults, freely choose sex work as their occupation'.)

And so it went—one astonishing unfounded claim after another, one inexplicable break with past UN guidance after another. Where UNAIDS, the Office of the UN High Commissioner for Human Rights and the International Parliamentarians Union had issued guidance that clearly advised governments to review 'with the aim of repeal' criminal legislation and other laws that criminalize 'adult sex work that involves no victimization', there was not a single hint of this in the guidance note.

Nor was there any echo of the explicit warning of their earlier advice that 'criminalization reinforces the stigma associated with sex work and pushes sex workers to the margins of the society', or of the recommendation that 'where sex work has legal standing, laws against abuse and exploitation are more likely to be enforced, thus reducing the incidence of violence against sex workers, especially as perpetrated by corrupt enforcement authorities'.

The acquiescence to the Bush administration was so extreme that no mention was made that the worldwide evidence reviewed by UNAIDS over the past decade had showed how collectives run by empowered sex workers, such as the Durbar and Sangram/VAMP, produced the best results not just in stemming HIV rates and improving overall conditions, but also in tackling sex trafficking and child prostitution.

There is no shame amongst the shameless, I thought to myself, when—right on the heels of the guidance note fracas—the American press reported that former US AIDS Ambassador Randall Tobias, recently promoted to Deputy Secretary of State in charge of all American foreign aid, was a regular user of high-end call girls. 'Ex-AIDS chief in escort flap called hypocritical: Backed US policy that forbids aid to help prostitutes', the *Boston Globe* wrote.

The hypocrisy beggared belief. Apparently, the man who had ferociously led the Bush administration's efforts to eradicate prostitution around the world himself made regular use of sex workers! Tobias's attempts at defending himself included the tragicomic claim that he did not have sex with the women from the escort services, but merely had the 'gals come over to the condo to give me a massage'.

Within months, Republican Senator David Vitter, one of the fiercest proponents of 'family values' conservatism, was implicated in the same scandal, proving to be another regular client of the escort service used by Tobias. (Unlike Tobias, however, Vitter did not insult the public's intelligence by claiming that the women were only providing massages.)

Less than a year later, New York Governor Eliot Spitzer, a Democrat, resigned after a federal investigation exposed his double life as a regular client of high-end sex workers. Not only had Spitzer vigorously prosecuted escort services (of precisely the kind he later secretly patronized) in his previous post as New York State's attorney general—parroting Bush in calling prostitution 'modern-day slavery'—he had also inked the toughest anti-sex work law in the US during his first days in the Governor's office. This law equated sex work with trafficking, handing up to a year in jail to men who patronized prostitutes, regardless of whether the prostitute was a victim of trafficking, a move that led abolitionists to call him their 'hero'. Yet, in the past few years, Spitzer had spent as much as $80,000 on $1,000-an-hour sex workers.

The scandals led to the worldwide mocking of the Bush administration's anti-prostitution crusade. They showed the moral bankruptcy of its advocates, doing more to counter and discredit their views than all that had been achieved by our appeals to logic, evidence and human rights principles.

Even so, my exultation soon turned into disappointment when it became evident that these powerful men would not be held to account while the women implicated would surely be victimized. I was reminded of Doon School in the 1970s, when the witch-hunting prefects thrashed defenseless younger boys whom they themselves molested routinely. As was the case in that school boy world, the big and the powerful in the real world were also especially prone to priggish moralizing and staggering hypocrisy. (Quite apart from the prostitution-related scandals of Tobias, Vitter and Spitzer, UNAIDS's Piot was also discovered to be in an illegal romance with a highly paid consultant who had been hired at his insistence, while the World Bank's hawkish Bush-appointee Paul Wolfowitz had recently been brought down due to similar findings. And the Catholic Church was being battered by revelations that, for decades, it had systematically ignored rape and sexual abuse of tens of thousands of children by clergy worldwide, allowing serial abusers to continue to prey on youngsters.) As in the Doon scenario, they usually escaped punishment by virtue of their power and stature, while their victims were reviled and persecuted.

Thus, under US federal and state laws on prostitution and sex trafficking (which criminalize the buying and selling of sex), Spitzer, Tobias and Vitter should have faced criminal investigations and jail terms extending to several years. But nothing of the sort happened.

Though the scandal forced Tobias to resign from his top-level Bush administration post, he immediately became the head of the Indianapolis Airport Authority. Vitter continued as Senator after apologizing for having committed a 'very serious sin'. Spitzer became a political pundit, with a column in *Slate* and a nightly TV show. It was an indictment of America's vaunted boast that no one is above the law—rich, powerful men were indeed above the law, seemingly no less than in corrupt India.

But, in depressing contrast, as always, the sex workers and madams who catered to these powerful men were cruelly punished. A year after one of her former employees hanged herself rather than face trial, 'D.C. Madam' Deborah Jeane Palfrey, the middle-aged former escort who ran the service used by Tobias, Vitter and thousands of other affluent men, hung herself shortly before her sentencing, rather than suffer years in jail. In a handwritten note, she described her predicament as a 'modern-day lynching'.

17

The Most Dangerous of Times

The breadth and scale of the harm being done to sex workers by the Bush anti-prostitution campaign mounted each year. I saw this when I set out on the road again for researching this book after quitting UNAIDS.

Everywhere I went, in all the many places where American aid and might wielded outsize clout, there was only worsening persecution of sex workers, the imposition of ever-harsher laws, and massive cuts in funding for the valuable HIV prevention programmes in which sex workers themselves played a leadership role. The progress that had seemed imminent in India and elsewhere just a few years earlier had, instead, turned into terrible reversal.

Thus, in contrast to its expectation less than a decade back that sex work by consenting adults would soon be treated rationally as an accepted part of the global entertainment industry, the *Economist* now noted critically: 'The oldest profession is also the oldest pretext for outraged moralising and unrealistic lawmaking devised by man ... Outside a few pragmatic enclaves, attitudes are hardening. Whereas, ten years ago, the discussion was mostly about how to manage prostitution and make it less harmful, the aim now is to find ways to stamp it out. The puritans have the whip hand not because they can prove that tough laws will make life better for women, but because they have convinced governments that prostitution is intolerable by its very nature.'

It was the rare government, such as Brazil's, that had the political will to challenge the Bush administration's diktats, even if this meant losing many millions of dollars in American aid and being charged with promoting 'sex slavery'. More typically, governments began to consider anti-prostitution laws that toed the Bush administration line, which equated sex work with sex trafficking and child sexual exploitation, or moved to increase the criminalization of sex work in already existing laws along the lines of the US model.

India was amongst these, along with Bangladesh, Cambodia, the Czech Republic, Guatemala, Lithuania, Mexico, Nepal, Papua New Guinea, South Africa, South Korea and Zambia. And in these countries as well as many others, the anti-prostitution sentiment fuelled by the Bush campaign stoked government and public violence against sex workers of a concerted intensity that had never been known before.

In sub-Saharan Africa, the moralistic hysteria whipped up by American-financed hardline Christian groups led to sex workers being blamed for these countries' ruinous hyper-epidemics of AIDS, much as they had been accused in the early years when the disease first emerged. (Gay men were the other scapegoats this time around, with extremist Christian clergy in Kenya, Namibia and Uganda—often publicly abetted by visiting American preachers—urging their governments and followers to execute gay men.) Zambia launched a mass incarceration of young women suspected of selling sex, with the police publicly whipping sex workers while calling them 'bitches who are killing the nation' for spreading AIDS. In the Democratic Republic of Congo, twenty-nine cases of sexual violence against female sex workers by police or military, including rape, kidnapping and torture, were documented in just three months of 2007.

In Latin America, the Latin America and Caribbean Sex Worker Network documented the murder of thirty-four sex workers over just ten months. In Bolivia, violent raids culminated in the public lynching of sex workers.

In Cambodia, Laos and Thailand, scores of sex workers began to mysteriously disappear after the launch of the Bush anti-trafficking efforts. Subsequent investigations by human rights groups and journalists revealed that many of them were being held prisoner by private 'raid and rescue' organizations on the pretext that they were victims of trafficking and sexual slavery and needed protection. These organizations were funded by hardline US Christian groups and the Bush administration. Even larger numbers of sex workers were jailed in brutal conditions in governmental detention centres. Hundreds were deported to strife-torn Myanmar or troubled ethnic-minority areas in the region, after being imprisoned as illegal immigrants.

I witnessed firsthand the storm of abuse that had been unleashed in Cambodia. At the beginning of 2008, to avoid losing US foreign aid under the Bush administration's anti-trafficking campaign, the Cambodian government issued a sweeping law that outlawed prostitution by equating it with sex trafficking of women and children. The Bush administration commended Cambodia for the new law, and promptly removed it from its watch list of human-trafficking countries.

But, within Cambodia, the new anti-prostitution law unleashed a violent campaign against sex workers by the police, far more savage than the periodic sweeps of the past. The police—themselves well known to be regular users of sex workers—interpreted the law stigmatizing and banning sex work as a licence to exploit and abuse these women with even greater impunity than before. They had been given greater power to do so because the new law criminalized soliciting, which had not been an offence until then.

A large but unknown number of female and transgender sex workers were imprisoned in jails and so-called 'rehabilitation' centres—and even by the time of my documentation visit in April 2008, several months after the raids had begun, the whereabouts of hundreds remained unknown. This was confirmed by many domestic human rights groups, such as the Women's Network for Unity, working with sex workers.

The sense of fear was palpable, in strange contrast to the indolent French-colonial feel of Phnom Penh, with its colonnaded houses, the promenades along the vast, slow Mekong, and the elegantly attired Cambodians and expatriates. Not one sex worker was willing to be quoted, or even to meet anywhere that could put them at risk of being spotted with me, an outsider with a notepad.

I eventually interviewed sex workers in crowded cafes, pretending that we were friends meeting up. I kept to my promise of not taking written notes or taping the conversations. The women I met had sold sex off the street or from porn video shacks and brothels located in lower-income parts of the city. It was clear from what they told me that even more than in India, sex work was one of the few earning options open to impoverished women in Cambodia, one of Asia's least developed countries, because hundreds of thousands of young men and women were in desperate competition for even the lowly-paid jobs in tourism and sweat-shop garment manufacturing, the only other existing industries. They told me that ever since the police crackdown began some months ago, they had been subjected to extortion, beatings and rape by policemen. Until then, the police had never acted in such a concerted, harsh fashion against them.

Most had stopped working because the police now demanded bribes of fifty or more US dollars, ten times more than what they used to extort before the enactment of the anti-prostitution law. Their children and parents were destitute, they told me, as they depended on the women's daily earnings to eat and live.

Two of the women had been held against their will for several months at a rehabilitation centre, prevented from contacting their relatives despite having IDs proving that they were in their thirties. Even frantic pleas that they at least be allowed to phone their children had been denied. Each one of them had friends who were still missing—they had no idea where they were, and were too scared to look for them. Later, I hired a local motorcyclist to drive me through the neighbourhoods where they had worked earlier—whole stretches of eerily empty bamboo huts that once housed low-price karaoke bars and brothels, but were now sealed off. The only living creatures in sight were stray dogs and cats.

Just as astounding as the all-pervading sense of fear was the conspiracy of denial. Barring sex workers, human rights groups and a few journalists, everyone else in Phnom Penh acted as if not one sex worker had been beaten, raped or made to disappear in recent months. Human rights abuses were so commonplace in Cambodia and so intertwined with the corrupting over-reliance on foreign aid that the UN and donor governments habitually looked the other way.

UNAIDS's Cambodia office, despite being the first place that Cambodian and international sex workers' rights groups had turned to for support, joined in the public silence, as did its Bangkok regional headquarters. It was only some months later that the UN Office of the High Commissioner on Human Rights began to investigate the abuses in government detention centres, and though its reports were never made public, the findings were known to include evidence of suspicious deaths, rape, torture, and illegal restrictions on freedom of movement.

As it happened, at the time of my research in Cambodia, UNAIDS's governing board meeting was being held in Chiang Mai, just a few hundred kilometres away, in neighbouring Thailand. Would Peter Piot criticize the campaign of abuses being inflicted on Cambodian sex workers in his opening speech to the board? I really didn't expect so, given Piot's past record of failing to challenge the Bush administration. Moreover, US AIDS Ambassador Mark Dybul was currently chairing the UNAIDS governing board. I doubted that with Dybul in this key post, Piot would take the Bush administration to task.

And so it was: there was not even a single word mentioned about the dire situation of Cambodia's sex workers in Piot's speech, or in the discussions that followed in the days of the board meeting. UNAIDS's fall to being an accomplice in Bush's war on sex workers was absolute.

It took many months of protesting by human rights organizations, particularly the Asia-Pacific Network of Sex Worker Organizations, before the Cambodian government suspended its violent campaign against sex workers. Now the evidence of abuses, so studiously ignored by UNAIDS and other international organizations, came to the forefront.

It was finally revealed that hundreds of sex workers—as well as drug users and beggars—had been held in inhuman conditions at so-called 'rehabilitation' centres, including the government's infamous Prey Speu detention centre on Phnom Penh's outskirts. They testified to daily beatings and rapes, custodial deaths and suicides to bring an end to the torment. The *Economist*'s correspondent wrote from Phnom Penh in the summer of 2009, 'Barely legible on (Prey Speu's) grimy walls a few weeks ago were cries for help and whispers of despair from the tormented souls once crammed into its grimy cells. "This is to mark that I lived in terror under oppression," read one such message.'

India was a prime target of the Bush administration's war on sex workers. In 2004, the US State Department put India on its 'watch list', one of the worst tiers in its unilateral annual ranking of nations according to their performance in combating human trafficking, especially that relating to sex trafficking.

India's Congress-led government moved swiftly to placate the Bush administration. In May 2005, the Ministry of Women and Child Development, headed by Renuka Chowdhury, proposed far-reaching amendments to the Immoral Trafficking (Prevention) Act—the primary Indian law governing sex work and trafficking—incorporating all the points held dear by the Bush administration and abolitionist campaigners.

The amendments would effectively change the law from the ambivalent criminalization of sex work that had existed since the first version of the anti-trafficking act was enacted in 1923, to heavy-handed prohibition of sex work along the lines of the Bush administration's ideas conflating sex work with sex slavery. Modelled on laws already in force in Sweden and New York state, it would also criminalize paying for sexual services on the grounds that clients were abetting trafficking and sexual exploitation. Anyone found to even be visiting a brothel faced up to six months in jail and a fine of Rs 50,000.

And though the amendments were ostensibly aimed at emancipating sex workers, it was clear that the overriding intent was prohibition at any cost, even that of immeasurably worsening the abuse of the women. Thus, one astonishing clause would sanction raids to forcibly remove even adult sex workers from their profession—in the past, only minors or adults who declared that they were victims of abuse or trafficking could be legally removed through raids and given shelter by government institutions. Another clause would increase the length of time—to an astounding seven years—that a sex worker could be imprisoned in corrective institutions.

I was flabbergasted that Chowdhury could defend these provisions, which overrode an adult's rights to self-determination so blatantly and inflicted such cruel punishments on sex workers. (Strikingly, over a decade back, the National Commission for Women had pressed to have precisely such clauses removed from India's anti-prostitution laws, emphasizing that they victimized sex workers.) The intent was clearly to make it impossible for India's sex workers to continue earning, even if they were adults who insisted that they sold sex willingly and had entered the trade free of exploitation, as so very many I knew had.

Chowdhury's proposed amendments set off a storm of criticism. Sex workers, collectives, including the Durbar and Sangram/VAMP, protested that they as well as countless others would be left jobless and destitute if their clients were arrested. They angrily criticized the provisions that allowed the removal and imprisonment of even adult sex workers who expressly stated that they were selling sex entirely of their own accord. 'This is typical of the patriarchal Indian state, which believes that women never achieve adulthood,' said Bharati Dey, the Durbar's Secretary.

AIDS service organizations and the Health Ministry's National AIDS Control Organization—now headed by a committed official with a specialization in public health, Kanuru Sujatha Rao—lambasted the amended bill for the damage that would be done to HIV prevention efforts. 'The criminalization of clients would force both clients and sex workers underground, worsening the already high obstacles to promoting safer sex in the commercial sex trade,' NACO wrote in an inter-ministerial memo. 'Moreover, with fewer clients and diminishing earnings, sex workers would find it harder to insist on condom use, resulting in escalation of STIs and HIV.' Human rights groups warned that the police would now turn to harassing and blackmailing sex workers' clients, in addition to exploiting the sex workers themselves.

Support for the sex workers came from once-inconceivable quarters, evidence that the efforts put in by sex workers and their allies over the past decades had positively influenced the thinking of officials even beyond the world of AIDS prevention. The Ministry of Home Affairs—responsible for implementing criminal laws through the police—stated that the amendments only worsened the confusion between trafficking and voluntary sex work. This would distract attention and resources from aiding genuine victims of trafficking and abuse, it said, candidly noting that the amendments were likely to encourage the police to abuse sex workers even more harshly.

Another reason for this broad opposition to the amendments proposed by Chowdhury was the fact that there was now a wealth of data and knowledge on Indian sex work conditions, rather than the utter ignorance of the pre-AIDS era. All of this contradicted the main argument put forward for the amendments—that India's sex workers were universally victims of trafficking.

Over the past decade, researchers on AIDS and sexuality had written thousands of papers and dozens of books on contemporary sex work patterns in India. Even the first autobiography by an Indian sex worker had been published by fifty-year-old Nalini Jameela of Kerala, leading to enormous sales in Malayalam as well as English. This knowledge base had improved yet further because of the Bill & Melinda Gates Foundation's $300-million HIV prevention effort in India, begun in 2003, which commissioned massive country-wide surveys and in-depth research on sexual behaviours to guide its work, particularly about sex work patterns.

Arguably, more was now known about sex work in contemporary India than in any other comparable country, in stark contrast to the absolute lack of knowledge when the epidemic first emerged in 1986 amongst Selvi and the other sex workers in the Madras reformatory. It was finally possible to reach conclusions based on hard evidence and an understanding of dynamic trends, rather than on punditry, ideology or imagination, or even—as in my case—the inevitably incomplete knowledge I was left with despite years of research.

The defining characteristics of sex work in 21st century India, as revealed by this vast body of research, not only ran counter to popular notions but also showed clearly that the overwhelming majority of India's three million or more women sex workers—roughly 1 per cent of the adult female population—entered this trade of their own accord. They did it to escape bad or abusive marriages, as a means of survival and as the best-paying alternative available to them, not from the kinds of criminal abuse that constitute trafficking.

Thus, far larger numbers of women in the eastern and peninsular states, from Bengal to Kerala—where women possess significantly greater autonomy and overall well-being than in the northern half of the country—turned to selling sex, contradicting the claim that sex work was overwhelmingly driven by the organized exploitation of hapless women. And for many of these women, sex work was neither a full-time nor a permanent occupation, but something they could turn to in times of personal or family crisis, or to supplement other sources of earning when that proved inadequate.

There were yet other striking results that ran counter to the notion that trafficking was the main supply chain for sex work. A vast majority of sex workers across India had begun the practice as adults, mostly when they were in their mid-twenties, not as teenage girls, typically after working at low-paid labouring jobs. And only a small minority of sex workers operated from organized places such as 'lodges' or brothels—the settings popularly associated with trafficking. In fact, the majority sold sex independently from public places or their homes, a trend that had strengthened with the affordability of mobile phones. This pattern held true even in the major cities, including Delhi, Kolkata and Mumbai.

Sex work was widespread in rural areas too, especially in peninsular India, with rural women turning to sex work at even younger ages than in urban areas because of the dire lack of economic opportunities. Only a small percentage of sex workers were from communities popularly associated with sex work, such as those of the devadasi tradition.

Also, in a major new trend, higher-end sex work had expanded as urban India was transformed by the booming economy. There were more men with cash to spend, and more middle-class women and men selling sex as the quickest way to making a buck. Cell phones and the Internet offered anonymity. In every city that I travelled to, even the mainstream newspapers were full of classified ads for massage parlours and 'friendship clubs', offering the services of both women and men. A web search for 'escorts' and 'call girls' produced thousands of sites, ranging from independent one-woman operations to large agencies offering women, men and transgenders of diverse nationalities.

All in all, this new wealth of research conclusively showed that given their illiteracy (with an average of two out of every three sex workers with no schooling), lack of employable skills and the Indian reality that over 90 per cent of people worked in low-paid informal jobs, selling sex was the only decently paid trade available to a vast number of working-poor Indian women. It offered earnings many times higher than what one would get from labouring in the fields or construction sites, or from working as maids or cleaners—hard labour that left them vulnerable to sexual abuse anyway. All the evidence indicated that a vast majority of women sex workers had turned to this trade of their own accord, based on an independent, autonomous calculus of what served their best interests—given the dismal lack of choices they confronted because of India's failure to make headway against poverty and the atrocious treatment of women. In no rational sense could their decisions or predicament be described as sex trafficking or sex slavery.

The research did not downplay the fact that trafficking into prostitution remained a sizeable and unacceptably cruel problem. But, clearly, the need to survive in India's harsh realities was the primary factor for women entering sex work.

There was nothing in this evidence to suggest that it was imperative for the good of India's women that this vital means of income be choked off or made more dangerous still by laws that punished them ever more harshly. To the contrary, the evidence indicated that reforms such as decriminalization and support for collective empowerment and legal rights were those needed urgently if the goal was truly that of helping the many women in India who sold sex. Simultaneously, vastly more had to be done to both protect and empower impoverished young women in backward areas, so as to tackle the broad factors that put them at risk of being trafficked, whether into prostitution or, even more commonly, other forms of forced labour and forced marriage.

Predictably, diehard abolitionists purposefully ignored all this evidence. The *New York Times's* Nicholas Kristof wrote in 2007, "There may be a sound argument for legalization and sex worker unions in Brazil and South Africa, perhaps even China. My sense is that in those countries, many women genuinely choose to be prostitutes because of economic pressures or opportunities. But in India, I have yet to find a single woman who made that choice—every single one of them first entered after being forced by a trafficker, her parents, or her husband.'

In a related column, sensationally titled 'The 21st-Century Slave Trade', Kristof charged, 'The brothels of India are the slave plantations of the 21st century.' About a woman that the controversial abolitionist group Aapne Aap had reportedly rescued from a Bihar brothel, he wrote, 'Meena's owners also wanted to breed her, as is common in Indian brothels. One purpose is to have boys to be labourers and girls to be prostitutes, and a second is to have hostages to force the mother to cooperate.'

Some years later, Kristof pronounced, 'India probably has more modern slaves than any country in the world. It has millions of women and girls in its brothels, often held captive for their first few years until they grow resigned to their fate.'

I couldn't recognize this barbaric and utterly lawless India, of millions of women held as slaves and forced to breed in brothels, that Kristof was writing about with such evident authority. His harangue reminded me of an American of an earlier generation, Katherine Mayo, the white supremacist and imperialist, whose 1927 book *Mother India* had variously accused Indians of being 'sex-ridden' and imprisoned by their 'slave mentality'. As it transpired, in just a few years, an international scandal about fabricated evidence showed Kristof's ranting about sex trafficking in Asia to be massively overblown.

Chowdhury also resolutely ignored all the hard data and evidence. She even ignored testimonials given by women from the Durbar and other sex work collectives. Years of see-sawing battle followed.

Chowdhury repeatedly brought the bill to the Union Cabinet and Parliament for approval. But opposition from the powerful Home Affairs ministry, allied with the Health Ministry and its AIDS control body, resulted in the Union Cabinet getting divided and the bill stalled. Even a review by a Group of Ministers failed to break the impasse. Thousands of sex workers marched to Parliament, urging that the bill not be passed into law.

In May 2006, Chowdhury introduced a slightly revised bill in the Lok Sabha, but opposition by other ministers now led to it being referred to a Parliamentary Standing Committee. The Standing Committee's report to Parliament urged Chowdhury to reconsider key amendments, including the two particularly controversial ones that criminalized the clients of sex workers and allowed for the lengthy imprisonment of sex workers who were 'repeat offenders'. (Eventually, the amendment bill lapsed in early 2009 with new national elections, to never be championed again by the Congress government now that President Bush was no longer in office.)

Though Chowdhury's bill had failed to be passed, testimony that India's democracy functioned at least in keeping the worst of outcomes from being realized into public policy, the regressive anti-prostitution debate fuelled a storm of violence against sex workers in many parts of the country. The violence was concentrated in states where the BJP, Shiv Sena, RSS and other obscurantist Hindutva groups were powerful.

In these groups, the Bush administration had receptive allies for its anti-prostitution views. Indeed, the US Christian right and the Hindutva groups, both intent on using politics to advance their bigoted take on religion, had eerily similar views about the need to curb the right of women to make decisions regarding their own bodies, their sexuality and reproduction. In the view of Hindutva's patriarchal leaders, Indian women had to be chaste and pure in their ordained roles of submissive wives and productive mothers of male children, as they embodied Bharat Mata, the sacred Hindu motherland that they were fighting to establish. There was no place in Bharat Mata for women who sold sex, particularly those assertive enough to insist that their rights as citizens be respected whatever their profession.

The Hindutva groups had begun persecuting sex workers even before President Bush's campaign fanned their animus. In 2002, in Nippani, a small town in Karnataka's northern Belgaum district, years of HIV prevention work by Sangram/VAMP were derailed by the local Shiv Sena and the police, when mobs attacked the collective's local office and assaulted sex workers. The local Shiv Sena leader told the press, 'Under the garb of the HIV/AIDS prevention programme, these women are promoting prostitution.' Nippani's police chief refused to accept a complaint by the women of VAMP, instead calling them 'bloody veshyas and not normal citizens', threatening to 'strip all the sex workers in the public square and beat them black and blue', and arrest them under anti-prostitution laws.

Now, with their views legitimised by President Bush and Western abolitionists, the Hindutva forces launched a sustained campaign against sex workers. What unfolded was far more devastating than even the terrible abuses sex workers had suffered in the first decade of India's AIDS epidemic. While the earlier mass raids and imprisonment had been knee-jerk actions fuelled by hysterical fears about the disease, the efforts this time appeared almost aimed at eradicating the women themselves, as if they were foul blots on Indian culture that had to be obliterated. In its scale and intensity of violence, it dwarfed even the parallel campaign being waged against gays and transgenders.

In the city of Surat, in late 2003, the police—under the BJP government of Narendra Modi—invoked the national anti-trafficking act and other laws to evict nearly seven hundred sex workers and their children from Chakla Bazar, even though the area had been home to sex workers for hundreds of years. The following year, the BJP government of Goa demolished the vast Baina brothels (which I had visited a decade earlier while with the World Bank), leaving hundreds of sex workers homeless in the midst of the monsoons. In Uttar Pradesh, brothels in Allahabad, Lucknow and Meerut were torched or demolished by extremist Hindutva groups.

Then there were the American abolitionists-led raids in 2005 in the small Maharashtra towns where Sangram/VAMP worked. That year, dance bars—featuring Bollywood-style mujras by fully clad women whom the men could admire but not touch or proposition—were banned throughout Maharashtra for allegedly being a front for trafficking and prostitution. Over a hundred thousand women lost highly paid jobs, forcing many to turn to sex work. Numerous women went to Middle Eastern countries to sell sex, facing an even higher risk of abuse and persecution.

In 2007, in Karnataka's Channapatana, with a BJP government in the offing, goons and the police brutally attacked sex workers who had gathered to peacefully demonstrate against police brutality. In Bihar, ruled by the BJP-allied Janata Dal United, mobs attacked sex workers in Sitamarhi town and burned down two hundred and fifty homes, while the police stood by.

Consequently, the first decade of the 21st century became the most dangerous of times for sex workers in India, instead of being an era of great progress, as had seemed likely just a few years earlier. Sex workers and rights campaigners who were facing the imposition of a brutal law, losing HIV prevention funds from USAID, and fearful of raids and worsening persecution, had to fight the Bush administration

Maryam Shahmanesh

Baina, demolished

and its hardline Christian allies, Chowdhury's Ministry of Women and Child Development, and the Hindutva forces from doing them even more harm.

The fight came from those who were least empowered. On a 2008 visit to Sangli, the small Maharashtra town where the sex workers' collective VAMP had sprung deep roots since 1992, the middle-aged sari-clad women—with a sprinkling of kothi men—told me about the terrifying mass raids, and how they had taken a more grievous toll on their morale than all the localized incidents of bigotry and oppression they had faced till then.

Sitting there amongst them, I thought to myself of the bizarre fact that a man born to enormous privilege—now the leader of the world's most powerful nation with nukes and drones and trillions of dollars in his control—was effectively at war against these impoverished and illiterate sex workers. The irony was that Bush professed to have the best interests of these women at heart—he claimed that he wanted to free them from 'sexual slavery'.

VAMP

Sangli's Gokul Nagar sex-work area

But the truth, of course, was that he and the other powerful men sitting far away in the rich world—whether it was US AIDS ambassadors Tobias and Dybul, UNAIDS's Piot, or the *New York Times's* Kristof—fundamentally didn't have any respect for these women. Consequently, they dismissed the sex workers' own accurate assessment of their lives as well as the legitimate solutions they put forward to solve their problems. (The women had thought deeply about the rights and wrongs of their work—one, Kamalabai, told me, 'What's wrong with us selling sex? Look, on TV and in the movies all they do is sell sex! All the stars wear short skirts and hot-pants, they show their legs and their breasts, they dance around—it is all to sell sex, to sell their bodies. The male stars too—what are they doing if not selling sex!') Like patriarchs everywhere, these elite men told these working-poor women exactly how they should behave—and when the women didn't obey, these men went to war against them, pressing for laws that would worsen their oppression, or demonizing them as villainous traffickers and brothel madams.

The fight against the Bush administration and abolitionists also came from two eminent Asian men. They were not radicals or human rights champions but pillars of the establishment—namely Chakravarti Rangarajan, the éminence grise of India's economic planning, and Ban Ki-moon, the recently appointed UN Secretary-General.

Rangarajan, an erstwhile governor of the Reserve Bank of India and key economic adviser to Prime Minister Manmohan Singh, might have seemed an unlikely choice to chair a blue-ribbon Commission on AIDS in Asia, in late 2006. What could an economist with narrow interests in macroeconomics possibly bring to an effort aimed at redirecting Asia's efforts against a disease transmitted by sex and drugs?

But Rangarajan displayed an extraordinary ability to grasp the peculiarities inherent to AIDS—such as the high rates of infection seen amongst outlawed populations, or the imperative need for human rights protection. I saw this first hand at a policy meeting held by the

Commission in January 2007, just a month after my resignation from UNAIDS. He did not appear perturbed by all the frank discussion of sex and drug use—even the matters of anal sex, condoms and lubricant that I inevitably had to cover in my presentation on tackling the raging HIV rate among Asian gay and bisexual men. Both his questions and comments convinced me that he was open-minded and humane.

I realized that my admiring appraisal of Rangarajan was well founded when, as a peer reviewer of the Commission's report, I read its close-to-final drafts in 2007. In place of the dishonesty and confusion that now blighted global policy reports on AIDS, as UNAIDS and other key institutions caved in to the Bush administration's bullying, the Commission had taken a rational position on everything that mattered—including the very issues that had become contentious because of the polarizing impact of Bush's ideological positions. It stated, 'At the national level, decriminalizing sex work, homosexuality, and the use of needles and syringes or drug treatment for injecting people is the most effective way to providing services for these marginalized groups.' There could not have been a sharper critique of the wrong-headedness of the Bush stance on prostitution or drug use.

On formally being presented the Commission's report by Rangarajan at the UN Secretariat in New York City in March 2008, UN Secretary-General Ban Ki-moon said, 'I look to Asian governments to amend outdated laws criminalizing the most vulnerable sections of society, and take all the measures needed to ensure they live in dignity.'

The substance and intent of Ban Ki-moon's statement was clear: he was urging the governments in his native Asia to free the most widely reviled and persecuted groups—whether sex workers, drug users or gay men—from the reach of criminal law, and treat them with the respect due to all human beings.

The launch on that spring day at the UN encapsulated how radically the world had changed in the half-century of my lifetime. Two elderly Asian men had the wisdom and the courage to insist that sex workers, drug users and other widely vilified people had just as much claim to justice as any other individual, while—in contrast—Bush, the President of the vaunted 'free world', and Piot, a European UN Under-Secretary-General (both significantly younger than the Asian men), opposed these legitimate changes.

An increasing number of the once colonized were finally freeing themselves of the stranglehold of abhorrent colonial legacies, of mindsets that belonged to our unfree past. And they—rather than the Western men who habitually laid claim to this mantle—were emerging as the world's leaders in the fight for greater freedoms, particularly for the people longest denied any claim to basic human rights.

But, despite all these efforts, the Bush abolitionist assault on sex work was so richly financed and so fueled by the powerful Christian right that the cause of justice for sex workers never recovered, in India and elsewhere, even long after his presidency ended. This was yet another of Bush's poisonous legacies to the wrecked world he left behind.

In the US, the anti-prostitution gag-rule remained in place through the Obama years, testimony to the depressing fact that the most populist, bad laws and policies are precisely the most difficult to end. Obama's attempts to amend how the gag-rule would affect the billions given annually in American foreign aid led Chris Smith, the hardline Republican who had authored that clause during the Bush administration, to accuse him of 'enabling sex trafficking and prostitution all over the world'.

Everywhere in the West, the notion that sex work had to be abolished because it was indistinguishable from sex trafficking, child prostitution and sexual slavery now had the power of a received truth not only among the reading public but also among decision-makers. This was so, despite the international scandals that had tarred leading figures of the abolitionist cause, including the *New York Times*'s Nicholas Kristof.

In 2014, a *Newsweek* investigation showed that Kristof had been duped for years by his lionized anti-trafficking partner, Somaly Mam, a telegenically beautiful Cambodian whom Kristof had called a 'heroine from the brothels'. After his praise helped her build a multi-million-dollar anti-slavery empire, Mam was revealed to be a con artist who had sensationalized the scale of sex slavery in Cambodia and elsewhere in South-East Asia to win fame and money.

The slew of epic deceits began with her own childhood history, laid out poignantly in her 2005 bestselling memoir, *The Road of Lost Innocence*. (With a glowing foreword by Kristof, the memoir was quickly published in a dozen languages.) Mam had claimed that she had been sold into a brothel as a young child, where she was imprisoned in a cage, raped and tortured. But the truth that now emerged was that she had led a happy rural childhood with her parents, ultimately training to be a teacher. And Mam's heartbreaking claim that traffickers had kidnapped and gang raped her teenage daughter, in retaliation for her anti-trafficking work, was now repudiated by the girl's father, who confirmed that she had eloped with her boyfriend.

Equally stunning, every one of the harrowing stories of young girls brutalized in sex slavery that Kristof had showcased in his *New York Times* columns were now revealed to be cases of outright fraud: they were ordinary girls whom Mam had recruited, carefully trained, and paid to lie about being sex slaves.

In the goriest of Kristof's trafficking pieces, hyperbolically titled 'If This Isn't Slavery, What Is?', a young Cambodian enslaved in a brothel at the age of thirteen recounted rapes, crude forced abortions, daily electric shocks, and being 'painfully stitched up' so that her 'virginity' could be sold again and again. The litany of savagery was capped by Kristof's description of how her right eye was gouged out by an angry pimp, soon growing 'infected and monstrous, spraying blood and pus on customers'.

But the truth was that the teenager had never been in a brothel, and had lost her eye in a childhood operation for a tumor, facts now corroborated by her eye surgeon and family. An equally brutal litany recounted by another girl featured in Kristof's previous column, in this case purportedly kidnapped from Vietnam and then 'offered to Western men and wealthy Cambodians', was also revealed to be a complete fabrication by Mam.

Kristof showed barely any contrition for these massive journalistic failures (particularly striking in the winner of two Pulitzer Prizes). Mam had 'hoodwinked' him, he insisted. The developing world presents unique journalistic challenges because 'ages, names and histories are sometimes elastic', Kristof now claimed, an assertion that sat oddly with his self-assured punditry on the far-flung nations that he jetted into. But rather than revisit his zealous conclusions about sex work, and question the efficacy of abolitionist strategies in light of the fact that he had clearly been wrong about a slew of basic facts, Kristof preachily urged his readers to not let Mam's serial lies ('this is about more than one woman') or the hypocritical follies of his other fallen abolitionist heroes (including former AIDS Ambassador Tobias and New York Governor Spitzer) undermine the noble cause of fighting sex slavery.

These scandals were quickly forgotten in the pell-mell churn of 24/7 news. Consequently, the popular confusion between sex work and sex trafficking remained intact almost everywhere in the industrialized world. Virtually the only firm advocates remaining for sex workers' rights were expert human rights groups such as Amnesty International and Human Rights Watch, progressive grant-makers like the Ford, Hivos and Open Society foundations, and public health specialists. An editorial in the *Lancet*, the influential public health journal, noted, in a January 2015 special issue on sex work and HIV, 'This Series calls on governments to decriminalise sex work ... Sex work is part of the human story. Accepting and embracing sex work—supporting those engaged in sex work to protect their health, bodily integrity and autonomy—should be our humane, as well as our pragmatic, approach to the reality of our human lives.'

But, when seen against the backdrop of the past decades, decriminalization and legal rights for sex workers now seemed unrealizable and utopian goals. Barely an iota of these goals had been secured in the thirty years that had passed since AIDS first began to take its killing toll on sex workers. (Tellingly, it was as far back as 1996 that the *Lancet* had first called for decriminalizing sex work.) And these had been the decades when the pandemic appeared to be overwhelming the world, and decision-makers were nervously receptive to considering exceptional things in an effort to check it. However, that window of opportunity had now closed forever.

Let alone the matter of securing broad human rights for sex workers, even the basic right of ensuring that they could protect themselves from AIDS had not been met. Less than 1 per cent of spending on HIV prevention focused on sex work. The funds directed towards sex workers' organizations were even scarcer. Consequently, even so late into the pandemic, only a tiny minority of sex workers across the world—probably less than one in five—had access to condoms and other HIV prevention services. Rates of HIV remained far higher among sex workers than other women in most developing countries.

There was no longer any global institution to lead the cause of the well-being and rights of sex workers in low- and mid-income countries, as UNAIDS had been doing until Bush launched his war on sex work. Though UNAIDS—under Michel Sidibé, Piot's successor—was now unstinting in vague rhetoric about supporting sex workers, it was wary of the enormous power of the Western abolitionist constituency. Hence, the organization ensured that vital human rights steps—particularly the foundational one of decriminalization—were gutted in a later version of the *Guidance Note on HIV and Sex Work* passed by the UNAIDS board in 2009. UN Women, established in 2010 to champion gender equality, was equally riven by ambivalence, aware that decriminalization and legal rights were critical to the well-being of sex workers, but cowed by the abolitionist stance of its wealthy Scandinavian donors. As for the Global Fund Against AIDS, Tuberculosis and Malaria, the leading source of donor funds for HIV-related efforts in developing countries, it found itself being headed by

Mark Dybul—the same man who had unapologetically led the Bush assault on sex workers, drug users and other defenceless people as US AIDS ambassador.

And, despite all the attention focused on the plight of sex workers in the decades since AIDS emerged, just a handful of countries had begun to treat sex workers more fairly. Germany, the Netherlands and New Zealand—and the Australian province of New South Wales—had removed laws that criminalized sex work. Canada's Supreme Court had struck down the host of laws that criminalized the very activities that sex workers had to do as part of their trade (such as soliciting), stating that they were not consistent with the sex workers' right to liberty 'in a free and democratic society'. Among developing countries, Brazil was the sole exemplar, with sex workers being accorded the same rights as other workers, including legal recognition of the profession and participation in the government pension fund.

But that was, for all intents and purposes, the sum total of progress achieved globally in these decades—despite the countless sex workers who had lost their lives to AIDS and the incredible efforts many had made to emancipate themselves as well as others. In the world's remaining countries, sex workers were either worse off or no better off than before AIDS emerged. Studying this record, I remembered Priscilla Alexander's despairing, frustrated cry all those years ago—in the 1994 article I had commissioned while at the World Bank—that where sex work was concerned, decision-makers seemed chronically unable to undertake rational policymaking, where human rights principles and the well-being of sex workers would guide them rather than puritanical ideology and unexamined prejudice.

As for India, all the vast promise of change I had seen since the mid-1990s had not amounted to lasting gains.

The extraordinary sex worker groups that dotted the country continued to make a huge difference to the safety and well-being of sex workers in the areas they worked in. But they were relatively few in number and the vast majority of sex workers did not have sustained help of any kind, especially because the hundreds of millions in international funding for India's AIDS efforts had evaporated now that the epidemic was found to be far from the gargantuan threat we had expected.

And though the sex worker collectives and supportive human rights groups continued valiantly to turn to the courts and sympathetic politicians to challenge the laws criminalizing sex work, there was no sign of a breakthrough. I realized that this was independent India's characteristic tragedy—that its governance perpetually betrayed the stunning opportunities for emancipation and progress thrown up by the democratic churning at the grassroots.

Instead, with the laws never having been changed, the old abuses of the past—the raids on brothels, the arrests and imprisonment of dozens of women—recurred with depressing everyday regularity, reported in newspapers across the country. With the new emphasis on anti-trafficking, the police insisted they were breaking up traffickers' rings and rescuing 'victimized' women. But, as in the past, the women were arrested, cursorily tried, and imprisoned in reformatories—making a mockery of the police's claims of helping them. (One of the most egregious examples was the arrest of a twenty-three-year-old actress, Shweta Basu Prasad, in late 2014 on charges of being a high-end call-girl. Basu was imprisoned for months in a Hyderabad reformatory. However, the police did not say a word about the wealthy clients she was allegedly servicing, a testimony to the hypocrisy and corruption blighting policing of sex work.) I often could not bear to read these newspaper reports, these constant reminders that sex workers remained as abused, wronged and vilified as decades earlier.

My despair reached its most intense phase when I met Kamala in the summer of 2013. She had agreed, though reluctantly, to meet me outside the women's reformatory in Chennai's Mylapore area. This is where, in a sense, it had all begun nearly thirty years ago—in 1986—when Selvi and five other HIV-positive sex workers were imprisoned here. This was also where Kamala had been imprisoned until recently, in a depressing parallel to Selvi's fate all those decades ago.

Kamala was waiting for me on the far side of the road from the reformatory's gates, the unbroken traffic clearly providing her with a reassuring sense of distance from the reformatory. She was thin, dark, middle-aged, dressed in a green-and-black saree of some shiny synthetic material, her hair tied in a neat plait.

'My years in the remand home were the worst of my life,' she told me. 'It was a prison. From the time I was arrested by the police in 2010, I kept saying to them that I was not a victim of trafficking or pimping, that I wanted to be free, that there was no reason to hold me. But no one listened. And they held me there for more than two years, till 2012.

'Right after our arrest, there were medical tests. We were herded into a van and taken to the hospital. On the way, the women officers told us that it was a medical check-up, that if we had any contagious diseases, we will be kept separately. I can't even imagine how they would be treated. Even the doctors and nurses who tested us looked at us like we were vermin. They addressed us insultingly, shouting orders like we were animals.'

There was a telltale strain of constant worry in Kamala's voice. It struck me that this abused woman had, ironically, the same first name as Kamala Nehru, mother of the most powerful Indian woman in recent times, Indira Gandhi.

She went on: 'I did not keep track of the number of times, but I must have been produced before the George Town magistrate's court at least twenty times. And each time I was sent back to the home.

'Perhaps I would have been released earlier, but when I was arrested, my husband was arrested too—booked as a pimp. He is not a pimp! He works as a guard. All he did was come to the police station on hearing that I had been arrested. Of course he knows about my work, but he never pimped me. He was sent to Puzhal prison for a month.

'My boys were suddenly on the streets, because, hearing of our situation, our landlady had thrown them out. They slept on the pavement at Broadway bus stand before a neighbour found them and took them into her house, even though she is as poor as us. She fed them every day. I will never be able to repay my debt to her. My boys had to leave school and start working at a mechanic's shop, even though they are so little.

'When my husband was released from jail, he found a lawyer to try to get me released. That lawyer took twenty-five thousand rupees from him—money that my husband had borrowed at a high interest! But that lawyer did nothing to help! He said he tried, but actually he did not do anything, just profited from our suffering.

'Sir, forget me. My suffering was nothing. I was better off than most of the women imprisoned there. My husband and children and neighbour would come to visit. There were so many women there who had no one coming to see them, ever.

'And the two women wardens were so shameless. Whenever visitors came, they would even take the biscuit packets they would bring us! They would also tell us to ask our visitors to bring sanitary napkins for them. They would then sell these or enter them in the accounts and keep the money. How can visitors come often if they have to spend so much money every time?

'These wardens took everything from me when I was first lodged there, even my jewellery and cell phone. When I was finally released, they gave me back the jewellery but did not return the cell phone, saying, "Give us one thousand rupees and we'll let you have it." But I did not have that kind of money, so I let it be and said nothing to them.

'When I was freed, my husband said to me, "We will manage with what we have. You must not do this work anymore." But he now has to work both day and night shifts as a watchman. He is very tired. And the boys' education has come to an end. They are both working and bringing in a little money every week. I want to help. But I don't know how. All I can do is manage the household expenses as best I can.'

I didn't tell Kamala about the emotions running through my head as I heard her out.I felt anger and despair. In the second decade of the 21st century, Kamala had suffered precisely what Selvi had suffered so many years earlier—years of imprisonment and abuse because of the old bad laws that left sex workers at the mercy of bigoted policemen and judges. This was the most damning proof of failure.

Decades had passed. Countless sex workers had risked everything in fighting for emancipation. Their circumstances had been discussed in innumerable articles and reports. UN organizations had made detailed recommendations. Millions had been spent purportedly on their behalf. And yet sex workers almost everywhere in the world were no closer to securing the most critical, foundational steps of just laws, basic rights and decent treatment.

18

Freedom—Won and Lost

Though we fared immeasurably better than sex workers, our fellow outlaws, we gay Indians also eventually found ourselves in a bizarre, dangerous limbo a decade and a half into the 21st century. The old oppressions and despairs still blighted our lives as before, even though we had won once-unimaginable things—even our freedom for a glorious but ephemeral moment.

Not a year went by that was not consumed by the unending twists and turns, impasses and reversals of the legal challenge to Section 377.

The Delhi High Court had dismissed the Naz Foundation's case in December 2004—three long fruitless years after it had been initiated—on the questionable grounds that its chief executive and listed appellant, Anjali Gopalan, was not gay and therefore had no legal standing to file a public interest challenge. It took another year before the efforts of Anand Grover, the lawyer representing Naz, made the Supreme Court instruct the Delhi court to hear the case promptly, saying it had erred in dismissing it.

Fortune was on our side now. A centrist Congress-led coalition had come to power in the 2004 national elections, ousting the far-right

BJP grouping that had stoked bigotry for nearly a decade. Thoughtful, rational leaders in the government as well as the bureaucracy were willing to consider the far-reaching social and legal changes that UNAIDS and other expert bodies said were essential to making headway against India's apocalyptic AIDS epidemic. (UNAIDS's revisions shrinking the epidemic's scale were still several years away.)

On World AIDS Day in December 2005, Prime Minister Manmohan Singh appealed for a freer public discussion on sexuality, emphasizing that this was vital for protecting younger generations from the escalating risk of HIV. The government's influential Planning Commission set up a task force to re-examine the laws that criminalized homosexuality and sex work. And then, in a breathtaking development in mid-2006, the Ministry of Health's National AIDS Control Organization filed an affidavit in the Delhi court in support of the Naz position of decriminalizing homosexuality—directly opposing the Ministry of Home Affairs. The affidavit emphasized that Section 377 was crippling HIV prevention efforts among India's large, pivotal populations of gay and bisexual men and transwomen, and consequently among their wives and women partners.

NACO's courageous move, which soon proved to be a body blow to the Ministry of Home Affairs' position, came about because it was now led by a senior bureaucrat with a deep commitment to public health—K Sujatha Rao—who had the backing of health minister Anbumani Ramadoss, a youngish politician who showed an unexpected interest in his responsibilities. (Rao and Ramadoss were also key figures in opposing the controversial amendments to the anti-prostitution law that would have intensified the criminalization and persecution of sex workers.) The judges noted in surprise: 'A rather peculiar feature of this case is that completely contradictory affidavits have been filed by two wings of Union of India.'

The Naz challenge was boosted further when Voices Against Section 377, a newly formed coalition of activist groups, filed a supporting intervention in court. Noting that 'the Constitution of India is one of the great emancipatory charters', their intervention emphasized that the Naz case concerned an 'invisible minority of Indians' who 'seek to unlock the assured liberties ... denied to them in an aspect of life that matters most to them: their own identity; their own sexuality; their own self'. The coalition brought together a broad swathe of civil society groups, ranging from those working on women's and children's rights to those focused on HIV prevention and yet others directly on gay and transgender rights, showing that the demand for decriminalization now had wide backing across Indian society.

And in September 2006, just a few weeks before the Delhi court was scheduled to begin hearing the Naz challenge, over one hundred and fifty prominent Indians released an 'Open Letter' urging that same-sex relations be decriminalized. This made headlines across the country, and it was a statement that the judiciary and the government could not ignore.

The Open Letter was the outcome of an effort I had begun some months earlier, while on holiday in India. (I was still working with UNAIDS in Geneva.) I had proposed to my friends Vikram Seth, the novelist, and Saleem Kidwai, the historian and co-editor of *Same-Sex Love in India*, that we demonstrate through a collective public statement that the most thoughtful, respected Indians felt that same-sex relationships had to be decriminalized as a matter of basic human rights. This would influence not just the courts and the government, but also public opinion. Both Anjali Gopalan of Naz and Anand Grover, the lawyer fighting the case, agreed with our strategy.

The Open Letter that we drafted, addressed to the government, the judiciary and India's citizens, stated: 'To build a truly democratic and plural India, we must collectively fight against laws and policies that abuse human rights and limit fundamental freedoms. This is why we, concerned Indian citizens and people of Indian origin, support the overturning of Section 377 of the Indian Penal Code, a colonial-era law dating to 1861, which punitively criminalizes romantic love and private, consensual sexual acts between adults of the same sex ... In the name of humanity and our Constitution, this cruel and discriminatory law should be struck down.'

It quickly won signatures from one eminent figure after another. There was the legendary freedom fighter Captain Lakshmi Sehgal, recently nominated to be India's President, who had led the Indian National Army's Rani of Jhansi Regiment in her youth. (Now in her nineties, she still worked every day as a doctor for the impoverished.) There was the activist Arya Samaj leader Swami Agnivesh, former UN Under-Secretary-General Nitin Desai, and former Attorney-General of India Soli Sorabjee. There were many great thinkers, journalists, filmmakers, artists and writers in the list.

Besides them, we consciously sought out signatories from traditionally conservative quarters where support could not be assumed, such as the armed forces, civil service, business and education. Among our supporters from these sections were former chief of the Navy Admiral Ram Tahiliani, Doon School Headmaster Kanti Bajpai, Planning Commission members Sayeeda Hameed and Kirit Parikh, and the éminence grise of the civil service in NC Saxena and JB D'Souza. All of India's secular, democratic, forward-thinking promise was represented here.

To our joy, Amartya Sen, the Nobel laureate in economics, offered to join us with a personal Open Letter. Sen wrote movingly, 'It is surprising that independent India has not yet been able to rescind the colonial-era monstrosity in the shape of Section 377... Today, 145 years later, we surely have urgent reason to abolish in India, with our commitment to democracy and human rights, the unfreedom of arbitrary and unjust criminalization.'

For me as well as many other gay Indians, these Open Letters marked a watershed in our conflicted and often fearful feelings about life in this country. The affirmations of support by highly respected individuals, almost none of them gay, meant that the India of 2006 was not the same country I had encountered as a young man in 1986, exactly two decades ago.

While I could now count on having innumerable allies and defenders if I faced any kind of homophobic persecution, I knew back then that scarcely anyone—except my family and close friends—would help. I wished my beloved friend Siddhartha had been alive to see this thrilling turning point—many of the people who hadn't even replied when he asked them for statements of support for *Less than Gay* in 1991 were now signatories to the Open Letter.

And the fact that the Open Letters led to widely supportive comments in the press and public discussions, barring a handful of hate-filled comments from obscurantist religious figures, made me realize that my long-held—if often flickering—hope that most Indians actually had a live-and-let-live attitude to same-sex issues was not misplaced. I also realized that the homophobic hatred that had swelled under the BJP's recent rule was not representative of public opinion. It was the work of the bullies in our society, particularly thuggish policemen and political and religious figures who used bigotry to advance their careers and power. Though they still had the power to do us immense harm, I now knew that they were a minority—and this filled me with hope.

So, for the first time ever, I felt I could return to live in India as an openly gay man without feeling constantly wary or besieged. (As it happened, I was to move back to India in late 2007, nearly a year after resigning from UNAIDS, as my relationship with my Geneva boyfriend had cracked under the stress of that upheaval.)

Even so, despite all these visible signs of public attention and the instructions from the Supreme Court that the case be heard speedily, the Delhi High Court did not give a date for the case. Two more frustrating years dragged by. By the time the court listed the case for final arguments, it was mid-2008.

A dozen day long hearings began in September, in front of Chief Justice Ajit Prakash Shah and Justice S. Muralidhar. With them, we were guaranteed an intelligent and impartial review, whatever the outcome. Shah had authored numerous progressive verdicts, while

Muralidhar was a former human rights lawyer. India's judiciary, to which every wronged community in the nation despairingly turned to in their search for justice and emancipation, was finally considering our grievance—and it had come after a decade-and-a-half of efforts by the ABVA group, Anand Grover and others to ensure that we were not denied this basic right.

On 7 November, I went for the final day of the hearings, held in the unprepossessing Courtroom Number 1. On that day, and in earlier reports from the hearings that I had followed attentively, the justness of our position shone through clearly. Everything was on our side—the evidence of the terrible damage done by this unjust law; the scientific affirmation that same-sex desires were a normal part of human diversity; the tremendous force of universal human rights principles; the past half-century's global trajectory of decriminalization and of according equal rights; and not least, the proof from the Open Letters that the most respected Indians urged an end to this archaic, alien law.

In that morning's hearing, as in the seven years since he had first filed the Naz petition, Anand Grover argued that the criminalization of adult, consensual same-sex relations violated constitutionally-guaranteed rights on numerous overlapping counts. Criminalization imperilled HIV prevention efforts, leaving gay and bisexual men and transgenders far more vulnerable to contracting this fatal disease, and violating their rights to health and to life. (Grover frequently cited UN recommendations, which the judges clearly paid close attention to, adding to my frustration that UNAIDS—kowtowing to President Bush—had so abjectly failed sex workers in practice even as it defended gay men in principle.)

Grover argued that criminalization also deprived these Indian citizens of the right to liberty, privacy and dignity. The Indian government had failed to prove any compelling grounds for selectively denying these rights to all those who had same-sex desires. And the harsh punishments prescribed under Section 377 for 'private sexual activity between consenting adults' merely because they were of the same sex also flagrantly violated the right to equality before the law, he stressed.

The lawyer representing the Voices Against 377 coalition, Shyam Divan, made a complementary set of arguments. The harrowing personal affidavits filed by gay men and women showed that Section 377 'subjects male and female homosexuals as well as transgenders to repressive, cruel and disparaging treatment,' said Divan. It 'degrades such individuals into sub-human, second-class citizens, vulnerable to continuous exploitation and harassment'. The harm done to them by Section 377 was all the more unconscionable for being provoked 'simply because they seek to engage in sexual conduct, which is part of their experience of being human.'

In a moving closing speech, Divan, who has an openly gay brother, said: 'The right to live with dignity is guaranteed to all persons ... Public morality is not a valid or sufficient justification to deny a person his dignity ... Indeed, in this context, it is the fundamental rights enshrined to protect minorities, including sexual minorities, that ought to prevail. Morality, by itself, in the absence of any other harm, cannot be a ground to restrict the right to live with dignity.'

I had closely followed the arguments of the three opposing parties—comprising the Home Ministry, a rabidly conservative politician, and a bizarre AIDS-denial group—from reports of the hearings. If there was any merit or even basic logic to their views I could not grasp it, reinforcing my growing conviction over the years that the 'moral majority' everywhere consists of irrational, aggressively opinionated cranks.

The Additional Solicitor-General representing the Home Ministry, P.P. Malhotra, argued that homosexuality must remain criminalized because it was 'neither known to nature, nor known to law'. He claimed that decriminalizing 'unnatural sex' would 'open floodgates of delinquent behaviour and be misconstrued as providing unbridled licence for the same'. This, as well as other bizarre statements by Malhotra—that consensual adult homosexuality was indistinguishable from paedophilia; that widow remarriage was a criminal offence—earned him sharp rebukes from the judges over the course of the hearings, at several points even being told to 'take this issue seriously'.

It was also clear from the judges' comments just how much the Home Ministry's stand had been weakened by the National AIDS Control Organization's cogently argued affidavit recommending the decriminalization of homosexuality in the interests of checking AIDS. Thus, whenever Malhotra argued that homosexuality should remain criminalized on public health grounds—saying, gays have 'sex with hundreds of persons, two hundred, five hundred, even more, it's more likely to transmit disease'—the judges would note that the NACO affidavit 'points to the contrary'. While I was relieved over Malhotra's arguments being so weak that even the judges could not hide their irritation, I was also aghast that such a visibly incompetent person could become the third-highest lawyer for the Indian government.

And then there was B.P. Singhal, a prominent Bharatiya Janata Party politician and younger brother of the leader of the extremist Vishva Hindu Parishad, Ashok Singhal. Singhal claimed to speak for a majority of Indians, insisting that they felt gay sex was 'inherently immoral, grossly unnatural ... the very antithesis of the lofty ideals, lofty values and lofty objectives' of Indian civilisation. It was astonishing to see how utterly ahistorical Hindutva ideologues were willing to be in defence of their bigotry—they were arguing that a colonial law dating back a hundred and fifty years was an integral part of Indian civilization.

Watching Singhal in the courtroom that day—a heavyset, forceful man in his seventies who seemed to be holding back an intense rage—I wondered at the kind of hatred that must have been impelling him to devote his waning years to this matter, filing pages and pages in court, and presenting himself without fail every day of these long court hearings. That day, in an angry intervention at the start of the hearing, Singhal vented: 'The mother of all harms to the human body comes from homosexuality.' I was fortunate to have come far enough to not be upset by his open display of hatred, to remember that the fault lay deep in him, not in us.

The arguments made by Singhal's lawyer were even more unhinged. 'Anus is not designed by nature for any intercourse, and if the penis enters the rectum, victim is found to get injury,' he pronounced, attempting to establish that male homosexuality was intrinsically injurious, even if between consenting adults. 'In the science of sexual physiology and anatomy, it is completely logical that intercourse is heterosexual, and any other way of releasing semen is unnatural.'

Singhal's lawyer hopped from one weird argument to another. Decriminalization would lead to a flood of divorces. It would shatter every member of the family. It would change the country's sex ratio. If the court were to decriminalize homosexuality on the grounds that it was the choice of two consenting adults, then why not also allow incest and the selling and buying of kidneys?

Gay men who 'didn't use condoms do not deserve sympathy or mercy,' he argued, adding that 'homosexuals enjoy group sex and even enjoy committing violence ... Drink and drugs are employed to obtain consent and increase enthusiasm. There is genital torture on anus, testis, blood letting.'

Rounding off the opposition was the bizarre AIDS-denial group known as Joint Action Committee Kannur (JACK). As far back as 2002, this fringe group had filed an intervention against the Naz petition on the incomprehensible grounds that while HIV was not the cause of AIDS—they didn't explain what the real cause was—Section 377 helped control the AIDS epidemic by discouraging 'rampant homosexuality'. It had since accused the prominent lawyers representing Naz and Voices Against 377 of financial corruption as well as other wrongdoings. These wild charges earned the ire of Chief Justice Shah, who acerbically noted that he had never seen 'such low levels' of arguments in court.

The hearings closed that day. And then, month after month, we waited impatiently for a verdict. While we feared the worst, we prayed for what we knew to be right.

Some seven months later, on the morning of Thursday, 2 July 2009, Justices Shah and Muralidhar ruled: that 'Section 377 IPC, insofar it criminalizes consensual sexual acts of adults in private, is violative of Articles 21, 14, and 15 of the Constitution ... Moral indignation, howsoever strong, is not a valid basis for overriding individuals' fundamental rights of dignity and privacy. In our scheme of things, Constitutional morality must outweigh the argument of public morality, even if it be the majoritarian view ... A provision of law branding one section of people as criminal based wholly on the State's moral disapproval of that class goes counter to the equality guaranteed under Articles 14 and 15 ... The criminalization of homosexuality condemns in perpetuity a sizable section of society and forces them to live their lives in the shadow of harassment, exploitation, humiliation, cruel and degrading treatment at the hands of the law enforcement machinery ... [Thus] Section 377 IPC grossly violates their right to privacy and liberty embodied in Article 21.'

I was free! The source of my sharpest and most abiding adult fears had been destroyed.

There was jubilation across India. Tears of joy were shed in Courtroom Number 1 of Delhi's High Court as the judgment was read out. People danced on the streets of every city. Countless crisscrossing e-mails shared the judgment's hundred-page text. We were free! We were no longer criminals. We had fought the bigots and won. We had helped make India a more just and promising nation.

I couldn't participate in the public celebration as I was with my father that day at his home in the Nilgiris. He was ailing from an aggressive brain tumour. But my celebration was all the keener for being alone with him. Holding back tears, my father told me he was overjoyed that he could live long enough to celebrate this day with me. To know that everything I had fought for had come about in his lifetime and mine. To know that I could no longer be persecuted because of this hateful law.

Now, he would no longer fear for me as he had done when I first returned to India from the US nearly a quarter-of-a-century ago. My father said he now prayed that one day soon I would win the right to officially marry the wonderful man—an Indian human rights lawyer—I had just begun dating. He could pass away peacefully now,

Provided by author

With Dad, on one of his last walks

he told me, knowing that I would be safe and stood a fair chance at happiness even if I continued living in India.

I was filled with immense love and gratitude for my lovely father. He had remained my unquestioning ally even when he was struggling privately to come to terms with my orientation. Without his backing, I probably would not have had the courage to fight back against homophobia as much as I did. And for at least a decade, he had clearly put behind him any lingering reservations about my orientation—a shift that was dramatically manifested in his frequent comments to my brothers and me that he wished only that I would someday find happiness with a good man.

So, my celebration alone with my dying father—this inspiringly honest, good-hearted and loving individual—at his quiet hillside home was immeasurably more wonderful than even being part of the public euphoria.

I had just one regret on that unforgettable day of emancipation—Siddhartha was not there to celebrate with us. With *Less than Gay*, nearly twenty years ago, he had made us see possibilities that had not even been imagined until then. How wildly he would have celebrated, that libertine intellectual activist, had he been alive that day!

That lucid judgment from Delhi's High Court, establishing the Constitutional reasons for decriminalizing same-sex relations, should have been the end of the constant fearfulness and stigma that we gay men and women had always known, and the beginning of a life full of hope for us in our own country. Not only was the decision unanimously praised by commentators, but—crucially—the Congress-led central government unequivocally said that it found no fault with the judgment and would not challenge it. Law minister Veerappa Moily called it 'well-researched, well-documented, well-argued'.

Seeing this reasoned behavior from the Congress' leaders, I felt enormous relief that the BJP was not in power; their track record of bigotry meant that they would surely have sought to have the High Court's decision overturned by the Supreme Court. The only criticisms, as expected, came from obscurantist faith leaders.

The sea change in attitudes that had been cemented by the court ruling was evident when an especially brutal incident of homophobia hit the headlines a few months later. A professor at Aligarh Muslim University, S.R. Siras, was covertly videotaped in his bedroom while having sex with another man, and then forced to quit his post by the university administration. The media and public commentators condemned the persecution, citing the Delhi court's ruling. The Allahabad High Court swiftly rebuked the university administration and reinstated the professor. But even all this support could not undo the personal harm done; Professor Siras committed suicide, and his lover was left badly burnt after trying to immolate himself.

So we felt reassured that the homophobic bigots had been proven to be a fringe minority in retreat in this vibrant, progressive India that was finally jettisoning so many bad legacies of British colonialism. We felt that people had forever understood the justness of our case, that public opinion was now overwhelmingly on our side.

And everywhere I travelled in those years, I saw astonishing evidence of how accepting Indians of every age were now of my orientation. This held true not just in major cities but also small-town Goa and the Nilgiris where I lived. The vast majority treated it correctly as an inconsequential matter that had no bearing on our professional interaction or friendships. If they ever broached the topic of homosexuality, it was only in a sympathetic spirit, to learn more about the difficulties I or the others they knew had faced.

Others embraced it. One of my most precious recollections is of my immediate neighbours in the Nilgiris, who told me that she and her husband were particularly happy that I had moved there as their teenage children would now have a role model in case they were gay. I could see that in this new India, homophobia was not widespread or intensely held, but was driven by a small number of bigoted bullies, almost all of them concentrated in hard-right political groups, extremist religious factions, and the police force.

Consequently, I did not worry when—in early 2012—the Supreme Court began hearing appeals against the 2009 Delhi decision. The apex court was certain to promptly uphold the rigorously argued High Court ruling. The government had refused to challenge it; none of the the fifteen petitioners had any standing in a Constitutional matter; and, not least, the petitioners were an embarrassment of cranks and nuts.

From the High Court case, there was the fulminant BJP-strongman B.P. Singhal and the AIDS-denialist group JACK. There was Suresh Kumar Koushal, an obscure astrologer worried that the decriminalization of homosexuality threatened India's national security because officers in the armed forces would now be emboldened to sexually abuse their troops. There was Baba Ramdev, a famed yoga teacher known for his outlandish views—in this case, he feared that the spread of homosexuality would damage India's population growth. There were obscurantist faith organizations, including the All India Muslim Personal Law Board (which advocates the strict application of the Shariat law to Indian Muslims) and the Apostolic Churches Alliance. Also on the list was the Delhi Commission for Protection of Child Rights, a government body headed at this point by a former high-ranking policeman with a predilection for moral crusades. Remembering the insane ranting of some of these groups during the High Court hearings, I couldn't help but feel sympathy for the Supreme Court justices who would be subjected to this drivel.

Arrayed on the other side were the Naz Foundation, which had filed the original public interest challenge in the Delhi High Court, and seven other entities, including the activist coalition Voices Against 377; a group of leading mental health experts; a group of legal scholars; a group of prominent academics; a group of parents with adult gay, lesbian or transgender children; and eminent film-maker and Member of Parliament Shyam Benegal, who has an openly gay daughter. These were highly respected people and groups, and arguing pro bono on their behalf were some of India's most celebrated lawyers.

And by now, global thinking about same-sex rights had advanced so much that if the justices looked abroad—at UN Secretary-General Ban Ki-Moon and President Obama advocating for the human rights of gays, or at the hundred-plus countries where same-sex relations were legal (including neighbouring Nepal) and the nineteen that recognized same-sex marriage—they would only find support for the Delhi court's ruling that 21st century India had to be a part of this momentuous advance of civilization.

I attentively read newspaper reports of the hearings as well as many legal briefs, both the ones seeking to reverse the High Court judgment as well as those from our side. But I decided against attending even one of the hearings, certain that this was merely a second act, with the outcome already determined in our favor.

The hearings ended in March 2012. We readied for a prompt judgment, but none came. Months passed, and then a year. Inexplicably, there was still no indication from the Supreme Court about a date for the decision.

Eventually, it became clear that the ruling would have to be issued by the end of 2013 because Justice G.S. Singhvi—the senior member of the two-judge bench—was retiring then. We surmised that Justice Singhvi was probably delaying the judgment for his last day in court to forestall any controversy. Though I was dismayed that over four years had dragged by since the Delhi judgment without a national-level decision being taken, neither I nor other observers were unduly worried. As long as the ruling was announced by summer 2014—when the national elections threatened to bring back the bigoted BJP in an anti-Congress wave—there was no reason for worry.

The judgment was finally listed for the morning of 11 December 2013, Justice Singhvi's very last day in the Supreme Court. That morning, gay men and women as well as transgenders—accompanied by their friends, relatives and supporters—gathered outside the

Supreme Court in the hundreds. Court 1 was full by the time Justices Singhvi and Mukhopadhya arrived at 10.30 a.m. At home in the Nilgiris, I sat glued to the Internet, checking online news briefs, as well as keeping an eye on the TV news.

At 11 a.m., two terse e-mails from gay activists present at the court appeared in my in box:

'They have overthrown the High Court judgment.'

'It seems they said Section 377 stands constitutionally. They have said Parliament must decide.'

I read those e-mails again and again in disbelief. This had to be speculation or mis-reporting.

I turned quickly to the TV news. There, a few minutes later, headlines confirmed that the Supreme Court had overruled the Delhi decision, with the judges saying, 'Those who indulge in carnal intercourse in the ordinary course and those who indulge in carnal intercourse against the order of nature constitute different classes; and the people falling in the latter category cannot claim that Section 377 suffers from the vice of arbitrariness and irrational classification.'

The sense of shocked, hopeless defeat would have been overwhelming but for the fact that there was widespread outrage across India and abroad. Newspaper after newspaper criticized the judgment in editorials, calling it 'disgraceful', 'retrograde' and a 'body blow to liberal values and human rights'. India's Attorney-General Goolam Vanhavati wrote an op-ed in the *Times of India*, saying that he had decided to break with precedent to write publicly because of 'the importance of the matter'. He then went on to call the court's ruling a 'tragedy'. United Nations human rights chief Navi Pillay said, 'Yesterday's Supreme Court decision in this case represents a significant step backwards for India.' (In telling contrast, BJP president Rajnath Singh welcomed the judgment, saying, 'We believe that homosexuality is an unnatural act and cannot be supported.')

The most moving criticism came from Leila Seth, Vikram Seth's mother and a former Chief Justice of the Himachal High Court. Through all the efforts Vikram and I had put in the past, including the Open Letters written in 2006 while the legal challenge was still before the Delhi High Court, she had—as a matter of principle—refused to influence her colleagues in the judiciary in even the slightest manner possible. But now she wrote in the *Times of India*: 'I have great respect for legal proprieties in general, and would not normally comment on a judgment, but I am making an exception in this case. The Delhi High Court judgment was set aside, Section 377 was reinstated in full, and even private, adult, consensual sexual acts other than the one considered "natural" were criminalized again.'

'As the mother of my elder son, I was extremely upset. But as a lawyer and a former judge, I decided to reserve my views till I had read the judgment. When I read it, it would be true to say that I found it difficult to follow its logic ... Both learning and science get rather short shrift. Instead of welcoming cogent arguments from jurisprudence outside India, which is an accepted practice in cases of fundamental rights, the judgment specifically dismisses them as being irrelevant ... But what has pained me, and is more harmful, is the spirit of the judgment. The interpretation of law is untempered by any sympathy for the suffering of others. The voluminous accounts of rape, torture, extortion and harassment suffered by gay and transgender people as a result of this law do not appear to have moved the court. Nor does the court appear concerned about the parents of such people, who stated before the court that the law induced in their children deep fear, profound self-doubt, and the inability to peacefully enjoy family life. I know this to be true from personal experience.'

Leila Seth ended by noting, yet more sharply: 'The judgment claimed that the fact that a minuscule fraction of the country's population was gay or transgender could not be considered a sound basis for reading down Section 377 ... But even if only very few people were in fact at threat, the Supreme Court could not abdicate its responsibilities to protect their fundamental rights, or shuffle them off to Parliament ... The reasoning in the judgment that justice based on fundamental rights can only be granted if a large number of people are affected is constitutionally immoral and inhumane.'

Surely this public outrage would force the Supreme Court to correct what was patently an egregious error, reflecting the vagaries and biases of at the most two particular judges? (The ruling on Section 377 seemed all the more inexplicable and rooted in personal bias when, a year-and-a-half later, another set of Supreme Court judges made a pathbreaking decision on transgender rights—recognizing a 'third gender' and ordering the government to provide them with quotas in jobs and education, in line with other minorities. In this case, the Supreme Court said: 'The spirit of the Constitution is to provide equal opportunity to every citizen to grow and attain their potential, irrespective of caste, religion or gender.') The court could use its review procedure to re-examine the case before a larger bench, given the fact that this was a Constitutional matter.

Within ten days of the judgment, the Congress-led government itself pressed for a review. In visibly critical language, the government listed seventy-six grounds to underscore that the judgment authored by Justices Singhvi and Mukhopadhaya had not fulfilled the apex court's responsibility for judging the constitutional validity of laws, 'especially a pre-Constitutional law', and was 'contrary to well-established principles of law laid down by this court enunciating the width and ambit of fundamental rights'. The government's plea was joined by Naz, Voices Against 377 and several other groups, each of them stressing that a larger bench should review the case.

However, on 28 January 2014, a Supreme Court bench rejected these petitions and decided that there was no reason to re-examine the original judgment.

Once again, I was a criminal in my own country, an outlaw for being who I was, with little hope for freedom in my lifetime.

Author's Notes

These short notes provide basic context as well as essential attribution and references. A full set of author's notes are available as a free e-book on both the publisher's and my websites, providing not just formal footnotes, references and links, but also commentary and suggested reading on several contextual issues that I've had to leave out of the book itself in the interest of narrative clarity.

In addition to the people whose insights have informed particular chapters of this book and who are thanked in those specific notes, I'd like to express my deepest thanks to my friends Joanne Csete and Aniruddhan Vasudevan, and my editor Vrinda Condillac, for discussions and advice that enriched my thinking across the entire book. It bears emphasizing that I remain solely responsible for the views expressed in this book, not the people I've acknowledged or thanked, who may indeed not share my views.

Chapter 1

Elite Calcutta was famous for striptease, can-can and drag performances until the 1970s. See, for instance, 'A merry journey', the *Telegraph*, 25 December 2011.

James Morris, born 1926, was already a renowned journalist and writer when he began to transition to becoming a woman, Jan Morris. In *Conundrum*, first published in 1974, Morris chronicles the 'conundrum' of gender she experienced, trapped 'in the wrong body'.

There is by now a rich literature on gender identity in children and adults alike, emphasizing the importance of parental/familial acceptance and support, and the individual and society-wide benefits of encouraging 'gender neutrality' (instead of the conventional emphasis on female and male). For insightful discussions, see, for instance: 'Once a Pariah, Now a Judge: The Early Transgender Journey of Phyllis Frye', Deborah Sontag, *New York Times*, 29 August 2015; 'How Changeable is Gender?', Richard A Friedman, *New York Times*, 22 August 2015; 'What's So Bad About a Boy Who Wants to Wear a Dress?', *New York Times*, Ruth Padawer, 8 August 2012; 'A Boy's Life', Hanna Rosin, the *Atlantic Monthly*, November 2008.

Chapter 2

I'm grateful to Krishna Kumar, Vikram Seth, Tarun Tahiliani, my father and both my brothers for discussions, over the years, regarding Doon and, more generally, schooling in India.

My criticisms of Doon are, in spirit and conscious intent, a criticism of the fear- and hierarchy-based educational traditions that are so pervasive in India that they are now arguably woven into our culture, with a poisonous impact not just on notions of masculinity and on gender relations but also on the treatment of the poor and powerless. So these are equally criticisms of other prominent schools like Mayo College, the Lawrence Schools, La Martinière and Scindia School—as well as a myriad of lesser known places—where physical and, often, sexual abuse, have been endemic. 'Ragging' in colleges is of course a closely related pathology.

For reports on physical and sexual abuse in other Indian schools and colleges, see, for instance: 'Losing their shine', Dev Lahiri, *Hindustan Times*, 30 August 2011; 'Bullying: A school teacher's perspective', Dev

Lahiri, *Times of India*, 1 June 2009. Lahiri is a former principal of both Welham Boys' School and Lawrence School, Lovedale, and a former housemaster of Doon. He writes, 'When I took over a school in 1991, I found that it was commonplace for senior students to entertain themselves by hanging little boys out all night from the first floor windows, to break their arms with hockey-sticks and to proudly autograph the plaster cast, to brand their slaves with electric irons all in the name of tradition.'

'Liberal streak', Edward Luce, *Financial Times*, 2 January 2004, provides a thoughtful discussion of Doon's strong points as well as of the difficulties of curbing bullying there. 'A bastion of tradition is restored', Jo Johnson, *Financial Times*, 9 June 2005, includes discussion of brutal bullying at Mayo College in the 1980s. In 'Catcher in the Rye', *Tehelka*, 7 October 2006, filmmaker Anurag Kashyap discusses his years as a sexually abused boarder at Scindia School, writing, 'Scindia was hell for me. The sexual abuse continued there for years. I hated myself. I couldn't understand why it was happening to me. I was often picked out, beaten, then taken to the toilets. To save myself from the beatings, I'd give in to the abuse.' Also see: 'Boarding school bullies', *Hindustan Times*, 5 May 2009; 'Is Hazing Worse in India?', Sudhin Thanawala, *Time*, 23 Nov 2007. Also look up CURE: Coalition to Uproot Ragging from Education.

Vikram Seth's Founders' Day address in 1992, the first notable public criticism of Doon, is available at doononline.net

The bullying routinely escalated to physical as well as sexual abuse ... From my discussions with alumni of Doon, Mayo and similar schools, it seems that bullying and outright physical and sexual abuse are longstanding, pervasive problems. My father wrote in his unpublished autobiography of his years at Doon in the 1940s, 'There was nothing really noteworthy in the five years I spent at the Doon School. Like in all boys' schools, bullying was the order of the day ... Homosexuality was rampant. As soon as an attractive-looking young boy joined, the seniors would befriend him and, before long, endeavour to seduce him. In case the seduction was resisted, the senior would have his life made miserable. Fortunately or unfortunately, this is what happened to me.' I never got around to asking my father to clarify whether this cryptic statement meant that he was sexually abused or had a consensual relationship with a senior. Nonetheless, these experiences doubtless contributed to my father's hostile views on homosexuality, which became empathetic only when he had to grapple with my orientation.

But so overpowering was the atmosphere of fear and so complete the lack of redressal mechanisms ... In the past decade, Doon has undertaken a range of reforms to specifically address bullying and, physical and sexual abuse, and, crucially, to ensure that students have access to on-campus counsellors. I have no personal knowledge of the impact of these changes, but hopefully they mean that students are now able to benefit from Doon's many good aspects. For a description of these changes—which include a comprehensive code of conduct for students that bars corporal punishment, unsupervised physical punishments, and the practice of 'fagging'—see Doon's website, particularly the publication *Codes and Policies*.

Chapter 3

I'm grateful to Rosemary George Marangoly for discussions regarding sexism as well as more generally the relations between men and women at St. Stephen's. She reminded me too of the Holi incident, which I had forgotten about. See also: 'Of chick charts, hen charts and other such women's stories', Saba Dewan, *Kafila*, 8 May 2012.

There was nothing in the India of the early 1980s to help a young man or woman deal with his or her homosexuality. The one notable exception was a sympathetic book by the mathematics genius Shakuntala Devi, *The World of Homosexuals*, published in 1977. But the enforced silence about homosexuality was so extreme that despite Devi's fame the book went barely noticed. I didn't know of it until I was in my twenties.

Chapter 4

For the medical profession's evolving understanding of same-sex desire, see Ronald Bayer's *Homosexuality and American Psychiatry: The Politics of Diagnosis* (first published 1987) and Henry Minton's *Departing From Deviance: A History of Homosexual Rights and Emancipatory Science in America* (first published 2002).

The history of regulating sodomy and 'deviant' sex in the US is covered in *Dishonorable Passions: Sodomy Laws in America, 1861-2003* by William N. Eskridge Jr. In 1986, the US Supreme Court unexpectedly upheld the legality of sodomy laws (still present in twenty-five states) in a case where two men in Georgia were arrested while having sex at home. Eventually, in 2003, the Supreme Court—once again hearing a case where two men were arrested while having sex at home (this time in Texas)—explicitly reversed its 1986 decision, calling its previous ruling 'demeaning' and saying sodomy laws were unconstitutional. See 'The Supreme Court: Homosexual Rights; Justices, 6-3, Legalize Gay Sexual Conduct in Sweeping Reversal of Court's '86 Ruling', Linda Greenhouse, *New York Times*, 27 June 2003.

Chapter 6

The most thorough source of worldwide information on human rights abuses of individuals because of their sexual orientation or gender identity is the yearly report by the International Lesbian, Gay, Bisexual, Trans and Intersex Association (ILGA), *State-Sponsored Homophobia—A world survey of laws: Criminalisation, protection and recognition of same-sex love*. See ilga.org and the excellent analysis by Aaron Xavier Fellmeth, 'State Regulation of Sexuality in International Human Rights Law and Theory', *William & Mary Law Review* 2008.

The overwhelming majority of laws criminalizing homosexuality were inherited or derived from colonial rule, particularly British colonialism. For an excellent analysis of the former British colonies, see *This Alien Legacy: The Origins of 'Sodomy' Laws in British Colonialism*, Human Rights Watch, 2008. For the British colonial impact in the

U.S., see Eskridge, op. cit. The majority of these laws focus on sex between men, though others criminalize specific sexual acts, such as anal and oral sex, regardless of the sex of the partners.

Almost everywhere, penalties for homosexual conduct have been—and remain—extremely harsh, including long terms of imprisonment (up to life), physical and chemical castration or hormonal treatment, physical punishment (including whipping), and execution. Until the late 19th century, many British colonies retained execution as the maximum punishment in their laws. As of 2015, eight countries, in Africa, Asia and the Middle East, officially legislate the death penalty for same-sex acts, notably all under interpretations of Sharia codes.

The irony was not lost on me that I felt safer in the US even though gays had until recently been persecuted there in the most brutal and systematic ways, and indeed still remained criminalized in many states. In fact, one of my gay Indian friends felt safer back in India than in the West, because as a graduate student in Canada in the late 1970s he had been arrested in a police raid on a gay bar and deported back to India.

Chapter 7

See 'Sexuality', *The Indians: Portrait of a People*, by Sudhir Kakar and Katharina Kakar, first published 2007, for an illuminating analysis of the 'wasteland' of both male and female sexuality in contemporary India, rife with shame, fear and coercion.

Chapter 8

In addition to published materials, the sections on Dominic D'Souza in this and later chapters are based on interviews in Goa with Raj Vaidya and Isabel de Santa Rita Vaz, in Mumbai with Dr Ishwar Gilada, Anand Grover and Ashok Rao Kavi, and in Chennai with Dr Suniti Solomon. The 2005 film 'My Brother Nikhil' is loosely based on Dominic. See 'Gay-Themed Film Tests Sensibilities in India', Somini Sengupta, *New York Times*, 6 April 2005.

In addition to the specific written materials cited, the sections on Selvi in this and later chapters are based on interviews with Shyamala Nataraj, B Sekar, Dr Suniti Solomon and Mary Thomas.

The events from the reformatory to the Indian government's public statement are detailed in an unpublished course paper by Sunil Suhas Solomon, Dr Suniti Solomon's son, 'From 6 to 6 million in two decades: The story behind the first six cases of HIV detected in India'. More critical assessments of Dr Solomon, officials of the Indian Council of Medical Research, and bureaucrats and politicians—especially the competition for fame that motivated many of this cast of characters—are presented in 'Avoid promiscuity', Sadanand Menon, *Sunday Observer*, 18 May 1986; 'AIDS: premature panic', Salil Tripathi, *Imprint*, August 1986; and, in 'Madras, India: Locking up prostitutes', Shyamala Nataraj, *The Third Epidemic: Repercussions of the Fear of AIDS*, Panos Institute, 1990.

And they were 'sexual' women, that last fact making them prey to particular scorn ... For an illuminating discussion about Indian 'anxiety around female sexuality' see Kakar and Kakar op. cit. They note that the 'inflexible checks' on female sexuality are evident in many contradictory dynamics, ranging from the idealization of both female chastity and the 'good mother' to the mix of ignorance, hostility and violence that typify men's sexual relations with their wives (instead of tenderness and eroticism); the paradoxical 'dark imagery' in myth and images that women are 'lustful and sexually rapacious by nature' and have to be curbed; and, in women's overpowering guilt and shame about sexual matters and their own bodies (particularly their genitals).

Chapter 9

For this chapter, my main sources have been *The Invisible People: How the US Has Slept through the Global AIDS Pandemic, the Greatest Humanitarian Catastrophe of Our Time*, Greg Behrman, 2004; *AIDS in the World*, Jonathan Mann et. al. eds., first published 1992; 'Poor man's plague', the *Economist*, 21 September 1991; and 'Jonathan Mann,

HIV/ AIDS, and Human Rights', Elizabeth Fee and Manon Parry, *Journal of Public Health Policy*, Vol. 29., No. 1, April 2008.

Chapter 10

I'm grateful to Priscilla Alexander, Joanne Csete, Melissa Ditmore, Anand Grover, Smarajit Jana, Shyamala Nataraj and Meena Seshu for illuminating discussions.

For the entire section on the development of WHO's first guidelines on HIV and sex work, I have drawn extensively on Karen Booth's fascinating paper, 'National mother, global whore and transnational femocrats: the politics of AIDS and the construction of women at the World Health Organization', *Feminist Studies*, 1998. (For exact attribution, see the full 'Author's Notes'.)

The guidelines *Making Sex Work Safer: A guide to HIV/AIDS prevention interventions* were eventually published only in 1993, because of delays that Alexander and Booth attribute to opposition faced by Alexander within the new leadership of the global AIDS programme.

Chapter 11

See 'Goan AIDS activist succumbs to virus', *Times of India*, 28 May 1992. The will is reproduced in *Dominic D'Souza: The complete story*, India Health Organisation (IHO), Bombay (No publication date given). The quote about his struggles to accept his orientation is also from this source.

Chapter 12

I'm grateful to Rustom Bharucha, Saleem Kidwai, Madhu Mehra and Jaya Sharma for discussions on various points in this chapter.

ABVA has made the full text of *Less than Gay* available freely online to the public, as befits a 'citizens' report'.

... the historical evidence showing that homophobia was a British colonial legacy ... For subsequent scholarly research on this matter, see the

following works, which unanimously conclude that overt persecution of same-sex relations and alternative gender identities began on the subcontinent only under British rule, though they differ in emphasis regarding how tolerant or accepting social attitudes were. In *Same-Sex Love in India: Readings from Literature and History*, editors Ruth Vanita and Saleem Kidwai stress that the relative tolerance of same-sex attraction is rooted in the most fundamental of Hindu concepts: the concept of rebirth absolves same-sex partners of blame because their mutual attraction is involuntary attachment that needs to be brought to a resolution in the present birth; and the belief that the universal spirit pervades all things means that in the ultimate analysis nothing is abnormal or unnatural. Sudhir Kakar argues, 'India has had a tradition of "benign neglect" of alternate sexualities, a tradition that is very much part of the Indian mind.' ('The judgment helps validation of homosexual identity', interview with Devika Sequeira, *Deccan Herald*, 23 July 2009.) Devdutt Pattanaik writes, 'Ancient Indian authors and poets without doubt imagined a state where the lines separating masculinity and femininity often blurred and even collapsed.' ('When gayness was out in open, not a matter of guilt', Devdutt Pattanaik, *Times of India*, 3 July 2009). Historian Wendy Doniger emphasizes that mutable androgyny and desire are a vital part of Indian mythology, with numerous deities and heroic humans alternating between being male and female alongside nonjudgemental allusions to a variety of sexual desires and activities. See especially *The Hindus: An Alternative History*.

The evangelical reformer who referred to Hindu gods as 'absolute monsters of lust' was William Wilberforce, quoted in 'Imperial deceivers', Kevin Rushby, *The Guardian*, 18 January 2003.

This tolerance ... was not destroyed by the spread of Muslim rule ... On the Indian sub-continent, Kakar and Kakar, op. cit., emphasize that the attitude of 'benign neglect' to matters of same-sex desire 'did not change materially in spite of the advent of Islam.' For analysis of the complex local and international dynamics that are resulting in worsening persecution of sexual and gender minorities in Muslim-majority nations today, see 'What Does Islam Say About Being Gay?', Mustafa Akyol, *New York Times*, July 28, 2015

The Habitual Offenders Act perpetuated the view of the Criminal Tribes Act ... In 1897, the Criminal Tribes Act was amended to expressly include 'eunuchs'—in the Indian context meaning hijras—who could now be arrested without warrant and imprisoned for up to two years. (The subtitle of the law now became: 'An Act for the Registration of Criminal Tribes and Eunuchs'.) Local authorities had to keep a register of all eunuchs 'reasonably suspected' of 'committing offences under Section 377'. Now cast as both a criminal tribe and a sexual deviant, hijras could be arrested merely on the presumption of sodomy. See Human Rights Watch, *This Alien Legacy*.

The text of the ABVA petition is reproduced in *Humjinsi: A Resource Book on Lesbian, Gay and Bisexual Rights in India*, edited by Bina Fernandez, 2002.

Chapter 13

For critical but contrasting views on the Bank/IMF's impact, see *The Lords of Poverty: The Power, Prestige, and Corruption of the International Aid Business*, Graham Hancock, first published 1989; *Globalization and Its Discontents*, Joseph E. Stiglitz, first published 2002; and *The World's Banker: A Story of Failed States, Financial Crises, and the Wealth and Poverty of Nations*, Sebastian Mallaby, first published 2004.

The criticisms of inflated salaries and profligate spending that erupted in the early 1990s are covered in 'How the World Bank cuts costs', the *Economist*, 14 April 1990; 'Breaking open the World Bank', Ken Ringle, the *Washington Post*, 25 September 1990.

... appeared as the lead front-page item in the fall 1994 issue ... 'Sex Work and HIV/AIDS', Priscilla Alexander, *Health Policy* 1994; Vol. 8: p. 1, 11–12. Washington, D.C.: The World Bank.

Chapter 14

In addition to specifically cited materials, the section on the development of the South India AIDS Action Programme (SIAAP) is based on discussions with Shyamala Nataraj, B. Sekar, Suniti Solomon, Mary Thomas and members of SIAAP's 'sangam' in Theni district, Tamil Nadu. The section on the work of the Durbar is based on discussions with Smarajit Jana and interviews over the years with numerous Durbar officials and members, including Bharati Dey and Sadhana Mukherjee. I'm also grateful to Ashok Alexander, Joanne Csete, Anand Grover, Smarajit Jana, Shilpa Merchant, Shyamala Nataraj, K. Sujatha Rao, Swarup Sarkar and Meena Seshu for broader discussions regarding sex work and HIV prevention in India.

See *Societal Violence on Women and Children in Prostitution,* National Commission on Women, Ministry of Women and Child Development, Government of India, 1996.

For the Durbar's development in its first decade, I've drawn extensively on the penetrating article, 'Going Brothel to Brothel, Prostitutes Preach about Using Condoms', Celia Dugger, *New York Times,* 4 January 1999. Another important source is 'Sonagachi: A Sex Worker Project in a Red Light District of Calcutta, India', *Female sex worker HIV Prevention Projects: Lessons Learnt from Papua New Guinea, India and Bangladesh,* UNAIDS, *Best Practice Collection,* 2000. For later material, I've drawn extensively from Prabha Kotiswaran's landmark study *Dangerous Sex, Invisible Labor: Sex Work and the Law in India,* 2011. (For exact attribution see the full set of Author's Notes.)

Chapter 15

In addition to the people quoted here, I'm grateful to Vivek Anand, Anjali Gopalan, Anand Grover, Ashok Rao Kavi, Saleem Kidwai, Sunil Menon, Shyamala Nataraj and Radhika Ramasubban for discussions, over the years, that informed this chapter.

... an extreme that far dwarfed even that borne by gay men ... See *Human Rights Violations against Sexuality Minorities in India,* People's Union For Civil Liberties, Karnataka, February 2001, and, *Human Rights Violations against the Transgender Community: A Study of Kothi and Hijra Sex Workers in Bangalore, India,* People's Union of Civil Liberties, Karnataka, 2003.

Several points about the transformative years of gay mobilization are made by Radhika Ramasubban in 'Culture, Politics and Discourses on Sexuality: A history of resistance to the anti-sodomy law in India,' *SexPolitics: Reports from the Frontlines,* editors Richard Parker, Rosalind Petchesky and Robert Sember, 2007.

It challenged the constitutional validity of Section 377 on several grounds ... Because most anti-sodomy laws derived from British colonialism make no distinction between homosexual acts committed with or without consent, or between homosexual acts committed by adults as opposed to adults' abuse of children, the Naz petition asked to 'read down' rather than strike down the Section 377, so that consensual homosexual acts between adults are no longer criminal under the provision, while leaving intact Section 377's application to non-consensual acts and to children (until India passes a modern, gender-neutral rape law, and provides express legal protection for male children against sexual abuse.). See Ramasubban op. cit.; and, *This Alien Legacy,* HRW. For an overview of the legal process and links to all the relevant legal documents visit lawyerscollective.org.

Chapter 16

For discussions about sex work and trafficking that informed this and the following chapter, I'm grateful to Joanne Csete, Bishakha Datta, Jean d'Cunha, Melissa Ditmore, Anand Grover, Andrew Hunter, Smarajit Jana, Shilpa Merchant, Cheryl Overs, Shyamala Nataraj and Meena Seshu.

For insightful discussions of the Bush administration's record on AIDS and human rights, see *Body Count: How they turned AIDS into a Catastrophe*, Peter Gill, 2006; and, *The Wisdom of Whores: Bureaucrats, Brothels, and the Business of AIDS*, Elizabeth Pisani, 2008.

See, 'US accuses NGO of trafficking', Rema Nagarajan, *Hindustan Times*, 29 September 2005.

Chapter 17

For discussions that informed my understanding of the situation in Cambodia, I'm grateful to Andrew Hunter, Tony Lisle, Cheryl Overs, Sophat Phal and Swarup Sarkar, and several activists and sex workers who wish to not have their names disclosed.

... there was now a wealth of data and knowledge on Indian sex work conditions ... See: Kotiswaran op. cit.; 'Demography and sex work characteristics of female sex workers in India', R. Dandona et. al., *BMC International Health and Human Rights*, 14 April 2006; *Prostitution and Beyond: An Analysis of Sex Work in India*, editors R. Sahni, V.K. Shankar and H. Apte, 2008; 'Harsh realities: Reasons for women's involvement in sex work in India', Niranjan Saggurti et. al., Journal of AIDS and HIV Research, 15 September 2011; 'India', *The Global HIV Epidemics Among Sex Workers*, D. Kerrigan et. al., The World Bank, 2013.

For discussions on Hindutva and women, see *Hindu Wife, Hindu Nation: Community, Religion, and Cultural Nationalism*, Tanika Sarkar, 2001; and *Everyday Nationalism: Women of the Hindu Right in India*, Kalyani Devaki Menon, 2009.

For insightful commentary on the polarized debate between 'abolitionists' and sex-work-rights activists see Kotiswaran, op. cit. and Saggurti op. cit., as well as these shorter articles: 'People-trafficking and people-smuggling: Drawing lines in a dark place; Coercing hapless human beings into sex or servitude is obviously evil, but defining the problem (let alone solving it) is very hard,' the *Economist*, 14 August 2008; 'Body invasion is de-humanizing', Gloria Steinem, the *Hindu*, 6 April 2012; 'Moralistic assumptions', Shohini Ghosh, the *Hindu*, 6 April 2012, in which the Indian feminist responds to Steinem; 'Gloria

Steinem vs Prostitution in India', Svati Shah, the *Huffington Post*, 28 November 2014; 'The Price of a Sex-Slave Rescue Fantasy', Melissa Gira Grant, *New York Times*, 29 May 2014.

For thoughtful critiques of Nicholas Kristof's simplistic writing on developing-country matters, see 'Half the Sky: how the other half suffer', Germaine Greer, the *Guardian*, 30 July 2010; and, 'The White-Savior Industrial Complex', Teju Cole, the *Atlantic*, March 2012. For Kristof's role in the Somaly Mam scandal, see 'The White Knight: Nicholas Kristof wants to save the world with his *New York Times* columns. Why are so many of them wrong?', Amanda Hess, *Slate*, 18 June 2014.

Chapter 18

For discussions that informed this chapter, I'm grateful to Vivek Anand, Sumit Baudh, Vikram Doctor, Anjali Gopalan, Anand Grover, Saleem Kidwai, Sunil Menon, L Ramakrishnan, Gowthaman Ranganathan, Vikram Seth and Aniruddhan Vasudevan.

For a brief history of the litigation process as well as comprehensive links to all the relevant legal documents, see lawyerscollective.org.

See 'A mother and a judge speaks out on section 377', Leila Seth, *Times of India*, 26 January 2014.

I have of course no way of knowing with any certainty whether, in whatever remains of my life at the age of fifty-four, the Supreme Court will reverse this decision (a curative petition is pending before it), or whether Parliament will choose to decriminalize homosexuality. The latter is highly unlikely; the former is a possibility.

Acknowledgements

This book owes everything to Jacob Gayle, then head of the Ford Foundation's global initiative on AIDS—I cannot thank him enough for his willingness to fund what I candidly told him would be a no-holds-barred account. Immense thanks go also to Roshmi Goswami, who led the foundation's efforts in India on sexual, reproductive and women's rights. I'd also like to record my appreciation for the Ford Foundation itself for its long history of fighting for the excluded groups and the embattled freedoms that other funders lack the courage to defend—bravo and don't stop!

I'm grateful also to Canada's International Development Research Centre for an unrelated research grant on poverty in India that nonetheless helped me with the broader research for this book. My thanks in particular go to Stephen McGurk for his patience regarding that project.

In Vrinda Condillac, I had the editor that all writers dream of—an engaged intellectual companion, a gifted wordsmith and the source of invariably challenging but infallible advice! I owe her thanks that words cannot express.

In Sumit Baudh and Aniruddhan Vasudevan I found not just brilliant collaborators and researchers but also enduring affection and friendship. India cannot go wrong when it has such brave and compassionate young people fighting for social justice.

For their comments, advice and encouragement while reading drafts or parts of the book, I am indebted to Sohaila Abdulali, Sumit Baudh, Rustom Bharucha, Corinne Brenner, Joanne Csete, Kiran Desai, Bharat Dube, Rosemary George, Anna Ghosh, Suzanne Goldenberg, Jimmy Jacob, Katharina Poggendorf-Kakar, Sudhir Kakar, V.K. Karthika, Saleem Kidwai, Krishna Kumar, Sankar Sen, Meenaskhi Shedde, Saudamani Siegrist, Manasi Subramaniam, Tarun Tahiliani, Ellen Tolmie, Aniruddhan Vasudevan, Kamala Visweswaran and Mithoo Wadia. Thank you all—immensely!

While writing this memoir I constantly realized just how blessed I am with family and friends, of the kind who make my heart sing in wonder and joy. They are far too numerous to name here—but I hope each of them will somehow know that I thank them for every small and great loving act that has made all the difference to my life. In Pratap and Bharat, I have had the great luck of having principled, caring and brave brothers—and I treasure the fact that our love has become ever richer and stronger as it has aged.

Much of this book was written while living in the Nilgiris, and so it is fitting that I get to record my affection for Sree, an individual of unparalleled loving-kindness, in whom I found another wonderful, steadfast brother; and for Bops and DJ, caring friends who made my father's dream of living his last years in the wild come true.

Not least, there are my infinite thanks to Lorca—the most faithful and fun of hounds, who made even tough days bearable—there's no doubt that you've lived up to the example set by your legendary namesake!